CERPHE'S UP

A Musical Life with Bruce Springsteen, Little Feat,
Frank Zappa, Tom Waits, CSNY, and Many More

CERPHE COLWELL
WITH
STEPHEN MOORE

Carrel Books

Carrel Books may be purchased in bulk at special discounts for sales promotion, corporate gifts, fund-raising, or educational purposes. Special editions can also be created to specifications. For details, contact the Special Sales Department, Carrel Books, 307 West 36th Street, 11th Floor, New York, NY 10018, or carrelbooks@ skyhorsepublishing.com.

Carrel Books® is a registered trademark of Skyhorse Publishing, Inc.®, a Delaware corporation.

Visit our website at www.carrelbooks.com.

10 9 8 7 6 5 4 3 2 1

Library of Congress Cataloging-in-Publication Data is available on file.

Cover design by Rain Saukas
Cover photo credit: © Joel Heiberger/*Washington Post*

ISBN: 978-1-63144-052-6
Ebook ISBN: 978-1-63144-053-3

Printed in the United States of America.

Dedications

I dedicate this book to my beautiful wife, Susan, my beloved parents, my favorite musicians, and my loyal radio listeners with love, appreciation, and thanks for allowing me to be a part of your lives.

—Cerphe Colwell

To my family, Margaret, Charles, and Suzanna, with love.

—Stephen Moore

Contents

Introduction

Ever since I was a child listening to my transistor radio—late at night buried under the covers—music has always been my true compass. I got chicken skin listening to Chuck Berry, Roy Orbison, and other early pioneers of rock and roll music. Then The Beatles baptized me with explorations. They gave me permission to be irreverently hip if I wanted to, and to reinvent myself at my will.

So I became a musician, an art student, and finally a broadcaster on emergent and transcendent freeform FM radio. Our daring "do it yourself" ethic at my first station, WHFS 102.3, was to *not* play top 40 hits. There was always a tension between artistry and commercial success in which we outwardly challenged broadcast conventions at every turn.

Freeform radio was a musical force and became a potent catalyst for social change. The counterculture fostered the birth of great music, a mosaic of creative drama, and I got to satisfy my relentless, creative impulses by playing whatever I wanted, including unknowns like the Bruce Springsteen band and Little Feat. My musical and personal crossroads were very self-indulgent but I was never cavalier about the good fortune that brought me to this pathway. A journey that continues after forty-five years in radio. I am extremely grateful.

Writing this autobiography has been enormously rewarding. It has given me a chance to relish and relive my multifaceted musical adventures and up-close encounters with some of the world's greatest musicians, and now share them with the congregation.

I am grateful to my wife, Susan, whom I love with all my heart, for helping me relive deeply personal moments I have shared and experienced with her throughout our sixteen years together. I am thankful to my friend Steve Moore for his eyes, ears, and spirit. He helped me document what's true about my work, and myself, and convey in words the spirit of American rock and roll radio, ever fast fading into myth.

I've been so fortunate to be friends and spend time with some of the finest musicians in the world. Their passion is inspirational, and I invite you to enjoy my experiences and savor the memories of a chaotic, energized radio industry intoxicated in the most powerful city in the world. I've never lost faith in the power of radio and why we still care about our brilliant musicians.

Remember the vibrations at the Capital Centre (or any large rock arena), the pin-drop quietness of the Cellar Door (or any other small, intimate music club), and the taste of the Dom Perignon and catering backstage (if you were lucky enough to slip past the guards)? This book might be like being on a long-distance phone call with old friends. It's a story of the birth of an industry, wild times, artistic drama, gifted musicians, and true love with an astonishing musical soundtrack that radiates creative restlessness.

I recently very much enjoyed *Wild Tales,* the very cool memoir of my good friend Graham Nash. He and many other exceptional singer-songwriters have published their autobiographies, and many of them were guests on my radio shows. Their examples helped me pull this collection of stories and interviews together, reminding me of so much I had forgotten in my rich and eventful life. The memories rush back.

So this book goes out to the truckers, the mad hatters, the ships at sea, and especially . . . (whisper) the little ladies of the night. Hang on. Here we go.

CHAPTER 1

Growing Up

In the beginning I was allergic to everything—except music.

My birth mother was from Boston. The only thing I know about her is that she asked a doctor to find me a new home. I have tried to discover who she was and what became of her, but she covered her tracks very well. My adoptive parents, Mabel Evelyn Chapin and Chester Fremont Colwell, were in their early forties. We lived in a modest house in the town of Winchester, a Boston suburb. I heard roosters crowing every morning, since our neighbor behind us had a barn. I smelled fresh hay when I raked the leaves with my dad.

Chester was an engineer for Cuneo Press of New England/ Ginn & Company publishers in nearby Cambridge, one of the most successful high school and college textbook printers in America. Mabel was an artist and housewife. Their only biological

Me, age nine
Credit: © Cerphe Archive

child had died one day after his delivery. He made it possible for me to become a Colwell. I am very grateful to that little departed soul.

My mom was a descendant of Samuel Chapin, who sailed from England to the colony of Massachusetts in 1642. For history buffs, Winchester was one of the towns that Paul Revere galloped through on his famed "Midnight Ride" through Cambridge and Boston. The late singer/songwriter Harry Chapin and I were second cousins. I still see Harry's brother, Tom, from time to time.

I loved my parents very much. They were supportive of whatever I wanted to do. There weren't many rules growing up in Casa Colwell.

Asthma-Cadabra

Asthma and allergies often kept me sidelined. It didn't help that Chester, or "Chet" as he was called, had a woodworking shop in the basement and was generating wood dust in the evening hours while he chain-smoked Winstons. My mom would yell at him, "Quit smoking in the house," and he'd joke, "I am not smoking in the house. I'm smoking in the basement."

Pop loved to smoke and take family road trips. In the summer, he'd pile us into our Ford Galaxy 500 and head to Lake Massasecum in Merrimack County, New Hampshire. In the fall, we'd drive through southern Vermont to enjoy the foliage. My mom, being a proper New Englander, dressed me according to the calendar, not the weather. Come September 1, no matter if it was seventy-eight degrees outside, it was wide-wale corduroy, flannel shirts, and cable knit sweaters for me. I'd be in the back seat swaddled in my hot garb with the windows rolled tight and Chet lighting one cigarette after another. Ugh.

In those days it seemed like every adult smoked. Our family doctor, whom we only saw when he made house calls, smoked while he took my temperature. Everyone on TV and in the movies smoked. Smoking was an addictive nicotine itch that many were scratching. I, too, smoked when I got to prep school, but I eventually learned that it's better not to scratch certain itches.

All that smoking, paint fumes, and a giant bowl of chocolate ice cream after most meals didn't seem to hurt my dad any. Pop lived to be ninety-one and was going strong right to the end, proving something I'd surmised years earlier. Chet was the exception, not the rule. And then there was my mother's devotion to hand-painted china. She had a very active kiln and elevated its use in our home from a hobby to a local home-grown business. Large boxes of plain white china arrived from Europe several times a year to be hand-painted and fired. We had a big table where students—young women like herself—came for lessons. They paid a small fee to learn how to decorate and bake china. It was a serious process that included dipping china in acid. Dad helped with this dangerous process, and his protective gear gave him the Dr. Frankenstein look. Dad installed

Mabel, Chet, and me. The Colwells, 1978
Credit: © Cerphe Archive/Robert A. Salazar

3

a button at the top of the steps for us to summon him if needed when he was doing his acid thing.

I suggested to my Mom that she charge her students more money for the china lessons, but Mother Mabel didn't care so much about extra money. She was an artist and she did it for the art. She loved sharing her talents with others. Again, she was a Chapin, whose family line has long been known for their artistry, music, and creativity.

My mom was a no-nonsense woman hailing from a lineage of no-nonsense women, but she had her girlish moments, too. Whenever I asked Pop for something, he usually replied, "We'll see." Mom would often say, "We'll see means yes," and look at me with a little grin. God, I loved those two.

I would eventually discover that the only Colwell in the house who liked making money would be me. The other two Colwells were pretty much satisfied with their material possessions, and fortunately, loving me was their greatest joy.

Odd Fellows and Dr. Spock

Dad was a devoted member of the International Order of Odd Fellows, a fraternal group originating in eighteenth-century England that helped people for the benefit of mankind. This was considered "odd" at the time. And you weren't supposed to draw much recognition to your humanitarian efforts. That's why other Odd Fellows, like President Franklin D. Roosevelt, comedic actor Charlie Chaplin, and the first US female dentist, Lucy Hobbs Taylor, to name a few, kept their membership on the down low. Dad's activity in the Odd Fellows was just one reason I often looked up to him as being somewhat "saintly."

My dad worked for a publishing company, so we had a nice library at home. Early on, I noticed a book around eye-level on the shelves with a cute baby on the cover. It was *Baby and Child Care*. On the flipside was a picture of the author, Dr. Benjamin Spock. I thought he looked a lot like my dad. Dr. Spock prescribed a new way to raise kids. He believed that parents' "natural loving care" for their children was the most important ingredient in the recipe for parenting. He urged parents to have confidence in their own abilities. Trust their common sense. He was convinced that parents' instincts were usually best. My parents followed his advice. I'm part of the Spock generation.

Now, let's fast forward to May 1, 1971. I had started my career as a radio personality/DJ with a Bethesda radio station, WHFS. By then, demonstrations against the Vietnam War were ever-present in the news of the day. People would come from all over the world to participate in the protests in the nation's capital. The May Day demonstration was huge. I covered the event for my station. Strange but true, the Beach Boys were one of the acts that played in West Potomac Park, where 35,000 protesters congregated. Other acts supporting the cause were Redbone, Phil Ochs, McKendree Spring, Livingston Taylor, Country Joe McDonald, and local bands like Claude Jones.

The protesters' goal was to close down the government, or at least traffic in DC. They didn't. But more than 7,000 protesters were arrested on the first day alone—the largest number of arrests in a single day in US history—with 6,000 more during the three-day event, for a total of more than 13,000 arrestees.

Many arrested protesters ended up behind a chain-link fence in a practice field used by the Washington Redskins at Robert F. Kennedy Stadium. By the fence, I suddenly caught a glimpse of Dr. Benjamin Spock. I knew he was against the war but was surprised he was locked up.

There he was in a gray suit, still looking a lot like my dad. I managed to get an interview with him through the fence.

Dr. Spock told me: "As a physician, I've helped parents raise healthy and happy babies who are now being slaughtered in a war that's illegal, immoral, unwinnable, and detrimental to the best interests of the United

States." As for the practice field, he said, "Calling this a concentration camp would be a very appropriate description."

I was one of those babies he spoke of. I too had been called for the draft but rejected for military service because of my asthma. Knowing I could have easily been one of those statistics, his logic really spoke to me. I remember his deep, comforting voice when I interviewed him. I felt grounded by what he said. I understood that part of who I was resulted from his ethics.

Cabin Boy

My dad built me a small cabin in the backyard when I was nine years old. This was a solid structure with concrete slab floor, pitched roof, and windows. I had shelves for my seashell and rock collections. My neighborhood friends, Larry, Rick, Bruce, and Kenny would hang out in my clubhouse. We got battery-operated walkie-talkies that could broadcast from a block or so away. My dad made us a "Fort Apache" sign, and we thought we were a cross between cowboys and pirates, a real badass club.

Everything was going great until my buddy Larry went on a summer vacation with his parents to Pennsylvania. He "borrowed" a few walkie-talkies, including mine.

I was so pissed when I found out that I unilaterally kicked him out of the club. I eventually got the walkie-talkies back, but he was still excommunicated from the Fort Apache badasses.

Larry lived directly across the street from my house, so it was impossible to avoid him. But he was out of the club for good. I barely spoke to him forever after. I came to discover that this is a Cerphe character flaw. For too many years I was like that: you got one chance with me, and that was it.

It would be later when I was at WJFK and had to manage G. Gordon Liddy, Don Geronimo, and Mike O'Meara that I learned to be more forgiving.

6

Young figure-skating champion Laurence Owen (deemed America's next figure-skating queen) was my next-door neighbor. She lived on one side of Smith Pond and I lived on the other side. As often as we could, the neighborhood posse, Laurence, and I would head to frozen Smith Pond to skate and goof around. To this day, I can't believe her skating-royalty parents (Canadian figure skating champion Guy Owen and nine-time US women's champion and Olympian Maribel Vinson Owen) were happy to see their daughter out there yukkin' it up with a bunch of preteen hockey players. But there she was, all grace and elegance, skating circles around us, and leaping clear of uneven ice and cat o'nine tails that had frozen hard into the surface. The rest of us weren't so lucky with those.

I once tripped and busted my elbow so hard on the ice that it grew to the size of a grapefruit. I walked home, thinking my sweater had bunched up on my arm. But when I peeled my coat off, what I found was a giant broken elbow in need of a cast. Not too long after that, Laurence, her mother and sister, and thirty-one other figure skaters, parents, coaches, and judges were killed in a plane crash on their way to the 1961 World Championships in Brussels. It still makes me well up thinking about it, but I know in my heart that beautiful Laurence is skating in heaven, leaping over cat o'nine tails on Smith Pond. She was so happy there: not an Olympian, not a champion . . . just one of the gang.

Crazy G

Celebrities in the town of Winchester were rare, but we had TV star Frank Fontaine, also known as "Crazy Guggenheim," the nutty drunk with the funny laugh in the "Joe the Bartender" sketches on the *Jackie Gleason* TV show. Frank lived with his wife, Alma, and eight kids in a very stately house on Highland Avenue. He'd cruise down the street in his 1960 baby-blue Thunderbird convertible, smiling, waving, and always with a great tan. The tan came from Miami, Florida, sunshine, where the Gleason show originated.

Frank dropped his act when Gleason asked him to sing. His rich baritone earned him a Number 1 album, the 1963 *Songs I Sing on the Jackie Gleason Show.*

He had to sell his twelve-room house in 1971 to pay an IRS tax debt. He died at fifty-eight of a heart attack in 1978. His stately house is now the Winchester Community Music School, providing musical education and performances for the community.

Other Winchester celebs were Mr. and Mrs. Schrafft, owners of a Charlestown, Massachusetts, candy company with over fifty stores. Artist Andy Warhol appeared in a Schrafft TV commercial in 1968. An interesting choice of spokesperson! Parents gave Schrafft candy as Christmas presents. It was delicious.

Imagine the excitement of us kids on Halloween going to the Schrafft house for trick or treat. Except they didn't give out Schrafft's candy there. They gave out *shit* candy. It seemed to be candy that survived many previous Halloweens. You could break your jaw trying to chew that crap. Are you kidding me? I should have gone *Full Metal Jacket* on the Shrafts for giving us bad candy. Couldn't you have spared some of the good stuff, Mrs. Schrafft?

I recently discovered that Brad Whitford, rhythm guitarist for the rock band Aerosmith, is also a Winchester native. Who knew?

As a kid, I listened to WBZ, a powerhouse Boston AM radio station with a 50,000-watt signal. Dick Summer was the evening DJ with his *Night Light* show. Summer had a live Venus flytrap plant in his studio. He would talk to the plant as if it responded to him. He'd create stories interesting enough to reel little ten-year-old me into his "theater of the mind."

Dick would go on to pioneer the softer side of album rock, and by 1968 was a big booster of "the Bosstown Sound" with local psychedelic bands like the Beacon Street Union, Orpheus, and Ultimate Spinach.

I'd be snuggled in my bed listening to Summer weave elaborate stories into song introductions on my Motorola transistor radio:

"What have I got to offer you? Not a Cadillac. This is Dick Summer on Night Light Radio 103 WBZ with my question: 'How would you spend your time if you knew next September would be the end of the world? How do you think the world might really end when it gets around to it? Or when it stops getting around to it, what would we say?'

"And don't forget to start spreading the rumor that the world will really end this September, and let me know the reaction of the people you tell this to. How would you spend your remaining days if the world really ends? Send your stories to me at WBZ. And here's how Gale Garnett will spend her last days. She'll 'Sing in the Sunshine' and get a nice tan."

I've valued these memories of Summer's work throughout my career. His creativity was an inspiration, an example of how a DJ could develop a distinctive on-air presence, create moods, and draw the listener in.

I'm with the Band

The 1962 *Dance with the Guitar Man* by Duane Eddy was the first record album I ever bought. I saw Duane on Dick Clark's *American Bandstand* TV show and loved his low, twangy guitar leads on songs like "Peter Gunn" and "Rebel Rouser." Inducted into the Rock and Roll Hall of Fame in 1994, Eddy was bestowed the title of "Titan of Twang" by the mayor of Nashville in 2000. Now, that's cool.

Many guitarists have credited Eddy as an influence, including Bruce Springsteen, Hank Marvin (the Shadows), Bob Bogle (the Ventures), Adrian Belew (King Crimson), and George Harrison.

Speaking of Beatle George, eleven years passed after the Fab Four made their 1964 US debut on the *Ed Sullivan Show* before I got to actually meet and befriend The Beatles' lead guitarist. Yet, it was only minutes after that show that I knew that I wanted a guitar and to join a band. The Beatles changed my world. It's hard to find the words to describe their impact.

I'm certainly not alone. Steven Van Zandt of the E Street Band once told me, "This was the main event of my life, and it was certainly the major event for many others, whether or not they knew it at the time. It was no less dramatic than aliens landing on the planet. . . ." Billy Joel once confessed, "The Beatles really synthesized what I wanted to do. The single biggest moment that I can remember being galvanized into wanting to be a musician for life was seeing The Beatles on the *Ed Sullivan Show*." Nancy Wilson of the band Heart cites this TV moment as "hearing the call to become a rock musician." She was seven years old.

Writer Kurt Vonnegut once observed that the "plausible mission of an artist is to make people appreciate being alive." When asked if he knew of any artists that actually pulled that off, Vonnegut replied, "The Beatles did."

Getting a guitar was the easy part. I needed only two weeks. My dad bought me a Sears and Roebuck Silvertone electric guitar. Mine was the 1448 model, in which the amplifier and speaker were built in to the guitar case. This was the starter guitar for thousands of beginners, including Bob Dylan in 1958 and Jimi Hendrix in 1956. Jimi named his Silvertone "Betty Jean." Pete Townshend used to buy them in bulk so he could cost-effectively smash them at the end of Who concerts. He wasn't about to destroy a pricey Fender Strat every night.

As for a band to join, I was lucky that some older friends started a group called the Luvlace Lads. I switched to playing bass. "Louie, Louie" became my symphony.

Skiing through School

When high school time came, I applied to Kents Hill, a Methodist-affiliated boarding school in Maine. One of my older, cooler friends had gone there and raved about it. He was usually right on most things he recommended. I was skipping quite a lot of school with the Luvlace

Lads, yet I was smart enough to realize I was spinning my wheels in public school. I needed a good education.

Founded in 1826 by an American Revolution veteran, Colonel Luther Sampson, Kents Hill is one of America's oldest continuously operating coeducational college prep schools. Colonel Sampson was a direct descendant of an original Pilgrim who had landed at Plymouth Rock in 1622. We're talking some *old* rock history here.

I loved Kents Hill. The students were friendly and innovative. We were part of the first generation that was turning on in the sixties—both literally, as in getting high, and philosophically to new ideas beyond the conformity of the fifties. The faculty encouraged the same values I learned from my parents, like altruism, compassion, and tolerance. And it was coed. The alpine skiing wasn't bad either. Hiking and biking trails of stunning natural beauty surrounded the 400-acre campus. At Kents Hill, I began to feel like everything was possible.

By senior year, I was lovesick. When I learned my girlfriend was attending American University in Washington, DC, I decide to follow her. We both started full-time classes at AU in September 1967. Because of my previous time at boarding school, my early college experience wasn't typical of many of my fellow students who were living away from home for the first time. But one new experience we shared was freedom. At Kents Hill, you attended classes, no matter what. The only excuses for missing class were (a) you were dying, or (b) you were dead. In college, you can sleep off too much weekend fun.

My room on the fifth floor of McDowell Hall was close to the elevators where the pay telephones hung like slot machines. Too close. The chimes of dimes and quarters dropping into those phones went on day and night as students phoned home. Those sounds and memories are etched in my mind. I'm always reminded of those days when I hear the opening of Pink Floyd's classic rock song "Money."

11

I enrolled as an art major and began taking life drawing, painting, and sculpture classes. I was tapping into my inner Leonardo da Vinci. Both female and male nude models were available for life drawing. They would drop trou—a new experience for me. My favorite was an older African American model, Geneva. Her bare body was sagging and weathered. It wasn't what would conventionally be called beautiful, but she was. I still treasure my drawings of Geneva.

These naked modeling experiences remind me of a quip by actor Sean Connery. When asked if he ever got an erection during a sex scene, he replied "I'm ashamed if I get aroused, and I'm sorry if I don't."

CHAPTER 2

Graduation Day

Music and concerts were popping in DC when I arrived. I learned my way around clubs like Mac's Pipe and Drum, Crazy Horse, and the Cellar Door. I would later know Jack Boyle, the owner of these clubs. There's more about the business-savvy Boyle and his Cellar Door Productions in Chapter 15.

I made friends who introduced me to their friends and soon we were all ricocheting throughout the scene. I actually auditioned for the band, the Hangmen as a lead singer. They had scored with their hit, "What a Girl Can't Do." Their drummer, Bob Berberich, later became Nils' Lofgren's drummer in his first band. At my audition I sang Smokey Robinson's "Tracks of My Tears." I was terrible.

Another early concert memory is when Chuck Berry came to perform at AU. A fellow female classmate slept with Chuck after the show. My friend was really stressed that people would hear about her one-nighter, especially the two people she called parents.

Chuck was well-known for blowing into a town expecting the concert promoter to provide two Fender Twin Reverb amps and a local band to back him up. Never a hard task, as just about every kid in the sixties had grooved to Chuck Berry. It was an honor to be asked to play with the legend. Chuck was also known for getting his fee paid in cash in advance of the performance. He would meet with the promoter several hours before show time and carry the cash in his guitar case back to his hotel room. Old school rock and roll economics.

Years later, at Georgetown University's McDonough Arena, DC's Bill Holland and Rent's Due were chosen to back Chuck, and I was invited to play on several of the opening songs. Chuck came out of his dressing room a few minutes before showtime and stood with us in the darkness backstage. We'd had no rehearsal and no time with Chuck beforehand to discuss sets. We didn't even have a set list. We all just figured he'd surely tell us before we went on. No such luck. The lights went down and we made our way to the stage. I was walking next to Chuck and asked, "What are you opening with?" He said, "A Chuck Berry song!" My heart flopped over in my chest. But then he hit the first few bars of "Johnny B. Goode" and we all jumped in. Thankfully, we knew Chuck's songs by heart, but it was still nerve-wracking not to have a plan. During the entire performance, the band had to watch Chuck's hands on his guitar to know what key the songs were in. I couldn't see anybody's hands so I was truly flying in the dark. Bruce Springsteen and Keith Richards tell a similar story about Chuck, so I'm in excellent company.

Natty Bumpo and the Fallen Angels were other bands I met and admired. Natty Bumpo had played with Jimi Hendrix at his 1967 DC debut at the Ambassador Theatre on 18th and Columbia Road, DC's short-lived answer to Bill Graham's psychedelic Fillmore Auditoriums. Jimi played five nights for a total of $1,500. Six months later, he packed the Washington Hilton ballroom for two shows. He picked up a $7,500 check, but on his way out through the secret exit—the same one that President Reagan used the day he was shot—Jimi said to the promoter, Durwood Settles, "I should have asked for a percentage."

The Ambassador occupied the same location as the old Knickerbocker Theatre. One of DC's worst disasters was the Knickerbocker's roof caving in from a snowstorm, killing 98 and injuring 123 attendees in 1922.

Both the theater architect and owner committed suicide in the aftermath of this tragedy.

The Fallen Angels were one of the more creative of the early bands I saw. Jack Lauritsen on guitar, Jack Bryant on lead vocals and bass, Wally Cook on lead guitar, John "Thumper" Molloy on drums, and Howard Danchik on keys. As an amateur guitarist, I was always enamored by the keyboard players. Dorm life wasn't that glamorous and Howard's parents lived in a Northwest DC neighborhood, not far from J. Edgar Hoover's house. I would hang with Howard at his parents' house and listen to music. He and I have remained good friends since those days gone by.

Claude Jones

Claude Jones was another great band in DC. They were our Grateful Dead. Here are some memories from the perspective of their manager, Michael Oberman:

"One day the band's drummer, Reggie Brisbane, came in to Chuck Levin's Washington Music Center and recognized me as the music columnist for the *Washington Star*. I had a small office in Chuck's store, shared with band booking agent Barry Rick. Barry was getting gigs for local bands like the Nowhere Men. I'd get office space for free because Chuck Levin wanted these musicians to come into his store and buy equipment.

"Reggie asked me to hear his band rehearse in their Military Road group house. I was blown away, especially by vocalist Joe Triplett, who sang lead on the Hangmen's "What a Girl Can't Do." I became their manager, while continuing to write my column for the *Evening Star* newspaper. Claude Jones was the sole band I'd defer to fellow *Star* writers Charlie McCollum and Boris Weintraub to cover.

"Claude Jones, collectively, was a socialist/communist group when it came to money and living arrangements. Every member of the band got paid $1 per gig. The rest of the money went to pay rent, food, cigarettes, and marijuana. They wanted me to live in their house to reduce my commission, but I wouldn't move in.

"We had a deal with a famous DC cardiologist, Dr. Michael Halberstam, who loved the band. He'd give free health care for everyone in the band in return for playing two gigs a year for him: one for a liberal political group and the other for a personal party he would throw. It was great because you could go to his office and he'd take care of your health, and then you might ask him for a script for Valium or whatever.

"I kept Halberstam as my physician after Claude Jones broke up. Unfortunately, in 1980, he was shot twice in the chest during a burglary in his house. He insisted on driving himself to nearby Sibley hospital despite being wounded. On the way there, he sees the burglar running through the neighborhood. Michael hops some bushes and runs him over. Turns out that the burglar was an escaped convict named Bernard Welch, one of the biggest cat burglars in DC history, with a home in Potomac, Maryland, that included a smelting oven where he could melt down the gold he stole. Dr. Halberstam died of his wounds. His funeral was attended by thousands of people who loved him. Welch got 143 years in prison, and died there in 1997.

"To friends and associates, Claude Jones was collectively known as the Amoeba. At any given gig, there might be five musicians on stage or there could be up to thirteen. Their roadie might hop on stage and sing 'Not Fade Away.' Keith Krokyn, their road manager, might play a guiro. We would sell out Mike Schreibman's Emergency club often. We had great original songs and much interest from record companies.

"There was so much interest that Mercury recording company Vice President Irwin Steinberg and President Irving Green flew in to hear them at the Emergency. After listening, they came to me and said, "We want this band.""

16

"So I agreed to meet them in New York to begin negotiations. The band, having this socialistic, anti-corporate philosophy, wanted a few of their band members to accompany me. This was a mistake.

"Mercury was offering $40,000 for an album deal with a second album option.

"Band members pretty much scotched the deal. They thought Mercury was part of 'the war machine,' and said so at our band meeting.

"I said, 'Guys, this is a lot of money, but if it doesn't work out, then your lives aren't over.' But the band said no to Mercury.

"One of the people who would have been involved with the Mercury deal told me about another fellow named Don Johnson (not the *Miami Vice* actor). Don had some money and loved Claude Jones. Don agreed to invest in the band so they could record an extended play (EP) record. With this underway, Don was pulled over during a traffic violation and the police discovered 2,000 hits of LSD in his car.

"Meanwhile Kroykn and I found a farmer, 'Old Man' Carter, who would rent a farm to a hippie band with a black drummer. It was a huge farmhouse and over 100 acres for $200 a month. The only caveat is that farmer Carter would keep some of his cows and peacocks on the land. So Claude Jones moved to this farm.

"The farm went really well until I get a call from Milan Melvin. Milan is Mimi Farina's brother-in-law, and Mimi is Joan Baez's sister. Milan says, 'We are looking for a farm near Washington. There are 165 of us called the Medicine Ball Caravan. We're traveling across the country and we have a bunch of music groups, including Alice Cooper. We want to pitch eleven 30-foot-high tie-dyed teepees. We're doing a concert in DC. And by the way, French movie director François Reichenbach will be along filming the entire thing.' By the way, the movie director's assistant was Martin Scorsese.

"The band thought this would be fun so we said we'd meet them outside a gas station in Culpeper, Virginia, to guide them to the farm. So the Caravan pulls up with a psychedelic painted bus flying Viet Cong flags, and a sign reading 'We've come for your daughters.'

"Warner Brothers was paying for the movie, and wanted us to take the entire Caravan folks for a nude swim on the nearby Rappahannock River.

"That was the beginning of the end for the Claude Jones farm. All of a sudden, there were state police in helicopters circling our farm every day. The cops told someone to tell us that if we weren't growing marijuana on the farm, then they would find some anyway.

"When Claude Jones gave up the farm, Nils Lofgren moved in."

Professor Gene Davis

Music at that time wasn't just a *part* of our lives; it was *shaping* our lives. We'd hear about imminent records by our heroes like John Lennon, the Stones, Joni Mitchell, and others and we'd wait weeks for these records to hit the stores. Then we'd rush out to buy the records and listen to them a hundred times to take it all in. Personally, I was a believer and I was trying to incorporate the spirit and the ideas I heard in the music into my daily living.

I also spent free time in college doing art history research. I was a regular at the Library of Congress or wandering around the Corcoran, Freer, or the National Gallery of Art.

I was also incredibly fortunate to study painting with arguably the most famous Washington, DC painter ever, Gene Davis.

A DC native born in 1920, Professor Gene's enduring fame is that he cofounded what is now known as the "Washington Color School" of abstract painting. You would likely recognize his iconic paintings, characterized by very colorful repetitive stripes. One of his most famous, *Black Grey Beat* (Acrylic, 1964) is in the Smithsonian American Art

Museum. Another outstanding work is *Sun Sonata,* composed of tubes filled with color backlit by a black light, commissioned by the College of William and Mary. Although never formally trained, Gene was an artist first, and my professor second. He shaved his head in the 1950s, so he had that Yul Brynner look ("because I thought it was a good thing to do," he would explain). He cruised the campus in a white Jaguar XKE. To me, he represented freedom. Proof that you should try to do anything you could imagine. Freedom in all of its possibilities and permutations was an idea that was in the air, and one that really drew me in.

Before art, Gene had been a Washington Redskins sportswriter and then a journalist covering Presidents Roosevelt and Truman. He was Harry Truman's sometime poker partner. He was a major influence in my life.

In 1985, he passed away at the age of sixty-four. I sincerely regret that I never circled back to tell him how much he meant to me before he died. I also regret that I never bought a painting from him back then. They go for upward of $150,000 these days. He probably would have given me one.

My experience with Gene has another prescient twist. He requested we bring in our favorite music to listen to in the classroom while we painted. I came in the next day with my copies of *Buffalo Springfield Again,* Jefferson Airplane's *Surrealistic Pillow,* and Paul Butterfield Blues Band's *East-West.* Another student brought in some forgettable poppy stuff, and someone contributed *Whipped Cream & Other Delights* by Herb Alpert and the Tijuana Brass to this strange brew. I remember thinking that our collective music experience would have been considerably better if I were controlling the playlist.

Radio Active

I next moved to a nearby Chevy Chase, Maryland, group house. One roommate was AU student Steve Walker, three years older, a theater major, and a right-on renaissance guy. Steve, more beatnik than hippie, wore a goatee. He was brilliant playing Lenny in AU's production of Steinbeck's *Of Mice and Men*.

Steve and I shared this love of new music. He had worked a very short stint at radio station WHMC-AM 1150 in Gaithersburg, Maryland, with DJ Barry Richards. Originally "the boss with the hot sauce" on stations WINX and WUST, Richards became a "heavy music" radio pioneer when his nightly *Underground Show* debuted in September 1968 on WHMC.

When Steve left WHMC, he invited me to check out his new part-time radio job at a Bethesda radio station up the street. It had a split format then in the winter of 1969: easy listening music like Frank Sinatra, Peggy Lee, the Dorsey Brothers, and so on during the daylight hours and from 7:00 p.m. to dawn, it was rock and roll or anything else the DJs fancied. The owners gave Steve a late-night shot at playing whatever he wanted. "Let the inmates run the asylum," so to speak.

Steve said, "Cerphe, I'm doing this WHFS show. You love music. Why don't you sit in with me? Maybe I can get you a job."

Never imagining being a broadcaster, I hitchhiked up Wisconsin Avenue (we all hitchhiked everywhere in those days, kids) and sat in with Steve at 'HFS for about two weeks. We brought our favorite records to play, and had a conversational "on air" style. It was the same way we talked in the group house we shared.

Speaking of style, I have never thought it was the sound of the voice that made a broadcaster special. It was their attitude and what he or she said and played that I cared about.

Steve taught me everything about radio, like how to cue a record and run those ancient turntables at 'HFS. I recall that he liked to play Blood, Sweat & Tears (before David Clayton-Thomas came in) and the Blues Project, to name two. I was mesmerized. Steve truly was my first radio mentor.

At that time, I never really listened much to the radio, including American University's famed WAMU, where the Joy Boys—Willard Scott and Eddie Walker—did their first student broadcasts. I never even visited the campus building where the WAMU studio operated. I mainly saw live music and listened to records.

I learned about Spiritus Cheese. They were Joshua Brooks, who had worked briefly as a traffic manager and producer at 106.7 WRVR in New York, Josh's friend Mark Gorbulew, and Mark's girlfriend, Sarah Vass, all Bard College grads. The three decided to start a radio show and figured someone would hire them. WHFS didn't exactly hire them, but rather sold them time on the station. Their show earned a new crop of listeners to 'HFS. So many, in fact, that the *Washington Post* ran a story by Paul Richard on the success of Spiritus Cheese. Richard reported that the station had jumped from 800 listeners a night to 22,000. Their popularity persuaded the station management to shift from piecemeal popular to a full-time progressive radio format. 'HFS revoked Spiritus Cheese's buying time, and hired them as full-time DJs. Mark and Sarah soon left 'HFS but Josh stayed for eleven years.

After two weeks hanging with Steve on-air, he brought me in to meet one of the owners: Jacob "Jake" Einstein, a former Baltimore news guy, older gentleman, and genuine character. I got the impression that Jake had problems with Spiritus Cheese.

Jake hired me on a handshake. That's how I began my radio career at station WHFS: Washington's High Fidelity Stereo radio. To show how loose it was, I didn't know that you needed a Federal Communications Commission license to be a broadcaster. Jake never asked me. The station was fined $1,000 by the FCC when they discovered that nobody bothered to confirm that I did or didn't have a broadcasting license.

It was obvious to me that I had a lot to learn about doing radio.

CHAPTER 3

Childe Harold:
Wild Billy's Circus

Nineteen seventy-three was a transformational year in America. The Vietnam War ended and the troops came home. The Senate Watergate hearings began, and President Nixon told the nation he wasn't a crook. The Apollo moon landings ended.

And all over the world, events grabbed the headlines. Egypt and Syria attacked Israel on Israel's highest holy day, Yom Kippur. Arab oil producers hiked prices. The value of the dollar dropped 10 percent. Secretariat, one of the greatest thoroughbred racehorses of all time, became the first Triple Crown winner in twenty-five years. And get this: the Bahamas gained independence from Great Britain.

Yes, it was a long time ago. Musically, all of the ex-Beatles had solo Top Ten hits: "My Love" (Paul), "Give Me Love" (George), "Mind Games" (John), and "Photograph" (Ringo). Roberta Flack scored big with "The First Time Ever I Saw Your Face" after performing for years at Mr. Henry's bar on Capitol Hill. Another DC native, Marvin Gaye, followed his masterpiece "What's Going On" with the sexually evocative *Let's Get It On* album, the best-selling record of his Motown tenure.

Yet another Washingtonian, jazz genius Duke Ellington, published his autobiography, *Music Is My Mistress* (Ellington wrote that he took his first piano lessons from a Mrs. Clinkscales. You can't make this up.) Bob Marley—with Eric Clapton's help—shot the sheriff and introduced reggae to an international audience. Edgar Winter's "Frankenstein" galumphed to the Number 1 spot on the Billboard 100. Pink Floyd released *Dark Side of the Moon*. A double-billed Grateful Dead and Allman Brothers concert rocked RFK Stadium.

With shoulder-length hair and making $125 a week, I was "broadcasting from high atop the Triangle Towers" in Bethesda, Maryland, from 7:00 p.m. to midnight. It was my third year of an eight-year run helping the 'HFS mission to expose listeners to progressive music.

The artists we were playing at the start of 1973 included Little Feat, the Paul Butterfield Blues Band, Tom Waits, Mahavishnu Orchestra, Bruce Springsteen, Sonny Terry and Brownie McGee, Paul Horn, Jerry Jeff Walker, The Allman Brothers Band, Jean-Luc Ponty, Emmylou Harris, Leo Kottke, Eric Dolphy, and the *Steelyard Blues* movie soundtrack. The price for any one of the entire stock of 45 rpm singles at nearby Record City on Fairmont Ave was fifty-five cents each.

Early on at 'HFS I emceed a Leon Russell concert at the old Painters Mill venue in Owings Mill, Maryland. Elton John was the opening act.

Elton was basically the new guy opening for Leon, who had been a studio musician for years but became a big deal after after George Harrison's *Concert for Bangladesh*. I took pictures of Elton backstage. I really liked his early music. *Tumbleweed Connection* is a masterpiece. Critics

Elton John at Painters Mill Music Fair, 1973.
Credit: © Cerphe Colwell/Cerphe Archive

23

agree and it's listed among *Rolling Stone*'s 500 greatest albums of all time. By the way, Bob Dylan played a sold-out show at Painter's Mill in 1991. Mary Chapin Carpenter's guitarist John Jennings opened for Bob. Then the place burned down two weeks later. Sadly, John passed away on October 15, 2015, from a prolonged battle with kidney cancer. Among his many credits are the eight albums he produced for Carpenter.

Other DC radio stations like WWDC, WEAM, WPGC, and WINX were killing it (not) with "Dueling Banjos," and "On the Cover of the Rolling Stone" by Dr. Hook and the Medicine Show.

Ragamuffin Gunner

In 1973, one of our CBS record reps, Earl Rollison, brought us copies of a new record. It was *Greetings from Asbury Park, NJ,* by an artist that none of us had heard before: Bruce Springsteen. I was hooked after one song. Like Bob Dylan, Bruce was a storyteller with a cool look and a poet vibe but also wasn't like Dylan at all. Bob is a chameleon who invented himself from a small-town Minnesota upbringing. Dylan's songs had a broad perspective and sounded like they were written for all of us. The subjects of Bruce's early songs were specific people playing out life's struggles and triumphs, and like a good novel, they created vivid pictures in your mind. He sang about cars, girls, and redemption and it spoke to me on a deeply personal level. One of the songs on that album, "Growin' Up," was a musical vignette of what my cohort and I were experiencing in the moment. It also held the promise of what was to come.

Bruce's next album, *The Wild, The Innocent & The E Street Shuffle,* featured the songs "4th of July, Asbury Park (Sandy)," "Incident on 57th Street," and the romantic, cinematic "New York City Serenade" with lyrics as haunting and melancholy as an Edward Hopper painting.

At that time, there were just a handful of radio stations in America like WHFS playing Bruce and other new, progressive, and freeform music. In Philadelphia, there was WMMR. The guy there doing what I was doing in DC was Ed Schiaky. Ed loved Bruce like I did and followed all his concerts in Philly and Jersey. Ed also befriended a young and then-unknown Billy Joel. Ed played Billy's first album, *Cold Spring Harbor,* on WMMR, and the two became friends. Other artists he helped along their way were David Bowie, Janis Ian, and Yes. Ed passed away in 2004 and took with him some of the greatest stories in rock and roll.

On Cleveland station WMMS 100.7, "The Buzzard" was Kid Leo. In addition to Bruce, Kid Leo is credited for breaking many artists in the Cleveland market, including Southside Johnny, John Mellencamp, Roxy Music, Cyndi Lauper, the New York Dolls, and the Pretenders.

While at WMMS, Kid Leo was also instrumental in bringing the Rock and Roll Hall of Fame to Cleveland. You can see his on-air work as part of the permanent radio exhibit in the Rock Hall. Today, he is program director and afternoon disc jockey on Little Steven's *Underground Garage* on Sirius XM Radio (Channel 21).

On New York's WABC was Vin Scelsa. On Boston station WBCN was a DJ named Maxanne Sartori. She was a huge Bruce fan and had Bruce and the band in the studio for a very early interview.

We were all part of the very small first group of on-air Bruce disciples and, with the exception of WMMS, we were all East Coast stations. Other stations had modified playlists, which means they didn't have to play specific songs in order, but I don't think any were as freeform as WHFS. I walked into the studio every day with a stack of records under my arm and said and played whatever the hell I felt like.

I once caught two thugs trying to steal my car. I grabbed a black and very real-looking squirt gun from under the car seat and chased them down a Georgetown street in my clogs. I caught one and beat the shit out of him. That was in the morning. That afternoon all the songs were about cars and thieves and fighting in the streets. Bruce's songs made me feel like he was writing and singing about what he saw and felt and believed in too. I had a brother-in-arms.

All of us would have agreed that Bruce had a seasoned bar band sensibility. Rockin' a bar band was his job with early groups like The Castiles and Steel Mill since 1968.

"I made a living in New Jersey doing the bars and playing what other people wanted to hear," Bruce told me later when I interviewed him on my program.

Bruce had broken up Steel Mill in 1971 to move to New York City to play his own music solo in clubs. That's where he found and signed with his manager, Mike Appel. Mike got Bruce an audition with the legendary John Hammond II, record producer and talent scout, who had already discovered legends like Billie Holliday, Pete Seeger, Count Basie, and Bob Dylan. After Hammond signed him to CBS, Bruce returned to the Jersey shore to re-form his band and cherry pick the best players he knew. I have often thanked bluesman John Hammond, Jr., for his father's amazing ear.

Bruce emerged from this bar band genre and began writing his own songs. Quiet, introspective ballads like "Mary, Queen of Arkansas" and musical narratives like "Sprit in the Night," which tells the story of a group of teenagers, Crazy Janey, Mission Man, Hazy Davy, Killer Joe, and Wild Billy reveling in youth and friendship at Greasy Lake. *Greetings from Asbury Park, NJ* had texture. It was a youthful blend of pessimism, optimism, and romanticism. It also had accordion. In 1973, the only place you'd hear accordion was on *The Lawrence Welk Show* and in polka bands. But there it was, on Bruce's debut album, with E Street Band's Danny Federici playing his heart out . . . beautiful, haunting, and different. *Outside the box* wasn't a term we used back then but it's appropriate. I found the album more than interesting. It was intriguing and addictive.

"Blinded by the Light" was a standout song and intended to be the hit single. It didn't land at first but later would be a hit for the UK band Manfred Mann's Earth Band. Little Steven joined Bruce's E Street Band in 1975. Today, Steven and I have a running joke about how Manfred

Mann's English accent made the lyric "revved up like a deuce" sound like "revved up like a douche."

Listening to *Asbury Park,* I thought Bruce was a passionate, gifted performer with something new to offer, and I began playing all but two tracks of the new record on 'HFS; "Spirit in the Night" was my favorite. Bruce was influenced by Bob Dylan and Van Morrison, but it was his conception and imagination of growing up in America that made him magnificently different. Freedom and liberation weren't just slogans in his Bruce's lyrics. You can't write songs unless you immerse yourself into the story. And Bruce was a prophetic light in 1973. He had his own trajectory. In a culture saturated with marketing—everything and everybody is for sale—but not Bruce. Bruce was and is our musical steward, someone who took a stand. He uses his gifts as a musical force articulating what many of us feel.

Soon I realized by listening to my fellow 'HFS jocks' shows that they too were Bruce fans. The station staff rarely met together unless some major problem needed to be addressed. Like when someone had been eating in the studio and left food crumbs or coffee stains on the turntable. I'm only half kidding.

At 'HFS we were all spending an enormous amount of time looking for new music, going to clubs, meeting people, and listening to bands. Shortly after playing his record on my program, I was thrilled to learn that the Bruce Springsteen band (not yet the E Street Band) was booked for three nights at my favorite music club, the Childe Harold. Jennis M. "Jack" Strickland, who passed away in 2010, was the booking agent who hired Bruce.

The Childe Harold opened in 1967 at 1610 20th Street, named after Lord Byron's poem about a world-weary young man's travels. The bar soon caught on as an influential hometown club when live local music was introduced in 1970. Intimacy was guaranteed because occupancy was only about 120 people. The marijuana smoke was so thick in the bathrooms you'd get a contact high just taking a whiz. The drinking age was 18. There was no shortage of patrons getting hammered regularly.

According to the *Evening Star* newspaper, the upstairs was designed by Luther Burbank McKean, who also did local DC clubs Chadwicks and Charing Cross. Large mirrors on the walls made the place seem bigger than it was. Pine paneling and gold leaf wallpaper gave it class and an elegant feel. But it was the deep respect the patrons felt for the performers that made it so special. Mostly, you always knew you were going to see and hear something exceptional when you walked up the front steps to the door.

"The place was incredibly popular," remembers former bartender Jim Collins. "The music scene in DC was hitting its peak. It was in the Dupont Circle neighborhood of intellectual think tanks, leftover beatniks, and hippies, like everyone at Food for Thought [a nearby café that opened in 1973 that featured live folk music]. It made for an interesting mix of people, and the bar was in the middle of it. It was a great time to live in DC." Today, Collins researches population issues at a Stanford University think tank.

Vice President Walter Mondale's daughter, Eleanor, would sometimes tend bar at Childe Harold. Her brother, Ted, was a steady customer. Jon Stewart did an early stand-up comedy show for a small audience that included Ethel Kennedy and a few of her children. One night in 1975, Beach Boy Mike Love showed up at singer Wendy Waldman's Childe Harold show. I met my first wife, Scarlet, there. She was a bartender.

The late bluegrass musician Liz Meyer recalled playing for $75 a gig plus cheeseburgers. Over the years, the menu reflected the scene. There would be the "B. Springsteen," homemade crab cakes, the Washington Redskin "G. Starke," turkey breast and bacon, the "Bonnie Raitt," BLT with curried chicken on rye, and the "Emmylou Harris," avocado, bacon, and mayo on whole wheat. There was once even a "Cerphe" vegetarian club. My sandwich wasn't a big hit back then. It came and went. I wish it had been a tofu burger.

Upstairs in the main banquet room you could get cloth napkins and Beef Wellington. The earliest print ads in the *Washington Post* and *Evening Star* before live music would just advertise "The Childe Harold: Beef Wellington" along with the phone number. I wish I could confirm the food quality, but hey, now I'm a vegetarian.

Wild Bill Heard

Childe Harold owner, William Augustin Heard Jr., born September 2, 1931, was a hard-living, chain-smoking, whiskey-drinking raconteur. After hours, Wild Bill, as he was called, sometimes with *Washington Post* writer Nicholas von Hoffman in tow, held court with friends, staff, and lucky insiders. Galliano liqueur and Dom Perignon would sometimes flow until 7:00 a.m. Survivors would end up in the kitchen eating the cheesecakes.

Bill's sandwich was appropriately named the "Wild Billy Burger," a filet mignon on an English muffin with Béarnaise sauce on the side.

"Wild Bill" was a big guy at six foot two and two hundred pounds, with a loud, gravelly voice. He was an ex-Army paratrooper and one-time racecar driver. An amateur guitarist, he earned his local reputation as an out-of-control brawler at other DC bars. He was kicked out of numerous bars until he invested inherited money from the John Deere fortune to buy his own place. He wanted a place of his own where he could drink and hang out with musicians.

Wild Bill.
Credit: © Bob Coleman

Bill was very cordial to me and loved all of us at WHFS. Why not? We gave him a lot of radio real estate by promoting the performers at his place. Bill had an "outlaw-on-the-lam" quality that made you feel skull-duggery was afoot, but he was lovable at the same time. There was always some kind of bruise or bandage on his face from bumping into shit, fall-ing down, getting into fights, and all of the above. He was real character. He could be your kindly "Master of the House" host one moment and then throw a beer mug at you the next.

"He once threw a barstool at me and I caught it in mid-air" recalls guitarist Phil Fox. Peter Bonta, a founding member of the superb Rosslyn Mountain Boys band, shares this story:

"One night after we played, I was at the bar getting paid with our fid-dle player, Bob Spates, standing beside me. Bill Heard wanted another drink and Pete Bell, the bartender, had just cut him off. Bill got belliger-ent and fired his Old Fashioned glass at Pete. Somehow, my head got in the way. The glass smashed and broke against the back of my head. As I started blacking out, my last thought was, 'I'm getting robbed.'

"I came to about thirty seconds later. Bob Spates said he saw my pupils dilate and turn to pinpoints. He thought I'd been killed. Wild Bill was totally freaked and insisted on driving me to the George Washington Hospital ER. To give you an idea of how bad off I was, I agreed to let him drive me there in his drunken condition. I was diagnosed with a concussion and had to carry a card in my pocket for a week informing one and all of my injury. Bill paid the ER visit bill and was so relieved I never sued."

Pete Bell adds, "Bill half-heartedly tried to hide it, but he was a sweet-heart most of the time." Jim Collins quips, "They broke the mold when they made Bill Heard. We hope."

Bonta offers another story: "I was living at Bill's place and we were on a four-day drinking binge with a couple of beautiful girls that we had recently met. As we drove through the Virginia countryside drunk out of our minds, DUI not being a big deal in those days, Bill was in the backseat with one of the girls and he started ragging at me about my driving and he wouldn't let up. I pulled the car over on a deserted road and we got out and started fighting much to the dismay of the girls who were under the impression that we were best friends. I knocked Bill into a ditch and jumped on top of him, got my hands around his neck and started screaming at him as I beat his head on the ground, 'I'm the only friend you got in the whole world' and he said 'I know, I know.' We both broke out laughing and the girls just stood there in shock.

"So we get back to DC and climb up the fire escape into the kitchen of the Childe Harold, snorted a little coke, and went into the back bar/dining room. Bill grabs a bottle of Galliano, starts drinking, and sees a very somber table of diners. He walks over and stares, and then recognizes Senator George McGovern, who had just been defeated in the 1972 presidential election. Bill starts screaming, 'It's the loser, it's the fucking loser,' over and over and over. 'How does it feel to be such a fucking loser?' At that point either the cooks or myself dragged him out as the McGovern party sat in stunned silence."

Bill's alcoholism eventually took its toll. It trumped his business skills because his place only seated a small crowd, yet he insisted on hiring increasingly expensive national acts. Profits were not impressive. He began giving shares of the business to Hossein Shirvani, who had started as a waiter and ended up owning the Childe Harold when Bill finally pulled out.

Bill's obituary reported that he was living in his car in 1990 with a half-gallon of vodka in the trunk. Hitting rock bottom, he checked into a VA hospital in West Virginia for help. He quit drinking and spent his remaining years in AA helping other alcoholics get sober. When he passed away, his church bestowed a plaque that named him "Custodian, philosopher, and minister to the down and out." Bill died from emphysema and pneumonia at age 70.

One of the people who booked all the great music at the Childe Harold was Judy Keyserling, a Beaufort, North Carolina, native with a great Southern drawl and armed with a master's degree in business from Georgetown University. Dixie Dee Ballin, whose band the Fabulous Touchtones played the regular Tuesday night slot for years, remembers Judy as "smart as a whip, well-traveled, cultured, and could hold her own with anyone."

"Judy had a great sense of humor and we spent a lot of time laughing in her office on the second floor of the club. Judy had great taste in music and should get the credit for bringing in many of the older black players from the South to perform," says Dixie Dee.

I kept up with Judy after she moved to booking events at the Ontario Theatre and then on to administration for the Capitol Ballet. She passed away in 2012. I appreciate what Judy and the other booking and admin staff at the Childe Harold did because I have the greatest memories of enjoying Woodbridge, Virginia's Emmylou Harris, native DC guitarist Danny Gatton, Falls Church, Virginia, guitarist Tom Principato, Garrett Park, Maryland's Nils Lofgren, and many, many others.

I was also thrilled by up-and-coming national acts like Bonnie Raitt, David Bromberg, Chris Smither, and Al Jarreau. Please see Appendix, page 271, for a complete list of Childe Harold performers, courtesy of the authors' memories and our friends in the 70s D.C. Area Music Scene Facebook group.

Those were the days.

CHAPTER 4

Springsteen: Spirit in the Night

I clearly remember that 1973 night driving down from 'HFS to see Bruce Springsteen make his DC debut at the Childe Harold. Other area shows that night included Carole King at Merriweather Post Pavilion, the J. Geils Band at University of Maryland, and Deep Purple at the Baltimore Civic Center. But it was Bruce I had to see.

When spring hits Washington and the trees are blooming, there is a distinctive sweetness in the air. With my car windows down and the warm breezes flowing in from the Potomac, the weather inspired a feeling that a magical evening at the Childe Harold was in store. The Bruce Springsteen band's lineup in 1973 was "Big Man" Clarence Clemons (saxophone), Garry Tallent (bass and tuba), "The Phantom" Danny Federici (organ, accordion, and later, virtual glockenspiel), "Mad Dog" Vini Lopez (drums), and David (Davey, as Bruce called him) Sancious (keyboards). Even though Davey had played on the record, he missed the first leg of the tour. DC is where he caught up to make his debut in the live band lineup.

I arrived at the Childe Harold in time for the band's sound check. *Washington Post* music writer Richard Harrington and the *Evening Star's* Michael Oberman were already there. Bruce was bearded and skinny. The band, except for Clarence, was casually clothed in jeans and T-shirts.

The Boss, in 1973.
Credit: © Paul Kasko

There was nothing pretentious about them. The two African American guys in the band (Clemons and Sancious) were very cool. Seeing a multiracial band was the exception to the rule back then. It was refreshing for me because they were great players. Today David Sancious plays in Sting's band, having left Bruce's band at the beginning of the *Born to Run* sessions to pursue solo and other projects.

I introduced myself to Bruce with some small talk about how much I liked the album and added:

"Hey, you want to be on the radio for an interview?"

"Yeah!" Bruce quickly shot back.

Bruce agreed to swing back to DC in a few days. He'd bring the band and some instruments and do a radio concert. I was elated.

I learned that Bruce was concerned then about record sales. *Greetings from Asbury Park, NJ* ended up selling only 25,000 copies in the first year. Bruce had studied the band business well. His talent was matched by his ambition. He knew that "good" is never good enough for the record companies. Even if you're Number One, you haven't been Number One long enough. His early knack for understanding the business of rock and roll, along with his practice of handing out band pay in the early gig days, is one reason he earned the nickname "The Boss."

Just two weeks before the Childe Harold gigs, Bruce had begun recording his second album, *The Wild, the Innocent & the E Street Shuffle.* It was released later that year in September, with very positive reviews but poor sales. Bruce's set lists for Childe Harold were selected from these two albums plus a few covers like Stevie Wonder's "Superstition," and the old Crystals' hit, "And Then He Kissed Me," which Bruce gender revised.

My friend JB Alison played bass with Liz Meyer and Friends and was there for all of the Childe Harold shows. He and Liz, along with the brilliant guitarist Danny Gatton, and Maryland State fiddle champ Jeff Wisor opened for Bruce's second two shows.

"Bruce was strange to me at first," JB recalls. "I had heard his debut album. I didn't dislike the record but I figured he was just another guy from New Jersey with a good band, reaching for the stars."

JB was wrong. We were both floored when Bruce and the band lit Childe Harold on fire.

"Wow, this guy and the Big Man had it going on. I became a devoted fan after his first set," says JB. "Bruce had a Telecaster guitar with a Les Paul 'Humbucker' pickup added between the standard Tele pickups. That was unusual then because it wasn't like the traditional Telecasters that Roy Buchanan and Danny Gatton were playing. This middle humbucker gave his Tele a fatter, more rocking, less country sound."

JB and the late Gatton, one of most remarkable guitarists ever, were close friends. JB drank beer, ate crabs, and built cars with him. Danny approached JB after Bruce's first set.

"I don't know what the big deal is about this guy," Danny said. "He's not a very good guitar player."

JB laughed because this was typical of how Danny rated everyone: based on guitar prowess.

"It's not about Bruce's guitar playing," JB replied.

As JB became a bigger fan of Bruce, he was able to make Danny listen to Bruce's second album. On one song, Bruce hits a clunker note. Like a trouper, Bruce left it on the record.

Danny listened to the record quietly. When that one single off-note exploded, he yelled, "What the hell was that?"

JB replied, "Danny, I think he left that note in on purpose—because Bruce doesn't give a shit. It's not about the guitar solo, but rather what he's trying to say." I agree with JB here, and add *it's what Bruce was trying to do*. Keep the magic of the moment.

Of these early days, Bruce told me, "I was looking for some way to put my music to some service on a nightly basis. You go into a town, you play a little music, you leave something behind. That idea connected us to the local community. It was a very simple idea, but it really resonated with me."

It was obvious by Bruce's performances at the Childe Harold that his train was rolling. He had a big heart that you could more fully sense in some of the newer, not-yet-recorded songs like "Rosalita," and especially "4th of July, Asbury Park (Sandy)." *Los Angeles Times* writer Robert Hilburn later observed, "The Sandy verses are whispered as if he was singing into his girlfriend's ear."

In "Rosalita," he imagines a record company giving him a big advance, so girlfriend Rosie's dad better get behind their romance. Bruce actually wrote "Rosalita" in 1972, when this "big record advance" was a fantasy. "Rosalita" would be Bruce's second set closer until 1984.

My view on his appeal would evolve as his concert venues expanded; once people experienced him on a big stage in concert, they found a passion that translated. Everyone in the audience *got* him. You have to see Bruce in person to reap that passion and understand why he is phenomenal. You can almost hear it on the records, but you have to see him perform to fully appreciate his power. Onstage, he is fearless and real, morally courageous and spiritually awake.

CBS promo man Earl Rollison—who gave me that first Bruce album—was at the Childe Harold shows. Earl agrees:

"It was a struggle promoting Bruce in the early days because he needed a proper stage to express himself. The small venues were not greatly helping him. And even though Columbia Records was the number one powerful label back then, there were only a couple of stations in the country like 'HFS that were playing Bruce, and radio play was important to his future. If it wasn't for Cerphe and 'HFS, it's possible that Bruce wouldn't be where he is today. Bruce and CBS are thankful.

"What made that time exciting and the music so good is that record labels spent much time trying to find great artists to sign and promote. They don't do that now. Today, aspiring musicians have to "look the part," or have a video and so forth. They seek out the labels.

"People with great musical talent then like Bruce and Billy Joel would be found. These artists had to work very hard to get established. And play a lot of shitholes, pardon my French. It was much like what a country artist did. They'd play 364 shows a year and take one day off. They became very good at their craft.

"Another example of this is the British Invasion after The Beatles. Most of the American acts were more like garage acts and hadn't performed on stage that much. The English acts had been working on stage every night of the year for quite some time. So when they came over to the States, they could perform on stage. The only American act that was working like that was the Four Seasons."

Bruce's band was exceptionally rehearsed and tight, playing an astonishing 138 dates alone from 1972 to May 1973. He was the owner-builder-driver of the band: passionate, engaged with the audience, sometimes even playful and goofy. He had no expectation that you wouldn't like his material because this was the best that he had to offer. He had a rare confidence.

The upstairs Childe Harold dressing room was always party central. Bruce wasn't interested in partaking in the party favors. He quietly hung with his band and wasn't in the inner office using the big mirror. He was focused on delivering a great show.

The band netted $750 for three nights. Bruce split the gig revenues equally among all the band members, as he has always done, which is kind of rare in the music biz. Bruce's Childe Harold gig contract was tacked to the wall behind the bar and hung there until Childe Harold closed for good in 2007. Today, it is the Darlington House, a popular Italian restaurant. A small section of the downstairs bar has a few rock photos framed on the wall and a poster of Emmylou Harris playing the Kennedy Center inscribed, "To Childe Harold, there will always be a place in my heart for you."

Shortly after the 1973 Childe Harold shows, *Rolling Stone* magazine ran a review of *Greetings from Asbury Park, NJ*. Music writer Lester Bangs—cited by many as "America's Greatest Rock Critic"—wrote a strongly favorable review. He thought the music was "breathtakingly complicated . . . bracing as hell" from a "bold new talent" and "Watch for him; he's not the new John Prine."

Locally, the *Evening Star's* music critic, John Seagraves had a different view:

"Greetings from Asbury Park (Columbia). All the kudos end here. It's been awhile, thankfully, since I've heard anyone as heavy handed as this, your troubadour, who makes such dramatists as Jacques Brel sound totally dispassionate. And none of it works. The most dreadful LP that I've had the courage to play to its entirety in months—an annoying, cloying abomination."

The late Seagraves wrote some beautiful music reviews. Unfortunately, very few involved rock music. John's son, Mark, today a TV reporter for WRC-TV explains, "The thing to understand about my dad is that he was a jazz guy. He usually wrote rock music reviews when the newspaper's regular rock critics weren't available. I never asked him if he ever changed his mind about his Bruce review before he passed away but I did ask him about his original slam review of Jimi Hendrix. My dad still thought Jimi was doing musical masturbation on stage."

Bruce in Studio

Just as we agreed, Bruce and the band showed up to do my radio show. He said the band got lost on the way to the studio and drove around the Capital Beltway twice.

He was a shy and unassuming guest. I asked him about how the recent positive press in *Rolling Stone* made him feel, and did he believe it?

Bruce answered, "It feels good, but I only believe what I read *to a degree.* It's a strange situation because I've been playing in bands for like nine years all over, and now, when I read something about myself, I thought it would affect me more than it does. It was almost nicer when I just thought about this happening."

"Do you still live in Asbury Park? What goes on there besides people listening to New York City radio's Murray the K?" I asked.

"Yes, we're still in Asbury Park. It's pretty nice." Bruce said. "But nobody goes there anymore. The average age is old people, very old.

"Still, there are a lot of bars and you can play there as long as you play what they want. We played all of them but last time, with our new music, we couldn't get gigs there no-how. So these cats [pointing to his band sitting in the studio] found this place called the Student Prince. It wasn't doing any business. None. Like ten people there on a Saturday night. We asked the owner if we could play for the door. So we started playing there and slowly built up a following."

Asbury Park's Student Prince club was where Clarence and Bruce teamed up. Clarence was playing in the Wonder Bar on 1213 Ocean Avenue in Norman Seldin's band, the Joyful Noyze. Bruce was playing close by at the Student Prince. On a break, Clarence walked a couple of blocks to see Bruce's band.

Bruce tells a Steinbeck-like tale of how he and Clarence first met. I won't do it justice, but the Cliff Notes go like this. The night was stormy. Clarence opened the club door and it flew off its hinges and blew away down the street. Bruce and the band were on stage, staring at Clarence's hulking framed in the doorway.

Clarence told Bruce, "I want to play with your band."

Bruce replied, "Sure, you do anything you want."

The first song they jammed on was an early version of "Spirit in the Night." Even though Clarence had come up playing in soul bands, he was a rocker. He wanted something new besides just playing James Brown all night long. And Bruce was looking for that soulful horn.

Following my 'HFS interview, Bruce and the band launched into a short set, starting with an instrumental "Satin Doll," with everyone yelling "Switch-a-rooney" in the solo segue back to the basic verse. Cute.

Just like he did in the Childe Harold shows, Garry Tallent played tuba on "Wild Billy's Circus Story." Then they played "Growin' Up" and "Mary, Queen of Arkansas."

On 'HFS, Clarence dedicated "New York City Serenade" to his buddies at Maryland State College, which he attended in 1961. That's where he joined his first band, the Vibratones, playing R&B covers. After college, he moved to Newark, New Jersey, and continued playing music at night. His day job until 1970 was working as counselor with emotionally disturbed boys at the Jamestown Training School.

"C'mon up to town so we can get drunk together" was his 'HFS studio shout-out to his school pals in southern Maryland.

With the radio show over, I walked Bruce and the band across the street for coffee at the Psyche Delly bar. Nobody in the front, where they sold sandwiches to go, knew who these guys were.

I found out later that the Childe Harold wasn't the first gig that Bruce played in the DC area. It was in April 1973 when Bruce learned that the band that had been hired to back Chuck Berry at a Cole Field House show at UMD had canceled. Bruce called the promoter and offered his band for free. Bruce also opened for Chuck playing songs from *Greetings*. Some heckler yelled, "I didn't pay five bucks to listen to your shit." Bruce shot back, "Well, the next time you see me you're going to be paying ten bucks."

In October, 1973 I was very pleased to receive a letter from Bruce's manager, Mike Appel. He wrote, "Just a short note of thanks for all the help you have given us with the promotion of Bruce Springsteen's album. . . . You have been playing "Kitty's Back" heavily. For that, we can't thank you enough. As you know it is extremely difficult to break a new artist on the air. An artist such as Bruce needs that extra airplay so that it is possible to show a great amount people what extraordinary talent he really is. Again, our thanks for your being so instrumental in the success of our artist."

I was invited to hang at the Record Plant in New York City during a recording session for Bruce's fourth album *Darkness on the Edge of Town*. I got a chance to watch his second drummer, "Mighty" Max Weinberg, hit a single drumbeat over and over as the engineers tried to tweak the sound. Over and over. This didn't impress my girlfriend, Alice, that much.

Max joined the E Street Band in 1974 when original drummer, Vini Lopez, departed. I started a great friendship with Steve Van Zandt at the studio when he came back to work in Bruce's band in 1975. Years later, he would portray Tony Soprano's consigliere, Silvio Dante, in HBO's epic series *The Sopranos*. More on that later.

When I visited New York City in 1977, Clarence

Clarence and me at Peaches Records, Rockville, Maryland. 1983.
Credit: © Eva K. Graham.

offered me his Seabright, New Jersey home to stay in. His New Jersey home was modest and colorful with a voodoo vibe. This was perfect because I was still trying to impress Alice. A trip to New York City, where I could bunk at the Big Man's place, was big-time cred. He told me he'd be away with an airline stewardess the first night so "just sleep in my bed," was how he put it. And Alice and I did.

On that visit, I brought Clarence a three-record set—*The Saxophone: A Critical Analytic Guide to the Major Trends in the Development of the Contemporary Saxophone Tradition*—on the jazz label ABC/Impulse. It included Sonny Rollins, John Coltrane, Charlie Parker, Eric Dolphy, Pharoah Sanders, Gato Barbieri, and other saxophone greats. He loved it.

The next night, Clarence, his stewardess friend, and Alice and I dined at a local seafood restaurant. Clarence ordered lobsters for us. When the meals came, three of us got normal-sized lobsters, but Clarence was served a three-foot, thirty-pound lobster. Just kidding. It wasn't that big but it was the most humongous lobster I had ever seen.

Clarence said all his favorite seafood restaurants in Seabright had a running competition on which could procure the biggest lobster for him. The Big Man was clearly "Mayor of Seabright." We all knew that Clarence had a big appetite for everything. Life, love, sex, drugs, food, and rock and roll.

Clarence passed away in 2011 at age 69 from complications of a stroke. Bruce posted a moving eulogy on his website stating that he and Clarence became each other's guardians. Bruce helped Clarence succeed in the world where "it still wasn't easy to be big and black," while "C," as Bruce called him, protected the Boss in a world where "it wasn't so easy to be an insecure, weird, and skinny white boy." But, standing together we were badass, on any given night, on our turf, some of the baddest asses on the planet."

Bruce Returns to DC

The Bruce Springsteen band officially changed its name in September 1974 to the E Street Band and would return to the Washington, DC area throughout the mid-1970s: seven shows over the next three years at Georgetown University's Gaston Hall (with John Hall's band Orleans opening) and McDonough Arena, two nights in 1975 at Carter Barron Amphitheater in Rock Creek Park, a show at the Painters Mill Music Fair outside Baltimore, and a 1974 Shady Grove Music Fair show with comedian Robert Klein opening. By the time Bruce and the E Street Band rolled into McDonough in 1975, on the heels of releasing their breakthrough album *Born to Run* and appearing on both *Time* and *Newsweek* covers, everyone in the audience knew this band was conquering the United States.

The band's contract rider for refreshments at McDonough included six cases of Heineken, four gallons of vodka, one bottle of Courvoisier, six bottles of good red wine, cases of cokes, fruit juices, sandwiches, coffee, and more. "By this time, Bruce had accumulated a huge entourage of insider friends and he always did his best to entertain them backstage," Earl Rollison confirms.

Bruce also remembered his Childe Harold friends by sending over a dozen tickets for staff and fans for the 1975 Georgetown University show.

In July of 1975, at one of Bruce's concerts at the Carter Baron Amphitheatre in Rock Creek Park, continued intermittent rainstorms kept postponing the show. In between squalls, staff would come out and use push brooms to sweep the water offstage. I was the emcee. Bruce was backstage pacing like a tiger, waiting for the National Park Service to give the green light for the show to go on. Eventually, it did, to the relief of the rain-soaked but completely thrilled audience. The editor of this book, Patty Johnson Cooper, was also at this show and remembers Bruce taking the stage with the retreating storm's lightning still flashing in the sky.

Future of Rock

Ron Oberman was a music columnist for the *Washington Star* newspaper. He left the *Star* to become assistant director of publicity for Mercury Records when they were headquartered in Chicago. Ron's brother, Michael, took over the column.

Ron went on to become the director of publicity for Columbia Records when *Greetings from Asbury Park, NJ* was released. Ron called his brother to let him know that Bruce would be playing the Childe Harold. Michael attended the show and said "hi" to Bruce.

"Oh man," said Bruce. "You are Ron's brother. You'll have to be Little O.B. because Ron is Big O.B."

After the *Asbury* record didn't sell well, Columbia was ready to drop Bruce. As director of publicity, Ron was friends with many rock journalists, including *Rolling Stone* writer Jon Landau. Ron was very vocal on why Columbia should keep Springsteen. He touted Bruce to anyone who would listen to him, "We must keep Springsteen."

So he invited Jon Landau to see Bruce live at Harvard Square, in Cambridge, Massachusetts, on May 9, 1974. After the concert, Landau wrote a strong review of Springsteen's show, including the famous quote, "I have seen the future of rock and roll and its name is Bruce Springsteen."

Sell Out

From 1978 through 1985, the E Street Band starting selling out Landover, Maryland's Capital Centre, an 18,756-seat sports arena

Getting out of the way after introducing Bruce. 1980.
Credit: © Jeffrey Snyder/ Cerphe Archive

44

that opened in 1973. Fans would gather the night before tickets went on sale and party hard in the parking lot. Sometime after midnight, you'd get a number, and then try to make it home for some sleep. You'd return by 9:00 a.m. the next day, when the ticket office opened, and get in line according to your number to purchase tickets. It's hard to believe that getting tickets back then was such a hassle when we think how easy it is today online.

My invitations to announce Bruce's shows were an honor. Once during intermission after his first set at a Cap Centre show, a roadie urgently summoned me: "Come. The Boss wants to see you backstage right now." Something in the way he said it gave me a sinking feeling. Had I done something wrong? Said something on the radio to piss off the Boss? I was seated next to Clarence's parents and I revealed a nervous smile as I got up to follow the roadie to what was sure to be my doom.

As we walked down the backstage corridor, I heard music coming from the end of the hall. It got louder as we approached. The roadie opened the door and there was Bruce sitting on the couch with his feet on a coffee table listening to a boombox blaring "Be My Baby," a Phil Spector song by the Ronettes.

When he saw me, he turned the volume down and said, "Sit down." He asked me how I liked the first set and what I thought of his pacing and choice of songs. There is no playbook or algorithm or framework on how to construct a stage performance. You've got to work from your heart and gut to capture the attention of the audience with the right combination of old and new material. I told him that he had nailed it. He signed a *Darkness on the Edge of Town* album to me, with the inscription "To Cerphe. Good Intro!" That made me feel really good.

Born in the USA Controversy

One day after an August 1984 Springsteen show at the Cap Centre during the *Born in the USA* tour, *Washington Post* columnist George F. Will

45

left me a phone message at DC 101 where I was on air at the time. His message read "Questions about Bruce Springsteen."

I didn't return his call, but I did keep that message for many years. Two days later, George's syndicated column, "Bruce Springsteen: The Blue-Collared Troubadour" extolling the virtues of Bruce's lyrics, his work ethic, and serious stature among fans was published in papers across America.

However, the conservative columnist's interpretation of Bruce's political leanings struck me as wishful thinking. He wrote, "I have not a clue about Springsteen's politics, but flags get waved at his concerts as he sings about hard times."

Will concluded, "If all Americans in labor and management, who make steel or cars or shoes or textiles, made their products with as much energy and confidence as Springsteen and his merry band make music, there would be no need for Congress to be thinking about protectionism."

Soon after the column, President Reagan, in full campaign mode for his reelection run against Walter Mondale, gave a stump speech that included Bruce:

"America's future rests in the message of hope in songs of a man so many young Americans admire, New Jersey's Bruce Springsteen. And helping you make those dreams come true is what this job of mine is all about."

Bruce's lawyer sent a cease-and-desist order to the president for trying to use "Born in the U.S.A." during his campaign. It was only the second time a cease-and-desist order was exchanged between a musical artist and a presidential candidate. The first one was between 1964 Republican candidate, Barry Goldwater, and Broadway producer David Merrick, over the song, "Hello Dolly." Goldwater wanted to change it to "Hello Barry." Merrick threatened to sue. He did, however, approve President Johnson's campaign request to change the name of the song to "Hello Lyndon."

Bruce commented on the "Born in the USA" episode in a 2005 interview with National Public Radio. Said Bruce: "This was when the Republicans first mastered the art of co-opting anything and everything that seemed fundamentally American, and if you were on the other side, you were somehow unpatriotic. I make American music, and I write about the place I live and who I am in my lifetime. Those are the things I'm going to struggle for and fight for."

George talked about that concert thirty-two years later for this book: "I had met [band drummer] Max Weinberg a couple of times. I think he was interested in public commentary at the time. I'm not going to get him in trouble by accusing him of being a conservative. I didn't know if he was or wasn't, but he seemed to like what I did, and I liked his work too. I went backstage and met Bruce that night at the Capital Centre. He was cooling off between sets. I gave him a copy of one of my books. I think I signed it "Born to Write." He thought that was funny. And we went on our merry way. It's a long-ago and far-away memory now."

For the record, I've never discussed politics with "Mighty" Max Weinberg, but I do know he campaigned for John Kerry in the 2004 presidential election. I sometimes wonder if I could have prevented some of the drama surrounding George's column if I had simply returned his phone call. I would have set him straight that Bruce was no conservative. I had already watched Bruce, with no cameras around, loading and unloading bags of food at the Capital Area Food Bank warehouse in DC around Thanksgiving 1980. I was promoting the Food Bank with public service announcements on my WAVA radio show and found out about Bruce being involved and lending a hand (literally!). This was an act of kindness on his part, repeated in cities throughout his tour. No publicity, no cameras, no press. The courage of Bruce's convictions goes beyond his songs.

I was asked by his management not to promote Bruce's involvement in the Food Bank in advance but did mention it after the fact. It is difficult for Bruce to do things publicly beneath the radar, but this certainly remained low-key, as did a private party a couple years later at the River Bowl on River Road in Bethesda, Maryland. Go figure. The E Street Band loves to bowl.

CHAPTER 5

Van Morrison: Astral Weeks

Among other things, I was playing bass guitar in 1968 with my occasional band, the Luvlace Lads. I was driving around Boston one day listening to WBCN, my favorite station. I heard a report that singer-songwriter Van Morrison had moved to the Boston area, and was living in Cambridge and forming a band. I thought to myself that's interesting and cool because I loved Van Morrison. His early 1965 hit "Mystic Eyes" with his first UK group, Them, was a compelling blues song and very unusual for the time. The instrumental beginning of "Mystic Eyes" is almost half of the song. The opening harmonica solo crescendos after a full minute.

In 1966, Van explained to American reporters that "Mystic Eyes" was inspired by a walk in Nottingham Park past a graveyard wall. Van said, "A group of children played next to it. Life and death beside one another, so close and yet so different. And then I thought of the bright lights in the children's eyes, and the cloudy lights in the eyes of the dead."

Still, George Ivan Morrison, born in Belfast, Northern Ireland, on August 31, 1945, wasn't widely known in 1968, although his classic song, "Gloria," had already achieved status as a bar band staple. Covered in America by Chicago band the Shadows of Knight, the song climbed to Number 10 on the Billboard charts in 1966, eventually sold a million copies to earn a gold record, and became an eternal pocket anthem for bands worldwide. The American version altered one of Van's lines, "she comes into my room, then she made me feel alright," replacing it with "she called out my name, that made me feel alright," thus winning airplay on radio stations that had banned Them's original version.

At gigs, musicians would often improvise different imaginative—and sometimes raunchy—scenarios for the quiet middle part when Gloria "walks down my street, comes up to my house, knocks upon my door (four drum shots), calls out my name, and makes me feel alright." The call-and-response chorus "G-L-O-R-I-A" was penetrating. Not since Muddy Waters's 1955 "Mannish Boy" with the lyric "I'm a man, I spell M-A-N" has this "spell it loud and proud" energy been so effective in driving a song home to the bone.

Van would become a household name when "Brown-Eyed Girl" (original title, "Brown-Skin Girl") dominated the charts in 1968.

Back to my story: a few days later I'm driving in Harvard Square, Cambridge, and I come to a red light. Standing on the street corner is Van Morrison. Van the Man! It was very dreamlike. Then I see him cross the street. I park the car as quickly as possible and run back to look for him. But Van is gone. He's nowhere to be found. Of course, in my mind I had already put Van's band together for him, and I, needless to say, would be his new bass player.

What I didn't know is how close I came to maybe making my passing dream come true. Van was planning, arranging, and rehearsing a new acoustic-based project, which would prove to be more innovative and artistically challenging than previous Van recordings like "Here Comes the Night" and "Baby, Please Don't Go."

He was indeed living in Cambridge and jamming with local musicians, and making friends that included Peter Wolf, later the lead singer of the J. Geils Band but then the overnight DJ on WBCN. Wolf's radio character "Woofa Goofa" was a hyper-hip jive talker with cool tunes and a lot of blues. Van gave him notes on what songs to play on air and some-times took over Peter's phone for his business calls.

Soon Morrison had organized his band, the Van Morrison Controversy, with bassist Tom Kielbania (this could have been me!), drummer Joey Bebo, and a jazz-trained flute player, John Payne, all local musicians. The Controversy played at coffeehouses around town, and at an underground bar, the Catacombs, at 1120 Boylston Street, two floors down from a pool hall. This is where Van developed and honed his new music. Peter Wolf taped a few of the Catacomb sets, capturing—although few would ever hear the tapes—what was about to become Van's next album.

Then Van left Cambridge, taking Kielbania and Payne with him, to record his next project at Century Sound Studios in New York City, his second studio album, titled *Astral Weeks.* The esteemed bassist Richard Davis, who had supported jazz legend Eric Dolphy, took over on bass. Kielbania taught him some parts and helped give him the feel of the music. Jazz guitarist Jay Berliner and drummer Connie Kay, both veter-ans of the Modern Jazz Quartet, also played on the sessions. When Kay asked Van what he wanted him to play, Van replied, "Anything you want."

The studio band didn't rehearse, and there were no lead sheets passed around. Van recorded his parts in an isolated sound booth with only acoustic guitar. The band then added the other parts to Van's recordings. According to the players, Van hardly talked to them. I think he was just in his own world.

Astral Weeks is considered one of the best, most visionary rock records ever. *Rolling Stone*'s Lester Bangs cited it as a "mystical docu-ment" and perhaps the most important album in Bangs's personal life. Today, Elvis Costello still calls it "the most adventurous record made in the rock medium."

Despite the critical acclaim, it took thirty-three years for *Astral Weeks* to achieve sales that certified it as a gold record. In 1997, music historian

Andrew Ford compared *Astral Weeks*'s musical sophistication and commercial success to classical music: "neither instant nor evanescent: *Astral Weeks* will sell as many copies this year as it did in 1968 and has every year in between."

"*Astral Weeks* is not about me," Van told National Public Radio in 2009. "It's totally fictional. It's put together of composites, of conversations I heard—you know, things I saw in movies, newspapers, books, whatever. It comes out as stories. That's it. There's no more."

Van's contention that there is nothing personal or autobiographical about *Astral Weeks* is a little hard to completely accept. Van married his wife, Janet, while he lived in Cambridge, and the *Astral Weeks* liner notes include references to a woman coming from Cambridgeport and being loved on the banks of the river.

Michael Oberman interviewed Van shortly after *Astral Weeks* was released. Van told him, "The eight songs on the album 'are thematically related through the same characters and places.'" With the release of *Astral Weeks,* he picked up what was almost a cult following. The lyrics from the record have been studied and debated.

"One time, a guy came up to me and said that *Astral Weeks* had kept his family together," Van said. "Most of the things have seven meanings anyway, so I'm not surprised that people are always finding new things in it."

Meeting Van

Although I never got to interview Van, I have seen him in concert many times and did meet him once. The meeting was with an entourage of media at DAR Constitution Hall on October 23, 1974. Warner Brothers invited us. Backstage, Van seemed very cold. At five feet five he was a short, standoffish guy. He really didn't want to talk to anybody. I was okay with that. I got to meet him. It was cool.

So I go back to my seat. The lights go down. The voice of God comes over the PA system from backstage: "Good evening, ladies and gentlemen. Welcome to Constitution Hall. Please refrain from taking *any* photographs. Thank you. And here's Van Morrison."

Early in the show, a flash bulb goes off. Van stops singing, does a 180-degree turn, and walks offstage. I waited a few minutes, and then a few more. Nothing. The crowd starts mumbling. Because I had a backstage pass, I got up and went to see what was going on. I was curious. I got to his dressing room. He was sitting alone and weeping.

Now wouldn't that have been the wrong time to ask him if he remembered seeing me in Harvard Square at the red light in my mother's Ford Falcon Fastback?

His manager showed up and told me, "Not now," and I left.

From the many reports of erratic behavior, canceled shows, and his own admissions, Van has struggled with personal issues that have affected both his life and his music. You find the words "stage fright" in his newspaper reviews of the day, but on a good night it never looked like stage fright to me. Think about his star performance at The Band's *Last Waltz* singing "Tura Tura Lural" and "Caravan." But that night, when I saw him backstage weeping, he looked like he was a fragile guy, and I suspect he still is. And Van wants what Van wants. He has been uncompromising as an artist.

On that night in 1974, Van eventually returned to the stage and the show was impressive. He was backed by Peter Wingfield on keyboards, Jerome Rimson on bass, and Peter Van Hooke on drums. Besides playing and recording with Van, Wingfield played on albums by B. B. King and Paul McCartney, and backed the Everly Brothers for eighteen years on keys after their 1983 reunion. Rimson played with Steve Winwood, among others, and Van Hooke was drummer in Genesis cofounder Mike Rutherford's side project, Mike + The Mechanics.

Morrison sold out Constitution Hall four years later but abruptly canceled that show because of "exhaustion." But Van has indeed survived and prospered over the years and is still a major force in music, actively inhabiting a legendary career that encompasses an astonishing range of styles, but they have always been on his terms. He was inducted into the Rock and Roll Hall of Fame in 1993 and the Songwriters Hall of Fame in 2003.

His Rock Hall bio reads in part: "[Van's] travels have led him down pathways where he's explored soul, jazz, blues, rhythm & blues, rock and roll, Celtic folk, pop balladry, and more, forging a distinctive amalgam that has Morrison's passionate self-expression at its core. With a minimum of hype or fanfare, working with a craftsman's discipline and an artist-mystic's creativity, Morrison has steadily amassed one of the great bodies of recorded work in the twentieth century."

CHAPTER 6

Tea with George Harrison

Nineteen seventy-five wasn't a good year for ex-Beatle George Harrison. He was reeling from harsh, negative reviews of his first (and only) solo American tour, including two shows at DC's Capital Centre in December 1974, promoting *Extra Texture (Read All About It)*, his sixth studio album.

George talked with reporters at the Los Angeles press conference that kicked off the 1974 tour. On the subject of The Beatles, he was pretty adamant: "I can't imagine The Beatles playing together again unless we were all broke," he told the press. "Having played with other musicians now, I don't even think The Beatles were that good. Paul's a fine bass player, but he's sometimes overbearing. Ringo's got one of the best back-beats in the business. I'd join a band anytime with John Lennon and Ringo. But I wouldn't join a band with Paul McCartney. That's not personal; it's from a musician's point of view."

George does a WHFS station ID.
Credit: © Joel Heiberger/*Washington Post*

At the Capital Centre, his backup band included keyboardist Billy Preston, reed player Tom Scott, guitarist Robben Ford, and the double drumming of Andy Newmark and Jim Keltner. This tour was the first time George had appeared on an American stage since his 1971 Madison Square Garden *Concert for Bangladesh,* and it had been eight years since he had played with The Beatles at DC Stadium on their last American tour. Billy Preston was the more crowd-rousing player with his then-current hits "Nothing from Nothing" and "Will It Go 'Round in Circles."

For the new shows George chose to do only three Beatle songs: his own "While My Guitar Gently Weeps," "Something," and John Lennon's "In My Life." The omission of earlier Beatles songs, especially George's Beatle songs like "If I Needed Someone" or "Taxman," was a miscalculation. Fans certainly wanted to hear them and were disenchanted that he delegated so much stage time to Ravi Shankar's long sitar songs.

Moreover, chronic laryngitis took its toll with audiences and critics. He sounded bad. Word started to trickle in to the DC area that the first shows by George on the West Coast were disappointing. Tickets were still available on the day of the 5:00 p.m. and 10:30 p.m. shows at the Cap Centre. Tour promoter extraordinaire Bill Graham even attempted damage control on a WMAL-FM interview. Said Bill, "There have been some changes in programming where the songs come in. . . . George's concern is to stand on his own, and not rely on his reputation as a Beatle."

In sum, the local DC reviews of the Capital Centre shows weren't good. I can't report on the show because I was out of the country on vacation and missed it. And *Extra Texture,* the album George was promoting, wasn't very good either. Under the heading "Transcendental Mediocrity," *Rolling Stone* called *Extra Texture* a "disastrous album" to match the "disastrous tour," and a "shoddy piece of work."

Harrison's musical biographer, Simon Leng, described it as "a musical soap opera, cataloguing rock-life antics, marital strife, lost friendships, and self-doubt." The marital themes were based on his breakup with first wife, Pattie Boyd, whom he had met when the band filmed their first movie, *A Hard Day's Night*. In her 2007 autobiography, *Wonderful Tonight,* Pattie wrote, "That whole period was insane. Friar Park was a madhouse. Our lives were fueled by alcohol and cocaine, and so it was with everyone who came into our sphere. . . . George used cocaine excessively and I think it changed him."

And then his 1970 hit song "My Sweet Lord" became the center of a copyright infringement lawsuit. In structure and melody, music publisher Brite Tunes thought it was just too similar to their song "He's So Fine," written by Ronnie Mack and a 1963 hit for the Bronx, New York girl group, the Chiffons. After a high-profile trial, Harrison was found guilty of having subconsciously plagiarized the earlier tune. George unsuccessfully claimed to have used "Oh Happy Day," an old (and copyright-free) Christian hymn, as the basis for "My Sweet Lord's" melody. The final court verdict gave 40 percent of "My Sweet Lord" to the estate of Ronnie Mack through publisher royalties to Brite Tunes, but with an agreement that George retain the copyright for his song. In 1975, the Chiffons recorded it.

The Quiet One

In 1976, George swapped his business agreement with A&M records for a new contract with Warner Brothers. George embarked on a new and brighter musical project that became the album *Thirty Three & 1/3,* aptly named for George's age at the time as well as the speed that albums played in the olden days. Music critics gave a thumbs up on this one, noting a "return to form" for George and one of his strongest collections of songs since 1970's *All Things Must Pass.*

The album produced two hits: "This Song," a satirical, jovial take on his copyright drama from the year before, and "Crackerbox Palace," a whimsical song that was further augmented by a surreal promo video directed by George's friend Eric Idle of Monty Python fame. The promo video was aired on the TV show *Saturday Night Live* on November 26, 1976, with Paul Simon hosting. Paul and George sang "Homeward Bound" together. Beautiful!

I enjoyed the show and was glad to see that George was bouncing back into the spotlight with some new music and energy, as well as his trademark wry sense of humor. Imagine my excitement to learn that George was coming *in person* to Washington, DC, for a press party to promote *Thirty Three & 1/3*. I knew I had to be there.

Word went out to the DC press that a Warner Brothers party for George was being held at the Madison Hotel. My 'HFS DJ credentials got me into the event. With my long hair and hippie coat, I was a fish out of water among the regular, mostly "white shirt and tie" press crew who packed the aristocratic Dolly Madison dining room. There, a large stereo system was purring Indian music "personally programmed by George," according to a Warner's executive. In strolled George Harrison in a beautiful, hand-stitched beige sweater. He was radiantly healthy and happy.

The seating was arranged so that George held court with every reporter equally distanced from the ex-Beatle, so, presumably, nobody would get scoops.

George began answering questions with goodwill. One of the first questions, of course, was would The Beatles ever perform together again? George replied: "I won't say positively that it can't happen, that it couldn't happen sometime in the future. But it isn't really very likely to. They've seen very little of each other during the past eight years. It would be difficult. They'd have to get to know each other all over again. And a great deal of rehearsal would be required. And, really, what would be the point? It would be like going back to school eight years ago. What would be the point of it?"

Jack Lloyd, a reporter for *Knight's News* commented on George's reply in a December 12, 1976, *Salt Lake Tribune* article: "[George's] substitution for the word 'they' tells it all. Harrison appears to view The

Beatles from a distance, reflecting on the group's achievements from a point of view that is almost more academic than personal."

At the party, George was more interested in discussing his current work on *Thirty Three & 1/3:* "Some of the new songs are closer to the spirit of *All Things Must Pass*," he said. "That was my first album in 1970, although that was done with Phil Spector co-producing, so he had hundreds of people play on it, a really big production number. This new one has a more focused production, and it's very positive, very up, and most of the songs are love songs or happy songs. It doesn't compare to the last one. That one caught me in less than a happy mood."

As the press guys started in on what could be considered "strolling down memory lane" type questions, George took the opportunity to riff philosophically:

"The main thing that I felt from the sixties thing—the LSD experience early on and the meditation that followed—was the realization that all of the goodness and all of the strength that can support life is all coming out of love," George noted. "And it's not just as simple as one guy saying to a chick, 'I love you,' an emotional kind of thing. So often we say, 'I love you when . . . I love you if . . . I love you but. . . . But that's not real love. Real love is 'I love you even if you kick me in the head and stab me in the back, I love you.' Or just 'I love you unconditionally,' and that goes beyond everything.

"Now that is a pretty far-out love to try to conceive. And when I realized a little bit of love, then I realized how shallow it was. It's like saying, okay, I'm the greatest singer in the world. And then you start thinking, 'Well just how good am I? How many notes can I hit? What are my limitations? And then you realize just how limited you really are. It's the same way with love. You realize your limitations and then it's a process of learning how to develop."

George told us that he was considering a second US tour to begin in the spring of 1977, and that he wouldn't make the same mistakes he made on the 1974 tour. George didn't really describe what those previous mistakes were, other than "too many concert dates crowded into too tight a schedule."

The spring tour would never happen. None of The Beatles liked to tour anyway, and George wasn't all that interested. He was the first Beatle to suggest they quit touring because the fans were making too much noise to hear the music.

As he spoke to various reporters, all eyes were on George. Like lions stalking elk at a watering hole, you could feel the excitement and tension of those waiting to pounce on any opportunity to interact with a real, live Beatle. I too was watching George. The Beatles changed my life in every way—and there he was—not twenty feet from where I was standing. It was surreal.

As he talked to one of the suits, I noticed George looking at the Tantric Yoga button pinned to my jean jacket. He looked at the button, up at me and back at the button. Then something crazy happened. With his eyes fixed on me, he wrapped up his conversation and walked over. He said, "Hi, would you care to have a cup of tea?"

It's hard to express what this meant to me. Here was a Beatle asking me if *I would have tea with him.* And it was the Beatle that I most closely identified with. The Dolly Madison room was old and stately, the press was predictable, and George and I were young. We talked about meditation, yoga, and vegetarianism, and I asked him who he was listening to at the moment. Jeff Lynne was his response. Flashing forward to 1987, George would work with Jeff on George's *Cloud Nine* album and then again the following year with Jeff, Tom Petty, Bob Dylan, and Roy Orbison on a little side project called the Traveling Wilburys. We ended up yakking so much that we never got that tea. It's just as well, as it was probably Lipton tea that he wouldn't have liked.

Washington Post music writer Tom Zito wrote about my encounter with George: *"The winner (of all the press) was WHFS-FM disc jockey,*

Cerphe, who not only managed to cop a brief interview, but also shove a cocktail napkin in his hand and asked him to record a station ID:

"'Ello, this is George Harrison, and when I'm in Washington, I listen to . . . what is this?"

'WHFS"

'Yes, when I'm in Washington, I listen to WHFS in . . . where is this?'

'Bethesda.'

'Bethesma.'

'Beth-EZ-da.'

'Yes, Bethesda, Maryland.'

'Now do you think you can do it once again from top? I listen to Cerphe on WHFS . . .'

By this time, Tom Curtis, who is a jock on rival WMAL-FM was all but wrapping his mike cable around Harrison's neck, even joining in on the WHFS chorus. Miffed at Cerphe's coup, WMAL program director, Phil De Marne, was steaming enough to walk out of the room while George was playing some tracks from his new record. That prompted Ed Rosenblatt, a vice president of Harrison's new label, Warner Brothers, to scream 'I want to kick that guy right in the ass.'

So I met George Harrison. George liked me enough to talk with me and record a station ID. And for this, a Warner Brothers suit wants to kick my ass. That's show business, kids!

The late *Washington Post* photographer Joe Hieberger took two pictures of George and me. He had mentored Jacqueline Bouvier, a George Washington University grad when she interned as a *Times-Herald* newspaper photographer. This was before she became Jackie Kennedy Onasis.

After the party, there was a rumor that George had visited some property in Potomac, Maryland, with an idea of maybe buying a home here. I wish that had happened. He might have purchased a fixer-upper in Potomac for $3 million. He would add a state-of-the-art recording studio. Of course, he and I would become close friends and he'd ask me to invite my musician friends like Nils Lofgren and the Claude Jones band to record with him.

Hey now, maybe I'd play bass with him.

The End

George died at a friend's home in Los Angeles on November 29, 2001, at age 58 from lung cancer. According to Hindu tradition, his ashes were scattered in the Ganges and Yamuna rivers near Varanasi, India, by his close family in a private ceremony. His *New York Times* obituary by Allan Kozinn ran over 3,800 words, which is 1,000 words longer than this chapter. One paragraph illustrated George's creativity and dedication to his craft: "His solo for Lennon's 'I'm Only Sleeping,' recorded in 1966, shows his fastidiousness. To mirror the dream world quality of the lyrics, Mr. Harrison devised a solo guitar line, wrote out its notes in reverse order, and overdubbed it onto a recording of the song that was running backward. To complicate matters even more, he recorded two versions of the solo—one clean, one with the guitar distorted—and combined them. His contribution to the three-minute song took six hours to record."

Beatlemania First Struck the US on WWDC

Life magazine called the arrival of The Beatles in the United States number ninety-six among the one hundred most important events that shaped America. And it all started here in Washington, DC, with the first American airing of The Beatles record, "I Want to Hold Your Hand." The date was December 17, 1963, and the disc jockey was Carroll James of WWDC. I was fortunate to get to know CJ the DJ before he passed away from cancer in 1997 at the age of sixty.

Although Carroll wasn't the first to play The Beatles on radio—WLS in Chicago had played "Please Please Me" ten months earlier—James's early advocacy notably helped launch the Fab Four.

Presenting Carroll with a Capital gold record on the twentieth anniversary of The Beatles in DC, Wax Museum, 1984.
Credit: © Cerphe Archive

James received a letter from Marsha Albert, a fifteen-year-old junior high school student from Silver Spring, Maryland, requesting that he play a record by an English group called The Beatles. James recalled, "I went to one of the people on our staff, Jo Wilson, and asked her how we could obtain a recording by this group. Jo knew a representative for British European Airways and after a phone call a stewardess brought it over on a flight the next day. Fred Fisk [a long-time broadcaster also at WWDC] and I listened to it. I thought it was interesting but Fred didn't like it at all."

James then called Marsha and asked her to come to the studio to introduce the record. "She was scared to death. I wrote out an introduction for her and at 5:15 p.m. December 17, Marsha said, "Ladies and gentlemen, for the first time in America, The Beatles singing "I Want to Hold Your Hand." The switchboard lit up like the proverbial Christmas tree. The listeners just went wild. It was spontaneous combustion."

James played the record every day for a week, fading it down in the middle to say, "This is a Carroll James exclusive," so the other stations couldn't steal it.

Executives at Capitol Records in New York who had signed The Beatles to a contract were planning to release 200,000 copies of the record to the American market early in 1964. News of the record's success in Washington reached New York, and Capitol moved the release date up to December 26. The company arranged for three production plants—Capitol's own, and those of RCA and CBS—to work through the Christmas and New Year's holidays to press one million copies of "I Want to Hold Your Hand."

By the time The Beatles arrived in America on February 7, 1964, to appear on Ed Sullivan's TV variety show, Sullivan had received 50,000 requests for the 700 available seats for the debut. Carroll James and his wife, Betty, were invited by Sullivan to attend, and they accepted. John Lennon's wife sat with them. "Cynthia was overwhelmed by it all," said Carroll.

Sullivan greeted James backstage by saying, "You're the guy who's been saying that he discovered The Beatles. Well, you can forget that because I had them booked since October."

Maybe so, but Carroll takes his place in rock history, and Washington radio audiences were among the first in the United States of America to acclaim The Beatles.

CHAPTER 7
WHFS 102.3 – Side One

I've often said that if 'HFS radio station owner Jake Einstein hadn't hired me to join his staff, I might have ended up working as a barista at Starbucks. That may not be true, but Jake literally changed my life. He became my mentor, friend, and father figure. But our relationship grew to become contentious and complicated. I can still feel my blood pressure rise a little when I think of the late Jake. As Chrissie Hynde once sang, "There's a thin line between love and hate."

Jacob Einstein Jr. was born in Baltimore in 1917 and grew up on the Eastern Shore as one of thirteen children. He had that "Balmer" accent. They weren't Maryland Blue Crabs. They were "cray-abs." He wasn't of Jewish-Irish descent but rather "Jewish-Arsh," and when mad, he'd yell, "Stop doing *thay-at!*"

His first radio job was selling ads for Rockville, Maryland station WINX. He came to WHFS in 1964 as salesman, and his rise to station ownership is history.

Astrologically, we were both Leos. The lion's sign is fire, and we can often be powerful personalities. Jake was the cantankerous elder lion at 'HFS who acted as if he were the center of the universe. I was the younger hippie lion trying to establish some turf for myself.

We had loud disagreements and frequent battles. It wasn't always personal, since he yelled at everyone. A sign on his door read, IF HE AIN'T YELLIN' HE AIN'T SELLIN'. No matter where you were at the station—a soundproof studio or the men's room—you could hear when Jake was mad. I wasn't used to working, period, let alone working with someone so much larger than life. He also had the charming habit of taking the business card of someone he met for the first time, and using it to pick his teeth while the person's jaw dropped.

Robert Palmer. Getting ready to sneak Sally through the alley, 1975. Credit: Big Al Sevilla / All Access Photography

Once I had returned from doing an exclusive interview with the ultra-cool artist Robert Palmer, who had left his critically acclaimed group, Vinegar Joe, for a solo career. Palmer had a hit song with "Sneaking Sally Through the Alley," with a then-unknown backing band, Little Feat. I lugged a newly purchased tape recorder backstage for the interview. Palmer was surrounded by hot women after the show, much like his 1986 video "Addicted to Love." I really wasn't experienced with the new, complicated tape recorder. I returned to the station with what I thought was a great coup. Unfortunately, your buddy, Cerphe, wasn't the most savvy technical expert in town.

The next day, I played the Palmer interview on my show, but the sound was muffled. It actually really sucked, but "Hey now, it's Robert Palmer!" I thought.

Jake came barreling into my studio. He was returning from one of his three-plus martini lunches at the Chase restaurant on Jennifer Street. He had heard the poor sound quality of my interview and was fuming.

"Turn thay-at shit off," he bellowed.

"But Jake, it's Robert Palmer," I protested.

"I don't care who it is," he screamed.

With that, he grabbed a large glass ashtray and threw it at me. I ducked, and it hit the wall and fell to the floor. Looking back, I think he altered the trajectory a tad to miss me on purpose.

This incident was the beginning of my long and dwindling road that led to being fired by Jake.

But let's shift now to my beginnings and adventures with the greatest music radio station in our nation's capital's history. And for this approbation, we owe the ebullient Jake, who passed away at the age of ninety in 2007. We liked each other, we hated each other, we respected each other. Not easy to explain, but the thing that counts is what you heard on the radio.

Where I Worked

In 1972, WHFS was a five-thousand-watt FM station, the first station to broadcast stereo in the DC area, transmitting from a 150-foot antenna atop the Triangle Towers. The Towers was a fifteen-story apartment house at 4853 Cordell Avenue, right across the street from the Psyche Delly bar in Bethesda, Maryland. The studios were on the second floor of the high-rise condominium.

"Red," our uniformed security guard, sat at the front desk in the lobby. There was a swimming pool on the roof where the residents and guests would drink and smoke dope. Two-bedroom apartments went for $327 a month back then. That's about $2,000 today, adjusted for inflation. WHFS occupied the equivalent of three of those apartments.

You'd walk into a softly lit reception room and come face to face with a psychedelic painted gasoline pump. There were music speakers in the drop ceiling in the reception area, but the music was subdued until the studio door opened. Then it was blaring.

(L to R) Me, Weasel, David Einstein, Josh Brooks, Damian Einstein, and Thomas Grooms.
Credit: © Cerphe Archive

The *New York Post*'s late rock journalist Al Aronowitz wrote a long article about 'HFS when Jake hired Murray the K to join the staff. His description of the studio made it sound like an opium den. It wasn't quite like that.

Aronowitz is probably best remembered for introducing marijuana to The Beatles. It was on August 28, 1964, that Al brought Bob Dylan and The Beatles together at New York City's Hotel Delmonico. Al claimed it was his stash and The Beatles had never tried it. Ringo has confirmed Al's story and said that John asked him to be his "royal taster."

In the studio, we had one turntable to the left and two to the right. Above the turntables on the right was a stack of new albums. This was the new stuff, and 99 percent of that music wasn't being played in other US markets. Our music library was a walk-in closet.

There wasn't a lot of hustle-bustle going on. Mainly Jake yelling. People would come and go, and fans were welcome to visit.

Listeners would show up with food. Some would show up with drugs. Others showed up at night scantily dressed to shtupp. They were full-spectrum. One listener, a woodworker, once brought two beautiful tables to the studio. He asked if I wanted one. I gratefully said yes. I still have this table in my living room. I wish I could remember his name. I didn't consider this payola although he did want me to play Ronnie Wood. Just kidding.

The tenants were either oblivious or happy and amused when we radio guys would come and go with our rock star guests. ("Wow, oh look, honey. Frank Zappa's hair is really long.")

This isn't revisionist history, but there seems to be more importance placed on the memory of 'HFS in the building now than there was back in real time as we experienced it.

One day a box arrived at the station addressed to me. Inside the box was a beautiful hardcover copy of *Don Quixote,* arguably one of the greatest literary works ever. Quixote, with his companion, Sancho Panza, tries to revive chivalry in sixteenth-century Spain.

With the book were several capsules of what looked like excellent mescaline. Also included was a detailed letter on how I should use the hallucinogenic, what I should expect, when I would probably throw up, and so forth. I was very impressed with the thoughtfulness of this listener.

And, no I didn't do the mescaline. Although years earlier I had. Once with my then-girlfriend on a Cape Cod beach. She was from DC. Our trip was going great until she got fixated on the people around us on the beach with their Massachusetts accents ("Let's pahk the cah in Hahvihd Yahd.")

She got so psychedelically fixated that she thought they were all Kennedys, and we were intruders on the Kennedy beach. I had to talk her down.

WGTB

I had heard Georgetown University's progressive music station, WGTB, a few times while at American University, but they seemed like they were "preaching to the choir" in their politics a little too much and weren't my cup of tea. I preferred to let the music speak to the politics rather than me telling people what I thought they should think.

Steve Lorber was a student at Georgetown University when he got hired at WGTB in 1974. "The station was very political," Steve recalls, "although my show, *Mystic Eyes,* was all about the music. I liked the old garage sounds of bands like the Music Machine and the Standells, with the new progressive stuff like Genesis coming out." Steve is pretty sure he was one of the first DJs to play the Sex Pistols in the United States.

"We used to make fun of' 'HFS back then," Steve says today. "They were playing "granola rock" with music by Little Feat and Bonnie Raitt. And we were introducing avant-garde European progressive fare. We had a very strong signal, whereas 'HFS was sometimes hard to dial in to. And believe it or not, WGTB was very much under the radar for a long time as far as the Jesuits who ran the university were concerned."

Steve believes it was when the Hoya basketball program under Coach John Thompson started heating up in 1978 that the Jesuits decided that the political spin of WGTB, with their promotion of the Washington Free Clinic and gay radio programs, was over the line. "I think the leaders were hoping to use the radio station for sports, and this created what became the end."

WGTB had long been a thorn in the side of the university, and there had been ongoing back-and-forth tussles. Georgetown's then-president, Father Timothy Healey, finally shut down WGTB in 1978 and eventually donated the station to the University of the District of Columbia for a single dollar. UDC sold the signal in 1997 to C-SPAN for $25 million. When WGTB was sold, Steve was hired to bring *Mystic Eyes* to 'HFS, the last bastion of free-thinking radio in town.

Several things happened when I started working at 'HFS that helped me realize I was no longer a college student. I lost some of my adolescent arrogance by meeting my on-air cohorts and other musicians my age. I observed how they were operating, often with organization and purpose. I viewed 'HFS as a gift and an opportunity. I suddenly wasn't a kid anymore. I was working a real job making a little money. Underline "little."

I am just New Age-y enough to be annoying, so excuse me if I sometimes get cosmic here. I have always felt that reality arrives at just the right time. The main objective I think we all had at 'HFS, but certainly I did, was to let the music be the star. Music always came first. Every word, segue, and moment was intended to clue somebody in on the music. On-air, I didn't talk much about myself.

There were exceptions. If I were in love with a girl, then I would play every song associated with her name. It would be "What's the New Mary Jane," "Cross-Eyed Mary," "Along Comes Mary," "The Wind Cries Mary," "Proud Mary," and so on. Again, when I got a new car, I'd do as many good car tunes as I could find.

God forbid if we were depressed. You might start looking for a ledge after four hours of sad music programming on one of those days. I admit this was self-indulgent, but if done right, it could be compelling and creative. I would agree that the thing that Weasel, Damian, and I shined at were our theme sets. There was no shortage of records about girls, cars, relationships, the weather—you name it.

Murray the K

I mentioned before that I first saw Jonathan "Weasel" Gilbert and his friend, Steve Leeds, on campus while at American University. They'd show up together at shows I'd attend. Steve was running the WAMU radio station and Weasel was his roommate; both were involved in radio. Steve and Weasel grew up on Long Island, New York, and listened to

"Murray the K" Kaufman, the self-described "fifth Beatle," on New York City's WINS 1010 radio station when they were kids.

Weasel had been running the reel-to-reel tapes of many of the great ethnic radio shows at 'HFS on the weekends. These ethnic shows ran on Sundays from 1 p.m. to 2 a.m. and included Indian, Jewish, Italian, Arabic, German, Greek, French, and Korean variety shows. For the shows that weren't live, he would babysit the tape player and press "play." If there was a tape jam, then he was screwed.

In 1971, Murray the K came to Washington from New York to do a short-lived show on WWDC. Jake announced that he was hiring Murray to come to 'HFS. Steve Leeds came in to produce Murray's show, and Weasel became Murray's engineer. Weasel was more than thrilled the first time Murray asked him to "get John and Yoko on the phone to test volume levels for an interview."

Murray, with his on-air partner, Judy Black, would be at 'HFS for one year. He came and went. But he was always very nice to me. He once took me backstage to meet singer Tom Jones, and I got the chance to watch Tom struggle to get his butt into a girdle in order to slim his waist for the show. Otherwise, we at 'HFS didn't really see Murray that much. Murray and Jake were simpatico, and got along well. Murray would do his five-day shift at 'HFS and then return to New York on weekends to do a nationally broadcast show for NBC's *Monitor,* which led to a spot with a regular nightly show on WNBC. He passed away from cancer in 1982 at age sixty.

Johnny Holliday, later the radio "Voice of the University of Maryland Terrapins" in both football and basketball, had a WWDC morning show. He worked with Murray the K on New York City station WINS in 1964, Murray's heyday. Johnny described Murray:

"To me, he was like a Pied Piper, running his live shows at Brooklyn's Fox Theatre. Seeing him on stage at the Fox—dancing his heart out while the crowd went wild—led me to believe that here was a guy who could still do it with the best of them. He was electric and extremely charismatic. He'd come out with that little straw hat on, and V-neck sweater. Tight pants. Beatle boots. I wished I had that much talent that I could flaunt."

When we asked Johnny today what he remembers about the early WHFS years, he said: "I first heard about a radio station that had 'The Weasel.' Then I heard they had 'The Weasel' and 'The Surf.' But when I finally tuned in, the music reminded me of what we were trying to do in my previous job at KYA in San Francisco: play local music and build an audience. For KYA, the local musicians included Janis Joplin, Jefferson Airplane, and the Grateful Dead."

Weasel

Weasel got his overnight radio spot in 1973. I was doing evenings, and he'd follow me, so I saw him for a few minutes each night for many years as we traded shifts. Sometimes we'd banter on-air and sometimes we just nodded to each other.

Weasel was very creative. It was in his DNA. He would put together very inventive and often inspired set lists at 'HFS. Since Weasel was on overnight, he could go on and on unrestrained. And he had a very unusual voice. Very un-radiolike.

We both grew up listening to East Coast radio. Weasel's early radio influence included John Zacherle, who found big success as a spoofy Count Dracula–style character. His 1958 "Dinner with Drac" song was a novelty hit. As we write this book, he's still alive and well at age ninety-seven.

With Jonathan "Weasel" Gilbert in 2015. Credit: © Stephen Moore

In today's radio, you might have fourteen seconds to talk, but without constraints the 'HFS staff could go on for fourteen minutes or longer. Weasel could pull that off. He might see fingerprints on the studio glass and turn that observation into a monologue with music that went for an hour. This is a tricky thing to pull off. You never want to alienate listeners with too much talking, but Weasel was able to find the sweet spot by pairing good stories with astonishing details and exceptional music.

He also has a mind like a steel trap. He can tell you what he had for breakfast eighteen Thanksgivings ago. However, he doesn't have total recall. That was my dad (joking).

Weasel lived in the Triangle Towers and still does. He would watch everything that came and went at 'HFS and knew everybody's business.

Other than a few minutes of banter with Weasel when he followed me, I'd see him and my fellow jocks at Jake's staff meetings. These were held a half-block from the studio at the Holiday Inn of Bethesda. The Margolius family were co-owners of both 'HFS and this Holiday Inn. We could use it for free, and Jake was always a fan of free.

Jake was in charge, so these meetings were mandatory. This was no benevolent dictatorship. He would always have an agenda. Low on the agenda would be food crumbs and coffee stains in the studio. High on the agenda would be switching our on-air shifts around. He'd play musical chairs with our schedule. And being Jake, he didn't recognize air shifts the way Arbitron did: 6:00 to 10:00 mornings, 10:00 a.m. to 2:00 p.m. mid-day, 2:00 to 7:00 afternoon drive, 7:00 p.m. to

The one and only Jake Einstein.
Credit: © Cerphe Archive

12:00 midnight evenings, and overnight. Jake would slice the times up according to Jake.

Jake would create odd hours for us, like maybe 1:00 to 6:00 p.m., and switch us around for no apparent reason. Now, being a control freak is not necessarily a bad thing when you are running a radio station. You have to rein some people in. I had to do that to some extent when I was at WJFK in later years. I didn't enjoy it, but Jake did.

He would announce, "Okay, Damian, you're going on in afternoons, and Cerphe, you will be on at nights." I would ask, "Jake, when does this start?" and he'd say, "Today."

None of us would push back on Jake because there was always the nearby Little Tavern where we could be serving burgers if we challenged him. I think Weasel was especially grateful for his overnight spot.

No Competition

Josh Brooks would bring in bluegrass to his show. Weasel, Damian, and I were kind of doing the same things. I would listen to all of us and some- times it would just *sound so good*. I was sure the listeners were feeling it. It was a powerful way of communicating for those times. We were doing these tone paintings with music. We were creating moods. We were 'HFS, Home Grown Radio.

I never felt any competition within our cohort of DJs at 'HFS. Jake's son David was the program manager for most of the time I was there. He was older than we were. For me, he was a little hard to get to know. He had a love for jazz. The mid-1970s was great for him because there was the popularity of Stanley Clarke, Weather Report, Mahavishnu Orchestra, Herbie Hancock, and other fusion artists. David loved that stuff and incorporated this music into his show. I learned to appreciate fusion from David.

Adele Abrams joined 'HFS as a part-time weekend DJ in 1974. I liked Adele very much. She was a twenty-year-old UMD grad who had previously worked at the campus station, WMUC, and briefly at WINX-AM.

"I was going out of my frickin' mind at WINX playing songs like "Billy, Don't Be a Hero," every hour," Adele today admits. "This wasn't a great time for Top 40 music. My dream was to work at 'HFS. I had heard that they were looking to hire a woman DJ, so I sent them one of my WMUC air checks. This particular example of my work was made after a friend of mine had committed suicide. The music was very emotional."

David surprised Adele with a phone call invitation to join her at the Psyche Delly for an interview. After a few Heinekens, they ended up in an argument on which Miles Davis record was the best. She said *Kind of Blue* and he picked *Sketches of Spain*. Adele says she thought the interview ended badly. "Oh shit. I shouldn't be arguing with the program director," she thought as she walked to her car.

Nevertheless, she got the job at 'HFS from 6:00 a.m. to noon for her Saturday morning show, and would also be engineering the Sunday ethnic shows.

She says, "You have to understand that I was a stone fan of 'HFS in college. My radio career goal was to work there. The fact that I achieved this at age twenty was remarkable. I was in awe of Josh, Cerphe, and Damian while in college. There was a little hero worship going on from me when I arrived, so I didn't hang out with the full-time on-air staff much because I was starstruck."

Adele reflects: "David Einstein was in a tough position. Being the program director and also the son of the owner, he was trying to keep the business going while herding the cats, the crazy hippies he managed. He was ten years older than me. He wasn't flashy. He often wore a tie to work. He didn't have a device like Weasel's voice or Cerphe's smooth style. So I think he got overlooked. And because he was in a boss position, he really didn't get a chance to bond with others. It was kind of a weird thing. But he was very knowledgeable about music and we developed a close relationship.

"Jake next hired me full-time to also write the advertising spots that weren't provided by the agencies and other station promotions. He knew I had studied marketing and liked what I was doing for 'HFS. We meshed. He was funny. I got positive feedback from him, although he'd certainly tell me that my stuff was crap if he didn't like it.

"One memory stands out when I think about Jake. It was February 7, 1978. I was at work when I got a phone call telling me that my father had died suddenly. I didn't know what to do. I hadn't seen my dad for a long time as he lived in New Jersey. I walked in to tell Jake what happened and that I needed some days off.

"Jake was so empathetic. He gave me a big hug. Asked me if I was okay. He gave me money for a plane ticket to fly up to the funeral. He said, 'Take as much time as you need.' I tear up just thinking about this memory. This wasn't the 'If he ain't yelling, he ain't sellin' Jake. It was another side of him. And our relationship forever changed after that. He became almost a father figure to me. I loved him."

Today, Adele is the president of the Law Office of Adele L. Abrams, a full-service firm of nine staff that focuses on occupational and mine safety and health, employment, and environmental law. She is also a faculty member at Catholic University.

Suzanne Takes You Down

Suzanne Gordon was one of the first 'HFS staff people I had the pleasure of getting to know. Unlike other on-air guys like Damian, David, and Thomas Grooms, Suzanne was actually there when I did my show and we became good friends. She was 'HFS's first news director, hosting her "News of the Universe" segments five times a day.

I remember Suzanne as being authentically cosmic in those days. She was a young feminist, lived in a Hindu Ashram, loved our 'HFS music, liked science fiction, and had strong political views and a wide range of interests. She had the intellect and drive to be a great news broadcaster, and she had a pretty impressive fan base of listeners.

"I was involved in the rock and roll, political, and spiritual worlds. These worlds were sometimes in tension with each other, and some people didn't get it," recalls Suzanne.

Today, she is L. Suzanne Gordon, PhD ("I'm a doctor, baby!!" she told us when we talked for this chapter), a professor in the University of Maryland Communications Department. Her PhD dissertation, *Field Notes from the Light: The Meaning and Significance of Near-Death Experiences,* is available online through the University of Maryland.

A native Washingtonian, she attended Hart Junior High and Ballou High School in Southeast DC, sitting behind or near Danny Gatton in each year's homeroom class. "They seated us alphabetically, and Danny and I became close," says Suzanne. "I remember him coming in to class really dragging every Monday morning after a weekend of playing guitar. He was a very sweet guy. Later, I'd go see him at the Keg and other DC clubs when he had his band. I was so crushed when I learned of his death."

Gordon's first encounter with 'HFS came when she worked summers at the *Washington Star* advertising department in the late 1960s during college. Jake Einstein would call about every three weeks placing an ad for a secretary. "I knew he managed a radio station. But soon he started asking for me. And [from talking with him] the first thing I thought is that he would probably be a tough guy to work for."

Eventually, Jake persuaded Suzanne to come to the station part-time to help with their public service announcements (PSAs) and do promos for events. "I resisted working there full-time, but eventually accepted in 1973 and started my news broadcasts."

"David [Einstein] was an excellent program director. Damian was a brilliant music director. Jake had a good eye for talent, but overall I didn't like working for him," says Suzanne. "I think it was hard for most of us to work for Jake."

The station didn't have any regular newswire services like UPI or Associated Press, so Suzanne would either rewrite news stories (for example, the death of Chilean President Salvadore Allende) from other sources or write them herself from her own experiences (for example, compelling reports from attending antiwar demonstrations, or covering DC activist Mitch Snyder and his Community for Creative Nonviolence group's work on behalf of the city's homeless).

Though small in number, other women broadcasters were emerging in the very early 1970s, including Cathy Hughes, who was just beginning to create the urban radio format called "The Quiet Storm" on Howard University's radio station (WHUR), and native Washingtonian Connie Chung who graduated U-MD in 1969 with a journalism degree and was soon the Washington correspondent for the *CBS News with Walter Cronkite*.

Another memory I have of Suzanne is that she would share vegetarian recipes with listeners. She'd play Paul and Linda McCartney's "Cook of the House" to lead into this bit. This evolved into the WHFS Vegetarian Cookbook. Her idea.

Suzanne looks back: "It's been more than forty years now. Cerphe and David played my favorite music at the station. Cerphe was the master and the star at 'HFS. I think Jake became jealous of his rising star status. Cerphe made assembling the set lists an art form. Twenty minutes would go by, and then it would hit me, the theme here is baseball."

"I'd be sitting in a small room in my ashram with a little fan pushing the pot smoke out the window, listening to Cerphe and thinking, 'He's reading my mind.' I would call him up often and tell him what a great job he was doing. Cerphe is a warm, kind, and spiritually aware person. We were very brotherly and sisterly together, but I love that picture of us kissing near the record library."

All the Way with LBJ

Suzanne says she was a "little hoodlum" growing up on Atlantic Avenue in Southeast DC. However, a boyfriend introduced her to Luci Johnson, the vice president's daughter, and they became friends. Vice President Johnson invited her to his colonial home in the Forest Hills section of DC often. Luci would spend the night with Suzanne in her Southeast home, with her Secret Service agent always nearby."

At 'HFS, Suzanne would later report on the Vietnam War demonstrations and she certainly did not agree with LBJ's war, but about Johnson himself she says today, "The Johnsons were the real deal. He was a good man." She remembers attending a dinner with President and Mrs. Kennedy at which Suzanne was sitting close enough to Jackie to whisper to Luci that "Jackie has big, bony feet, too." That became an inside joke.

Regarding 'HFS guests, Suzanne picks musicians Herbie Hancock and "Wah Wah" Watson (Melvin Ragin) as her favorites. They were friendly and down-to-earth. She also recalls saying, "Hi," once to a stranger in the studio and as soon as he replied, she knew from his voice that he was Tom Waits.

Wonder Who's Coming?

The Triangle Towers was guest star central for rock musicians for sure. Another example is when everyone on staff was over the moon to learn that Stevie Wonder was dropping by the 'HFS studios to promote his 1972 album, *Talking Book*. This album was nothing but great, with two tracks reaching Number 1 on Billboard's Top 100: "You Are the Sunshine of My Life" and "Superstition." In town to play a concert at the University of Maryland's Cole Field House, Stevie did only two local radio stints: at 'HFS (David interviewed him) and with R&B radio station WHUR.

Stevie (whose real name is Steveland Hardaway Judkins) arrived at our station with a large entourage. He was gracious and happy. I was surprised that he was six feet tall and rather big. After his interview (sorry, no tape), Stevie said goodbye to everyone and moved to exit the front door of the station. I yelled, "Thanks, Stevie, for coming." He turned around to face our small farewell group and boomed, "I'll see you all later," and chuckled.

I bet he used that line a thousand times. He was just too cool.

And speaking of cool memories, it was announced in 2014 that a documentary film, *Feast Your Ears: The Story of WHFS, 102.3 FM*, was planned. Community enthusiasm for this proposed film—with associated support from musicians and media—reinforced how much the memory of 'HFS still resonates in the hearts of our listeners. I immediately gave my enthusiastic endorsement to this project and was very pleased to appear at several community fund-raising events to launch the project. The production team filmed my recollections for this documentary and I, like so many fans of 'HFS, look forward to seeing this movie.

CHAPTER 8
WHFS 102.3 — Side Two

There was much to learn about music in those days. The 'HFS staff were my catalyst. We'd turn each other on to the music that we were passionate about and that spoke to us. When I listen to tapes of us back in mid-1970s, I first think we sound so National Public Radio. We were serious about analyzing this music and sharing details like where it was recorded, who the bass player was, and so forth. And listeners responded favorably. They wanted

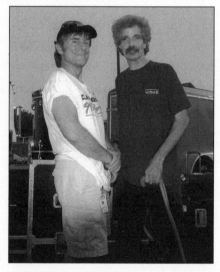

With Damian in 2013.
Credit: © Dan Rosenstein/Cerphe Archive

to learn the details, too. This radio interest in detail tended to evaporate as time went on. It's gone now. You won't be hearing, "And yes, Mike Bloomfield was using Ernie Ball flat-wound guitar strings . . ." For this you need to search Facebook groups like 70s DC Area Music Scene.

Damian Riley Einstein was very much into and knowledgeable about the blues and Americana music (before it was called that). Damian was the fifth of seven kids born to Jake and Rosamond Einstein in Denton, Maryland, on the Eastern Shore. Growing up, he discovered a box of 78 rpm jazz records by Dizzy Gillespie and Billie Holiday in his house and loved them. He began a career in graphic design and advertising until he heard Jimi Hendrix. After Jimi, music became Damian's mojo.

He started his radio career in 1970. His warm, wonderful vibe came through on the radio. He was a handsome young guy who was a radio star and also a great harmonica player. Damian's theme song was the "Two Step de Platin" by Ambrose Thibodeaux, a Louisiana French Acadian artist.

On December 13, 1975, Damian, with friends Ted Wagner and Tobey Nealis, then a carpenter who had worked for 'HFS, had been partying at the Psyche Delly bar across the street from the station. Tobey had just received his real estate license. I knew these guys well.

The news report headline was, 2 KILLED, ANNOUNCER HURT IN CRASH. At 2:50 a.m., their truck jumped a curb, crashed through a fence, skidded 140 feet across a field, and wedged under a walkway spanning a creek. The force of the impact sheared off the top of the truck.

I was devastated when I heard this news the next morning. We were all in shock at the station that next day. Both Jake Einstein and I shed tears together and prayed in Jake's office, hoping Damian would pull through. His prospects didn't look good. He was in extremely critical condition at Silver Spring's Holy Cross Hospital with head injuries, a broken jaw, and lung problems. Weasel was called in to identify the bodies of Ted and Tobey. I believe he was half-expecting to find me with them at the morgue since I hung out so much with Damian then.

Damian was comatose for ninety-three days. Bruce Springsteen and Clarence Clemons came to visit him while he was unconscious between life and death. The doctors told Jake that we shouldn't expect Damian to recover to lead a useful life. Brain damage, they said.

At first, I didn't think that Damian would survive. One of things that saved him I believe is that he has the tenacity that's hardwired into the Einstein genes. Both his dad and his siblings have that forceful presence. Being a middle child, he was probably influenced by both his parents, obviously, but also his brothers and sisters. He was the creative Einstein and, fortunately, a survivor. He awoke from the coma and during the two years following the crash, Damian proved the doctors wrong through determination, effort, and courage. And no doubt considerable pain.

When he returned in a wheelchair to a guest appearance on Josh's afternoon 'HFS show in 1977, Jake Einstein told the press, "The lesson to this whole thing is don't believe what the doctors say."

Damian picked "Cakewalk into Town" by Taj Mahal for his first on-air record since he was sidelined. The lyrics included "I had the blues so bad it put my face in a permanent frown, but now I'm feeling so much better, I could cakewalk into town." Damian said that God had helped him recover, jokingly adding "even though I'm a sleazy character."

From my perspective, Damian is imaginative and beloved. He is such a sweet guy. He is as witty, sharp, and wonderfully acerbic as he was before the accident. We share a goofy sense of humor. I learned a lot about blues from him. He's like the brother I never had.

Jake put him back on-air after the accident. He was somewhat hard to understand because of his serious injuries; and for new listeners who didn't know him before, this was difficult. But for those of us who loved him and understood what he brought to the party, we wanted him back on the air to do his craft. It was cruel and sad that this accident happened to someone who speaks for a living. It reminds me of the French jazz guitarist Django Reinhardt, whose fourth and fifth fingers on his fretting hand became paralyzed after burns from a fire. Or NPR's call-in show host, Diane Rehm, who has suffered with and overcome a neurological condition that affects the quality of her voice.

Jake Einstein, with a group of investors, had bought WHFS 102.3-FM in 1967 for $140,000. Twenty years later, he sold the station for $8.2 million to Duchossois Communications (pronounced "Duchey-Swah"), a division of Duchossois Industries Inc., a corporate giant with investments from race courses to defense manufacturing. Damian was ultimately, and not surprisingly, let go, with his disabilities cited as grounds. I was at WJFK when I heard that a rally to save Damian's job was developing. Nearly 10,000 showed up at Joe's Record Paradise in Wheaton, Maryland, for a "Save Damian" rally. Catfish Hodge, Freebo from Bonnie Raitt's band, and other musicians came out in support. I recorded a public service announcement at WJFK to promote the rally. The *Washington Post* picked up on it.

A support letter came from the "Friends of Damian Einstein." These "Friends" included Little Feat, David Crosby, Graham Nash, Nils Lofgren, and Bonnie Raitt. They wrote: "To remove Damian, or anyone, because of a supposed disability is, in our opinion, unconscionable. In focusing on Mr. Einstein's supposed disability instead of his tremendous ability to communicate and educate in a simple, eloquent manner, you have created an issue where an issue has never before existed. On the air and off, Damian Einstein is one of the greatest assets you possess."

Unfortunately, it was ludicrous for us to think that Duchossois was going to care about Damian.

But Damian didn't give up. With help from the Maryland Commission on Human Relations, he proved that his dismissal was discriminatory. The Maryland board agreed "that there was no reason to believe that Damian's speech interfered with his ability to perform and deliver a quality radio program." So on October 22, 1990, a year and a half after his removal, Damian returned to WHFS.

I've stayed in touch with Damian over the years and we still joke around and are always glad to see each other. He gets around fine with his cane. He and his wife, Patty, are happy.

Bonnie, Psyche Delly, and Root Boy

Early on, Jake would send us out to do radio shows remotely at various stores and restaurants. One time, I got assigned all week to the front window of Custom Hi-Fi, an electronics store on Wisconsin Avenue in Bethesda. They sold radios, turntables, speakers, and the like. I had met and interviewed Bonnie Raitt a few times, so I invited her to come to the store, and she did. So did Boz Scaggs, and the Nighthawks, who played inside the store.

'HFS was playing Bonnie's songs from her first two critically acclaimed albums, *Bonnie Raitt* (1971) and *Give It Up* (1972), but she still wasn't the commercial success that she became in 1977 with her hit song "Runaway" from her album, *Sweet Forgiveness*. And she wasn't a huge success until 1989's *Nick of Time*. Now she is iconic.

I knew a little about Bonnie's background from our early interviews. Her dad was John Raitt, the Broadway star of the movie *Pajama Game* and many stage musicals. Born in California, she went to school in Boston and ended up being more of an East Coast girl. Dick Waterman, also from Boston, was a promoter in the early 1960s of original African-American blues artists like Mississippi John Hurt and Son House. Dick persuaded Bonnie to pursue a musical career and became her manager.

"People have the impression that Bonnie came into the blues world because of me but that is not true," Waterman says today. "She had seen many blues artists in the Los Angeles area and she had learned to play every lick on the *Blues at Newport* album. What I did do was introduce her to blues artists and then she was on her own to absorb what they were doing."

One thing about Bonnie Raitt: she has a strong personality and she absolutely refuses to take any bullshit from anybody. "I was a strong girl and I am a strong woman," she would say. This attitude sometimes results in other people having less-than-pleasant experiences with her, but we got along fine.

Bonnie liked the DC area. Not only was there a music scene here, there was a strong blues scene going on. I know she learned a lot of slide guitar from Lowell George. You can argue that Lowell was one of the first slide guitarists to put leads on top of those New Orleans–type rock rhythms like "Dixie Chicken," and you can hear his influence on Bonnie's slide style. I watched her join Lowell at many shows.

When Little Feat broke up for a short time in 1974, Lowell helped local bluegrass dobro player Mike Auldridge (of the Seldom Scene) with his solo work, *Bluegrass and Blues* (Takoma Records), and on Bonnie's album *Takin' My Time*.

Both Lowell and Bonnie chose Fender Stratocaster guitars as their main gig rigs. Lowell bought stock 1970s Strats and modified them by replacing one pickup with a lipstick pickup from a Fender Telecaster. This added a higher ring to his leads. He also used a lot of compression on his leads, which produced that legendary sustain that became the hallmark of his sound.

Bonnie is the only female artist to have a Signature Fender Stratocaster guitar made in her honor. However, the two artists differed on slides. Lowell used an 11/16 Craftsman socket from Sears. "They don't break and you can get them easily," Lowell would say. Bonnie prefers a slide made from a Mateus wine bottleneck. At Lowell's memorial service, Bonnie called him the "Thelonius Monk of rock and roll."

One of Bonnie's gifts is that she has toured so many cities and hung out with so many musicians that she kind of knows everybody's town. Onstage, she'll talk about local restaurants like she's your buddy.

One of her earliest shows in the DC area was opening for John Prine for a week at the Cellar Door in 1972. *Evening Star* music writer Michael Oberman said, "Bonnie's vocals are a mixture of country blues and soul and her bottleneck guitar and piano playing seem to naturally blend in with the material she chooses." As usual, he got that right.

When Milos Forman filmed parts of his movie *Hair* in 1978 at the Washington Mall reflecting pool in front of the Lincoln Memorial, it was Bonnie and her band playing on a small side stage that helped recruit the many extras needed for the movie scenes. The concert happened at the end of the shoot, incentive for hanging around for the long takes and a way to move the extras from one place to another. They wanted everyone to run into the field where Bonnie's stage was. The field filling up and then full of people is the film's closing shot.

Bonnie is one of the best examples of an artist who really cares about the music, and she gives everything she has to bring you into her experience.

Chain Gang

Jake loved sending us out on "remotes," broadcasts outside of the studio walls in locations around town. "Remotes are good for us," he'd say. "They let us know who is listening to us, what sort of music they like, and they put the disc jockey in touch with his audience."

Honestly, I was never a huge fan of doing these remotes. But guess who was?

Weasel.

Weasel's radio shift was normally 1:00 to 6:00 a.m., so the remotes gave him a chance to have some fun up close with listeners. He once did a remote at Armand's Pizza, and playfully reported the fake special pizzas the place was "offering" on the night of his appearance: There was "Cerphe's Chewy Cheese," "Tom's Tummy Tickler," "Weasel's Insanity," "David's Fantasy Mushroom," "Josh's Country Pie," "Damian's Devious Delight," and "Hall's Hallucination."

Weasel was asked by a listener to play a song about pizza, and the only one he could come up with was Dean Martin's "That's Amore" ("when the moon hits your eye like a big pizza pie, that's amore"). 'HFS didn't have this tune in Weasel's record stack that night (or any other night, or day).

It would often be at these store remotes where Maurice, the Balloon Man, might float on by to join in on the fun. Sometimes, it seemed like the Balloon Man was everywhere up and down Wisconsin Avenue. You could often hear him chant his familiar "Make the ladies happy . . . make the children happy" while selling his balloons outside Martin's Tavern or the Roy Rogers (a.k.a. Drug Central) in Georgetown. We'd run his chant on the air. Sometimes, sports fans would recognize his voice selling beer at RFK Stadium during the sports games. Urban legend has it that Maurice was busted for selling something heavier than balloons.

Adele on Weasel

Adele Abrams remembers a remote with Weasel at the Float and Smoke, a waterbed store that also sold bongs and rolling paper in Camp Springs, Maryland. Jokingly, Weasel kept referring to the store as "Bed and Head." It was Weasel's idea to see how many people could fit onto a waterbed. People piled on. At some point in this contest, you could hear Adele say on-air, "Hey, somebody is biting my ass." Weasel and Adele always had a great banter going between them.

"Weasel was always something of an enigma," Adele admits. "We always got along great. The girls and I would 'squeeze the weas,' which was a running joke. He lived in the Triangle Towers then and still does. Several 'HFS staff had apartments back then and it was always party central.

"But off the air, Weasel is a very quiet and shy guy. He's never had a car and never driven. That's been a mystery to me. But on-air, he becomes the Weasel we all know."

Remote Game Changer

The big game changer in what a remote could do for Washington DC's local music started when Joe Triplett offered to build a stage for owner

Jim Anderson in the back room of his small carryout sandwich shop, the Psyche Delly. With a stage, Joe's band Claude Jones could play there. The address was 4846 Cordell Avenue, across the street from the 'HFS studios. In 1974, former Bambino's pizza chain owner Lou Sordo bought this property and further renovated it. Lou didn't know much about music or radio then, but he was a creative guy, and someone whose ego didn't stop him from asking questions, like "Why do these musicians need to have long hair to play music?"

Fortunately, Lou met up with Mark Wenner, vocalist and harp player with his newly formed blues and roots band, The Nighthawks. Mark told Lou that the Psyche Delly really needed music. "It's too good a space to waste," Mark said.

Lou took Mark's advice, adding a bar and installing acoustic tiles. Lou didn't just want to draw a big paying crowd, he wanted the individual bands he'd hire to build their own audience. This "play to the door" policy meant the musicians could earn money if they concentrated on building *their* audience to pack the small 150-person capacity club. This philosophy was different from most club owners back then. Lou was factoring in musical appreciation to the success of his bands, not just raking in dollars and cents.

Soon The Nighthawks, with Mark, Jimmy Thackery on lead guitar, Jan Zukowski on bass, and Pete Ragusa on drums, were rockin' the place. Lou suggested to Jake Einstein that WHFS air a live audio remote. Jake agreed but wanted to make sure Lou had professional sound. Lou rented a sound truck. The show was recorded and became the first of the *Live at the Psyche Delly* record series. The next live album featured Danny Gatton and the Fat Boys. This began the long symbiotic relationship between the Psyche Delly and WHFS 102.3.

Josh Brooks took the lead in representing 'HFS in person at the club. He hosted the Jump Parties with local bands in the cozy back room. He once wore a gorilla suit to introduce the iconoclastic Root Boy Slim, who launched his career from the club. 'HFS made Root Boy's "Christmas at K-Mart" a holiday standard. Soon The Psyche Delly became the Cellar Door of the suburbs.

"I first saw Root Boy at the Cellar Door," recalls Bill Danoff, the Starland Vocal Band leader who penned "Afternoon Delight," inspired by a drink of the same name at Georgetown's Clyde's Bar. "Root Boy blew me away. He was wearing a diaper and a leopard skin something over his shoulders, with those huge sunglasses. His band was incredible. I loved his songs "Boogie Till You Puke," and "I'm Not Too Old for You." We also ran into each other because we used the same pharmacy on MacArthur Boulevard. Offstage, he was Ken, short for Foster McKenzie. He was pretty legally medicated every time I saw him, but like so many others, was into his own trip with additional substances."

Once, Root Boy sat next to Bill in a Catholic church for drummer Bob Berberich's wedding. Root Boy invited Bill to follow him in the boy's bathroom in the adjacent church school where he laid out a few lines of coke. "I joined him but I'm an old Catholic boy and at the time, I kept thinking we're going to get caught and my career will be over."

Washington Post music writer Richard Harrington wrote the Psyche Delly's obituary when the club ended its live music in January 1983. Richard noted, "There was, in fact, a marked difference between the basic boogie and honky-tonk music of the 1970s and the often-dour New Wave sound of the early 1980s. The Nighthawks were the perfect example of a classic bar band working out of an exuberant blues and R&B bag and promising a night of blistering, barrelhouse fun: theirs was the kind of music that encouraged drinking and general carousing. . . . It also didn't help when Maryland raised the drinking age from eighteen to twenty-one last July. That cut off a large part of the Delly's natural constituency and sent it to bars in the District. . . ."

Today, 4846 Cordell Avenue is the address of Flanagan's Harp and Fiddle, an Irish-inspired restaurant that features live music. The Harp is also known as "The Home of Mary Ann Redmond," who plays there every Sunday. Richmond, Virginia, native Mary Ann is an astonishingly soulful singer who has won twenty-four Washington Area Music Awards (Wammies). With gifted Washington, DC, singer/songwriter Todd Wright, Mary Ann coauthored "Love Me Anyway," which Celine Dion covered as a duet with French singer Johnny Hallyday in 2012. That song, on Celine's CD *Sans Attendre,* has sold over three million copies.

Cerphe on High

Working on-air night after night had aspects beyond just talking and spinning discs that many people may not imagine. On occasion, I received calls from listeners who were very depressed. I think I talked them down from the ledge. We didn't become bosom buddies or anything like that, and I really don't know what happened to them. But at the time, I remember saying anything to keep them on the phone: "Hey, stick with me. I need to cue the next song." That type of thing. Sometimes I think about these calls; I sure hope everyone got through it okay.

And then there were the advertisements. Here's an example of one I did for the Joint Possession, a head shop just outside the gates of the University of Maryland.

"If you've been doing some of your best bogarting lately but you're still not getting enough, the Joint Possession in College Park has some good ideas for retaliation. The Joint Possession has bongs and tokers, water pipes and chillums, papers and roach clips, and all sorts of paraphernalia that will keep you doing your best bogart ever. And while you're doing that, you can read Zap Comics too. They have the whole collection at the Joint Possession at 7402 Baltimore Boulevard in old College Park, Maryland."

Ads like this may have attracted my fair share of listeners phoning in who just assumed that we were all stoned on air. We may have sounded like we were, but hey man, like that was the patois of our generation, baby. Generally, I think many listeners found me disappointing in person because they had in their mind that I was Cerphe, the party guy. Drugs, sex, and rock and roll.

The truth is that I was never a drinker or a stoner. I played soccer in high school, so the recreational drugs would have slowed me down. Plus I was asthmatic. Although I'll admit that I tried pot, coke, and hallucinogens when I got to American University, I became devoted to meditation and a vegetarian lifestyle. I've been that way for over four decades. That's why they call me the Guru of Tofu, the Sultan of Soy.

As I began trying to improve my spirituality in those early days at 'HFS, I invited Yogi Bhajan into the studio for an interview. He was the spiritual leader and entrepreneur who introduced Kundalini Yoga to the United States. Locally, his 3HO (Healthy, Happy, Holy Organization) Foundation owned the Golden Temple restaurant at Dupont Circle.

"The art of healing, the art of ecstasy, the art of God consciousness has millions of names in mystic terms," Yogi Bhajan told me. "It has to do with rhythm and reality. When the body is in rhythm, there is ease. When the body, or any part of the body goes out of rhythm, there is dis-ease."

I think we did twenty-five minutes together on-air, which is an eternity in radio.

Beach Boy Mike Love once came on with me to discuss Transcendental Meditation. We talked more about TM than music. We talked a lot. Again, that flexibility of time to talk on-air was a gift.

Years later at WJFK, I got a chance to again interview David Crosby, who was in the middle of his melodrama of drugs, guns, and potential prison. He had just been frog-marched off an airplane with a fantastic litany of contraband, and I was hoping to get a great interview.

My station manager agreed, but added, "Give him two minutes on-air." I don't think my manager cared much about what David did or didn't say; he just didn't want it to go long.

Fired Up and Out

In 1977, there was a Grateful Dead concert coming up at the Baltimore Civic Center. It was customary at 'HFS that when an important band like the Dead was coming to town, I might play an hour of their music a couple of days before the concert. Jake heard my show and came to me to object: "WHFS doesn't do this kind of promotion for upcoming shows."

I responded to Jake, "Are you kidding? Since when? None of us have ever had any direction on what to play or not play. It's why listeners tune in and it's what we've all been doing for the last seven years." Jake was just pissed because the concert promoter hadn't bought any airtime to promote the show.

He had written vague memos to me before with copies to the station's lawyer on this "artist promotion issue" he was hung up on. I was then young and naïve about how management works. I have figured out since that if they want you gone, then management starts a file on you.

However, on this day Jake showed up in his finest suit, tie, and gold cufflinks. That's when I found out I was fired. The suit and cufflinks were the giveaway. Everyone at the station knew that Jake liked to get finely dressed up to fire staff.

Because none of us had contracts or personal service agreements and WHFS was not a union signatory, Jake didn't need "just cause" to fire anyone. In fact, all of us at 'HFS were forbidden by Jake to join AFTRA/ SAG, the American Federation of Television and Radio Artists/Screen Actors Guild union. This was blatantly wrong.

There was major community blowback when Jake's ax fell on me. The newspaper guys called me from the *Washington Post,* the *Washington Star,* and others. Charles Young, a writer at the *Unicorn Times,* did a great story on my firing with the title "Out But Not Down."

Jake explained my exit to the *Washington Post* as "a long-time programming dispute . . . a difference of opinion between the station's idea of programming and Cerphe's. It has been coming for a year. It was inevitable."

I told the newspapers that Jake wouldn't tell me exactly why he fired me. After seven years at the station, I thought I deserved more than that. Jake routinely accused me of hyping things, and doing too much promotion for particular artists like Tom Waits, Bonnie Raitt, John Prine, the Grateful Dead, Frank Zappa, and Bruce Springsteen. I didn't consider playing good music as hyping; I considered it doing my job. I was turning listeners on to the music that I loved.

"Firing Cerphe was awful," Suzanne Gordon adds, "but Jake was always firing people. My associate, Charlie Gottenkieny, and I had a quote board on the back of our office door. We'd write cool things we heard by the staff or their guests. The quote that appeared the most was 'And another thing. You're fired.' Sometimes Jake would fire someone and then later in the day ask them to interview somebody, apparently forgetting that he had fired them."

Jake told the *Washington Evening Star* that WHFS had "a low-key esoteric taste in music but that Cerphe's approach had changed considerably from that format during the past year."

Say what?

What did change were the Arbitron April and May 1977 ratings for 'HFS. The station showed the strongest numbers ever, even beating album rocker station WMAL among women and men aged eighteen to twenty-four in the evening hours broadcast. This meant that my show surged in popularity during April and May. And at the end of May I'm let go.

Journalist Alex Cosper published an interview with Jake Einstein in the December 2000 issue of *Virtually Alternative.* He asked Jake, "Did you ever have input on what jocks played on the air at WHFS?"

The then-eighty-two-year-old Jake replied, "I didn't have input, I had denial. In other words, if I didn't like it, get rid of it. Sometimes, it got a little on the fine line of what I considered wasn't in the best taste, for lack of a better expression, and I'd take it off. I got in a couple of arguments. Columbia and I had a hot one at one time, I remember. So I just threw Columbia out of the station."

Looking back today, I think guys like Jake tended to pick on anyone who stood out. And that's exactly what I was trying to do. I wanted to attract every ear. I was dressing the part. Emceeing concerts. Building my audience. Getting ratings.

Again, we were both Leos. We both had tempers. And the lion is a cat. When cats get challenged, they sometimes arch their backs and try to appear bigger than they are. Jake would arch his body and fire you. It's possible that he was just resenting my rising popularity at the station. There was always a rage brewing in Jake, and he was definitely getting tired of dealing with me.

Although fired, I still had tickets to an upcoming 'HFS-sponsored event. I knew Jake would be there, so I bought a Boston cream pie from a bakery and took it with me to the event with a plan to smoosh it into Jake's face. However, when I got there, I saw that Jake had a very tall bodyguard, an off-duty Maryland cop, protecting him. I decided against risking getting pummeled by Jake's guardian angel.

After I said sayonara to 'HFS, I took some time to figure out what I was going to do. I reckoned I could continue doing my voiceovers and commercials.

Wrong. Jake made sure to let everyone know that he wouldn't be interested in buying any voiceovers or commercials by Cerphe. So Washington, DC, ad agencies effectively, if reluctantly, marginalized me because nobody wanted Jake Einstein as an enemy. Would you?

I still managed some freelance work and made some promotional appearances as "Cerphe (formerly of WHFS)." But I was deeply hurt by the firing. Remember, I never went to broadcasting school. I was an art major who by happenstance became a radio guy. I thought, "My God, if that's the way it is, then I don't want to be in radio."

Fortunately, I would get an Act Two in radio, thanks to WAVA radio station owner Alex Sheftell and his program director, Jim Herron.

Out of the blue, Jim, who was previously on air at WWDC, called and asked me if I'd come to the soft-rock station and "do anything I wanted." He offered Saturdays from 6:00 to 11:00 a.m. on WAVA 105.1. I would do the same freeform radio I did at 'HFS. I agreed and within a year, I was on permanent staff with an evening show, sharing the dial with my fellow WAVA crew: Jim Herron on mornings, Kelly Saunders and Gary Chase (formerly with DC 101), and overnight Lanie O'Dell (formerly from Richmond, Virginia's XL-102). DJs with last names, and working for a boss who was sane on a 50,000-watt flamethrower station that extended from Central Virginia through DC and Baltimore and reached Maryland's Eastern Shore.

I supported WAVA's music as it transitioned from "soft rock" to a more album-oriented rock (AOR) format. Although the set lists on my new show were not freeform, we were playing the favorite rockers like the Stones and Led Zeppelin and introducing new artists like the B-52s, Pat Benatar, and Dire Straits. The trip-tastic 1960s were over. The wonderful 1970s were turning into the New Wave 1980s. The Arlington, Virginia, studio of WAVA was a most happy home for me as my new on-air family began to build ratings against the top (AOR) station, DC-101.

I love radio.

CHAPTER 9

Stevie Nicks: Silver Springs

Stevie Nicks and I go way back to 1975 when Fleetwood Mac was an in-studio guest a few times. Stevie and Lindsey Buckingham had just joined Fleetwood Mac when they first visited me at 'HFS. Both were the American "new kids" in a very successful British band, so they let Mick Fleetwood and John McVie do much of the talking. Mick was way more articulate than John, who was either very stoned or had consumed tainted clams at Stuckey's on the interstate. He appeared to really not want to be at a radio station. Stevie and Lindsey repeated how excited they were at being asked to join the band, and I let them know that I loved their previous solo *Buckingham Nicks* album and suggested that the band perform material from it at the Cap Centre because 'HFS was playing it and listeners loved it. Stevie (still a brunette!) was wearing a peasant blouse and jeans, an early prototype of leather and lace (pun intended), but hadn't perfected her fairy outfit at this point. The seven veils would come later!

I joined them in the limo to the Cap Centre in Landover, Maryland. It was a memorable ride. On that occasion, John McVie inexplicably tried to jump out of the moving car as we briskly cruised down Wisconsin Avenue. He was halfway out of the limo, with Mick Fleetwood and I struggling to rein him in. We were lucky he wasn't killed. I still can't explain why he did this—what happens in the limo stays in the limo—but we got him calmed down and the show went on. That's rock and roll.

Stevie once told me that the Silver Spring, Maryland, exit sign on the Washington's doughnut of angst, the Capital Beltway, was the inspiration for the title of her song "Silver Springs."

Born and raised in Phoenix, Arizona, Stevie was a high school senior when she met her future love and musical partner, Lindsey Buckingham. He was playing "California Dreamin'" at a party and she started singing harmony with him. They migrated together to the San Francisco Bay Area to form a band called Fritz, opening for acts like Janis Joplin and Jimi Hendrix. Stevie points to them as her performance mentors. Her center-stage spotlight with Fritz was training for things to come.

Their shot at fame came when record producer Keith Olsen invited Lindsey and Stevie to Los Angeles for some recording at his studio, Sound City. These tracks became the *Buckingham Nicks* album. As luck would have it, drummer Mick Fleetwood of the British band Fleetwood Mac was looking for potential Los Angeles recording studios and visited Sound City. Producer Olsen chose a tape of "Frozen Love" from the *Buckingham Nicks* sessions to show the quality of his recording facilities. After listening, Fleetwood asked who the guitarist was. Olsen said Lindsey, adding he was one part of a duo and probably wouldn't leave his partner who was also his girlfriend. Soon, Lindsey and Stevie were in the band.

"Neither of us had ever heard of Fleetwood Mac," Stevie confesses, "so we went to a record store and bought their albums. I could see how we could add to their sound, how we could fit, although I didn't think they really needed me. But I loved all of them instantly."

Rock critic Bud Scopa reviewed their 1975 *Fleetwood Mac* in *Circus* magazine:

"From listening to Fleetwood Mac, you'd think this once-definitive British blues band was a Southern California pop group—and you'd be right. The three remaining English members—drummer Mick Fleetwood, bass man John McVie, and keyboard player Christine McVie—have moved to Los Angeles and traded in their first American member, guitarist Bob Welch, for a pair of Americans. Lindsey Buckingham and Stevie Nicks are largely responsible for making their new LP Fleetwood Mac's best since 1973's lovely *Bare Trees*."

Stevie was quoted by Sylvie Simmons in *Creem* magazine, describing the band: "I'm the baby of Fleetwood Mac—ha! I'm 33 years old, a very old baby, but it's hard for them to watch me walk away and do anything. Because everybody in Fleetwood Mac is possessive—including me. Everybody in Fleetwood Mac is jealous. That's why it's so passionate and always will be, because we never achieve boredom and there's always some fiery thing going on. It causes us a lot of grief, but at the same time it's never something that you don't find interesting. I can't really figure us out. It's a strange grouping of people."

Next came an emotional meltdown for the band. Christine divorced John. Mick's marriage went south, and Stevie and Lindsey's romance ended. But they still reported to the recording studio every day to create their triumphant second album, *Rumours*.

Rolling Stone critic John Swenson led his positive 1977 review of *Rumours* with "Rock and roll has this bad habit of being unpredictable. . . . But in Fleetwood Mac's case, the departure of guitarist Bob Welch— who'd reduced the band to recutting pointless and pretentious versions of old standards—amounted to the biggest break they ever had. With that and the addition of Lindsey Buckingham and Stevie Nicks, Fleetwood Mac suddenly became a California pop group; instead of laborious blues/rock jams they started turning out bright little three-minute singles with a hook in every chorus."

Stevie Today

Today, Stevie is back in Phoenix enjoying her life and status as a Rock and Roll Hall of Famer and composer/performer on the sixth biggest-selling studio album of all time, *Rumours.* I also lived in Phoenix for a short time and once saw Stevie in a Bed, Bath & Beyond store.

"I love Phoenix," Stevie confides. "People know me there and let me cruise around town and yes, Bed, Bath & Beyond is my favorite store. But I also love the Washington, DC, area. After 9/11, we were back there many times. We stayed in a hotel directly across from a fire department, so these days when I think of DC, I think about the 9/11 experience."

In 2004, Stevie started her charity Stevie Nicks's Band of Soldiers for wounded soldiers. Stevie, sometimes joined by bandmate Mick Fleetwood, visits wounded soldiers, giving out iPods loaded with her favorite music to raise their spirits. In fact, Stevie won the Outstanding Achievement Award at the 2015 USO of Metropolitan DC-Baltimore thirty-third Annual Awards Dinner on March 24, 2015. She holds the record for the most hours spent over a five-year period visiting combat-wounded service members. She recently told local DC News Channel 8, "I am more proud of this than Fleetwood Mac or any of the other things I've done."

Stevie has written some astonishing music, both as a member of Fleetwood Mac and as a solo artist. Songs like "Rhiannon," "Landslide," "Leather and Lace," "Stand Back," "Silver Springs," and "Edge of Seventeen." I once asked Stevie how she wrote music. What was her method? She explained: "When I finish a record, I pretty much move on because I don't really want to be influenced by anything on that last record. Once I finish a record, I don't go back and listen to it. I guess in my heart, I kind of think nobody else does either. I know that's wrong because people come and say this song made this [happen] for me, or this did that for me.

"For instance, one night at the end of our set and I was doing 'Edge of Seventeen,' I was walking across the front of the stage. When the song is almost over, I go across and shake everybody's hands. I got to the mid-dle of the stage and went around the monitor and put my hands down.

And all of a sudden, I was holding both hands of this little girl and she looked very ill. And I stopped in my tracks and stood there for about thirty seconds just transfixed. I didn't know what to say to her because it's so loud, the music and everything. I just held her hands and wanted to drop to my knees and give her a hug and say, 'Oh, stay with us for a moment more.' I came home last night and wrote a poem about her. I don't know who she was. I don't know if she was just having a terrible day or if I was right and she was really sick, or what. As soon as I got off that two-and-a-half hour flight I went straight to my room and got some paper and wrote a poem about her. I will put that poem to music. So that really is how I write. When something inspires me or touches me, then I can't wait to put it down with the emotion I had felt three hours before."

Thinking about "Edge of Seventeen" and other iconic songs in her catalogue, I wondered what were her favorite songs to perform. She replied, "The songs transfer back and forth from the bands I'm in. In Fleetwood Mac, we do 'Gold Dust Woman' and 'Rhiannon.' They are really great with Fleetwood Mac and they are really great with my band, too. I look at those songs and they really don't belong to anybody. People want to hear them, so whenever I play, I pretty much play those songs. And then I build the rest of my sets around those songs. It's also been very fun doing the thing with Don Henley recently. It has been like a 1950s review, because we come on and off, on and off in each other's sets. We start at eight o'clock and don't finish until 11:30. It was very difficult, the first three shows. It was like the hardest thing that we have ever done."

I met up with Stevie on their 2014 Fleetwood Mac tour at the Verizon Center. She was still on top of her game, singing her quintessential songs. "It is the love of my life," she says. "People say to me, what is your perfect evening? What would you do? For me, it's a room with an amazing view, over water, and a desk, and paper, and a really good pen, and some kind of inspiration. That is the moment I live for, as a writer. I pretty much dedicated my whole life to that. I didn't get married. I didn't have children, so that I could do this. And I could do my art uncompromised without having to answer to anybody else. That is what my life has been. It has been dedicated to putting those words on paper that I think will help people in some way at some point."

Magnet and Steel

Stevie has another connection with the Washington, DC, area. She was the inspiration for Walter Egan's 1976 hit song "Magnet and Steel." Egan, a Georgetown University grad, was the founder of local band Sageworth and Drums.

The Sageworth story begins in 1967 when Walter, with fellow GU students Peter Chowka (vocals and guitar), John Zambetti (guitar and backing vocal), Ralph Dammann, and later Tom Guidera (bass player), Matthew Sheppard (drums), and Annie McLoone (lead vocals), formed one of the best original bands in town. Egan credits Bill O'Brien, owner of Tammany Hall, for "keeping our struggling band working and fed when we really needed it." He also recalls performing while tripping at the 1970 Berlin Airlift, an all-day festival at RFK Stadium headlined by Detroit's Grand Funk Railroad with a long set by the then-unknown Allman Brothers Band.

"Tom, the guy who ran that festival, never paid us, yet, coincidentally, interviewed me on TV years later when my hit record came out. I asked him 'Where's the $365 you owe me?'

"Tom tried to make believe that there must be some mistake and kind of made mumbling noises with his surprised face!" Walter says.

Annie and Walter gigged together in the band until he headed to Los Angeles. Annie went to Boston and recorded her solo album *Fast Annie* in 1972. Walter was discovered in 1976 playing a "Hoot Night" at the Troubadour, and was offered a record contract. Sound City engineer Duane Scott in Van Nuys, California, hooked him up with Lindsey

Buckingham to produce Egan's first album for Columbia, *Not Shy*. Both Lindsey and Walter were both big Brian Wilson and Kingston Trio fans, so they hit it off immediately.

Stevie Nicks and Annie McLoone sang background vocals on the album. At that time, Lindsey and Stevie were working well together professionally but their personal connection had gone platonic. Egan explains: "Lindsey would join me in the studio during the day on production and tracks and then Stevie would come in at night and we'd do the vocals. I got to spend time with her alone. Given my affinity for female singers, I fell for her immediately. She became my girlfriend for a while, and when we broke up the next Christmas, she told me, 'You know, you are a lot like Lindsey.'" Walter (whose real middle name is Lindsay) replied, "I guess that's a compliment."

CHAPTER 10
Lowell George: FEAT!

Lowell George, founding member of the band Little Feat, was a very exceptional musician. Born in Hollywood, his father raised chinchillas and sold their furs to movie studios. His father's friends included Hollywood actor Wallace Beery and comedian W. C. Fields. Errol Flynn, the womanizing movie swashbuckler, lived next door.

Growing up with characters like these enabled Lowell to seem to know the story behind the story on everyone in Hollywood. He once told me that between scenes on the *Wizard of Oz,* the Munchkins, who had never been around so many other little people, did a whole lot more than represent the Lollipop Guild—they were having sex with each other at every opportunity. Someone on the crew would have to go around the set and round them up for the next take. Lowell liked to say, "They were getting it on big time" (drum shot). After he

With Lowell George, 1979.
Credit: © Robert Sherbow / Cerphe Archive

told me this, *The Wizard of Oz* took on a whole new life and made me love my favorite film even more!

Lowell could write, play, and sing. You can usually find two of these qualities in a gifted musician, but rarely all three. In 1973, "Crocodile Rock," by Elton John, and "Dueling Banjos" from the *Deliverance* movie soundtrack were the two songs dominating DC radio stations WPGC, WEAM, WEEL, and WINX: At 'HFS, it was "Dixie Chicken" by Little Feat.

I think the keys to the success of Little Feat were many: they had a rock and roll feel to their music that never relented and, in fact, intensified as they matured as a band. Then there were the syncopated, often quirky, Allen Toussaint–like New Orleans rhythms Lowell infused. The players added superbly crafted blues to the mix with Lowell's stingingly sustained slide guitar leads and exuberant vocals, and they never lost their sense of humor. Frank Zappa's drummer, Jimmy Carl Black ("the

Lowell and me in 1977.
Credit: © Robert Sherbow/Cerphe Archive

Indian of the group") is said to have provided the name of the band as a comment on Lowell's size nine little feet.

"Fat Man in the Bathtub" features a character named Spotcheck Willie who wants to score with a sweet Chiquita named Juanita. He hears her moan. The lyrics to this and many Feat songs are cool, witty, and very different.

Local musician Bill Holland once wrote about Lowell's singing, "Unlike many of his peers, George doesn't sing above the music—he pushes and slides the words right to the core of the melodic and rhythmic pulse. This may make it hard to distinguish the words sometimes, but ultimately, the effect produces a more powerful reaction to this listener."

Little Feat then featured Lowell as its main player with writing credits on ten of the *Dixie Chicken* tracks. Richie Hayward, on drums, had been with the band Fraternity of Man, whose "Don't Bogart Me" found fame in the 1969 film *Easy Rider*. "Don't Bogart that joint, my friend" became part of the counterculture lingo. In many films, actor Humphrey Bogart has a cigarette in his mouth but it doesn't look like he's smoking it. I think that's the origin of this phrase.

Pianist Billy Payne hailed from Waco, Texas, and was influenced by the gospel music of his childhood. Bassist Kenny Gradney had been with Delaney and Bonnie, the Shirelles, and other bands. Guitarist Paul Barrere was born in Burbank, California, and contributed to Little Feat's songwriting with such songs as "Feats Don't Fail Me Now" and "Time Loves a Hero."

On congas was Sam Clayton, brother of singer Merry Clayton, who was featured in *20 Feet from Stardom,* the Oscar-winning documentary about background singers and their impact on the music industry. Merry's vocal on the Rolling Stones's "Gimme Shelter" always raises the hairs on my neck. Speaking of the Stones, Mick and Keith were particularly taken with Little Feat, and asked them more than once to tour with them. Lowell turned down the offers, which royally pissed off their recording company, Warner Brothers. Warner execs thought they were just throwing away these enormous opportunities for world exposure.

One of the first reviews that Little Feat got in DC was by Michael Oberman in the *Evening Star:* "Some of Lowell's songs, like 'Willin', deal with trucks and life on the highway. Lowell says he likes to write about trucks 'because here are these people who are caught—stuck just like you and I are stuck. And here's this guy who enjoys himself, doing what he's doing, driving trucks. He loves it.'"

Playing in the Band

Frankly, the band played the Washington area frequently because this was the center of their early popularity. While most of the country was slowly discovering them, DC became a Little Feat town. I saw them at a free concert at West Potomac Park with Babe and other local bands, and many other shows, including opening for Bonnie Raitt and Paul Butterfield

(l to r), Paul Barrere, me, Lowell George, Kenny Gradney, Richie Hayward, Bill Payne, and Sam Clayton's knee.
Credit: © 1975 Dave Nutteycombe

at Georgetown's McDonough Gym, and playing with Liz Meyer and Allen Toussaint at two different George Washington University's Lisner Auditorium gigs.

It would be while sharing the bill with Liz Meyer that Lowell first got an earful of DC guitarist Danny Gatton. Lowell would later write in the liner notes of Danny's 1978 *Redneck Jazz* album that "Danny is the best guitarist in any style that I have ever heard."

Little Feat would next open for Three Dog Night, Souther-Hillman-Furay, and Jefferson Starship, and shared the bill with Dave Mason, for all four shows at the Cap Centre. Feat next came to the Warner Theatre with opening act the Pousette-Dart Band. By this time, everybody in the audience knew the words to their songs. By 1977, Little Feat would sell out six shows in a row at the Warner.

Word went out that Little Feat would be doing their first live recording at Lisner Auditorium. Tickets were sold at only two local record stores, Orpheus and Penguin Feather, and at the Psyche Delly bar. This concert, and one earlier at the Rainbow Theatre in London, is where the *Waiting for Columbus* double album was captured. The cost of recording was $11,000. Add another $10,000 of studio time to mix the tracks. Lowell then overdubbed most of the vocals and many leads. Released in 1978, this became the group's bestselling release.

You can hear me introduce the band on that LP and lead the crowd in the "Feat, Feat, Feat" chant. I checked the 2015 sales on Amazon, and it was Number 38 in Classic Rock sales, some thirty-eight years after its release.

Little Feat pianist Bill Payne commented that *Waiting for Columbus* "was the live album that had everything, from the highest of highs to the lowest of lows where the thing would come crashing down . . . there were many, many high points, and one of them would include having the Tower of Power horn section out there. In Washington, we were able to muster up some really amazing shows and performances, including a version of 'Mercenary Territory' from a sound check."

Lowell, with my '57 Porsche Speedster, on the night before he died.
Credit: © Robert Sherbow/Cerphe Archive.

After *Waiting for Columbus,* Lowell was hospitalized. We didn't know why. Following *Columbus,* Lowell produced the Grateful Dead's *Shakedown Street,* and then began work on a solo album, *Thanks I'll Eat It Here.*

This solo record received poor reviews, but Lowell toured it, including at George Washington University's Lisner Auditorium, and gave a strong performance. He came on my WAVA radio show to promote it. He looked awful that night. Bloated. His skin was yellow. We were all a bit startled. And worried.

The picture of Lowell pointing to the "Speedster" tag on my Porsche was taken after our WAVA interview. The next night, he played Lisner and returned to his $40 room at the Twin Bridges Marriott hotel in Arlington, Virginia. He had complained to his wife, Elizabeth, and road manager, Gene Vano, of chest pains after the show, and breathing problems later. But he told them he felt better the next morning. When Elizabeth and Gene returned to the room at 11:00 a.m., they found him unconscious. An ambulance was summoned, but he couldn't be revived. The news was initially reported that he died from a heart attack, but it was later revealed to be a heroin overdose. So sad.

Mike Schreibman, Washington rock promoter and president and founder of the Washington Area Music Association (WAMA), and Lowell were close. Mike did booking and promotion for all of Little Feat's local shows. Mike said at the time of his death that "Lowell was the most loyal person I have ever worked with. And in this business, that is rare."

The following is the one of many 'HFS studio interviews I did with Lowell George. On this occasion, he brought along his friend, Linda Ronstadt, who was then recording what would become her first Number 1 album, *Heart Like a Wheel,* at Silver Spring, Maryland's Track Recorders studio. Lowell was helping Linda with the album, in particular her version

With Lowell and Linda Ronstadt at Lisner Auditorium, 1975.
Credit: © Big Al Sevilla/All Access Photography

of his best-known song, "Willin'." Peter Asher, of the 1960s duo Peter and Gordon fame, was producing it. The day was March 3, 1974.

Cerphe: We'll do a few messages and get them out of the way. Actually, why don't you say hello?

Linda: Hi.

Lowell: Hello.

Cerphe: You're really here.

Linda: We really are.

Cerphe: We got Lowell an amplifier that will kill all amplifiers. A Silvertone amp.

Lowell: It's terrible. It's perfect.

Cerphe: I want you to know that this amp was used by The Kingsmen to record "Louie, Louie" in the garage.

Linda: It has history.

Lowell: This is the one that was in the garage?

Cerphe: It's the hottest amp.

Lowell: "Louie, Louie" sold a lot of copies.

Cerphe: I'm going to play it for you later.

Lowell: I'm ready.

Cerphe: I can tell you are. Linda, you were in town and then sick right after that last concert.

Linda: I was sick during that concert. I think I got the whole audience sick. I sounded awful. I had the flu. I couldn't sing at all.

Cerphe: That's not what I heard.

Linda: I was there and I thought don't be a prima donna. I can sing, but when I got on stage, I felt like a jerk. I canceled the next two shows.

Cerphe: It's a fine band you have now with Sneaky Pete [Kleinow].

Linda: Yeah, we got so we're playing real good on the tour. I was looking forward to playing this gig because Washington is my favorite town. And Lisner Auditorium is a great place to play.

Cerphe: And you have a bus.

Linda: Yes, it was the first time we had a bus. Me and Jackson Browne. But, God, I'll never do it any other way again. You get about three times the amount of rest. And you don't get those horrible sinus problems when you fly. I've been doing this a long time, but I've never gotten over being afraid of it, you know?

Cerphe: The plane thing?

Linda: Yeah, I'm a devout coward. Lowell likes airplanes.

Lowell: Yes, little ones.

Linda: The ones you put together with airplane glue.

[Lowell picks up his guitar and sings "Blowin' Away."]

Linda: Woo.

Cerphe: Wow.

Lowell: No second verse but that's alright.

Cerphe: The amp worked.

Lowell: You know I record on a little amplifier.

Cerphe: Have you seen those Pignose amps?

Lowell: Yeah, I have one on the bus.

Linda: They are good for hotel rooms, too.

Cerphe: They run on a flashlight battery, right?

Lowell: About eight of them. But you can plug them in, too. It was all those guitar player freaks in Los Angeles who'd have to fly to the East Coast to play concerts and they needed to bring an amp.

Cerphe: You had a bunch of guitars stolen from you.

Lowell: Actually, they sent them to Puerto Rico. I told them I had Puerto Ricans living in my building, and they sent them back. Everything was all right.

Cerphe: Did the guitars get a tan?

Lowell: Actually they wound up in the LA airport in a shed. So whatever good that was done to them—the vitamin D coursing through their veins—was lost. Every time I turn around, I'm having a guitar stolen, so I figure I'll start a production line.

Cerphe: We're stealing the guitar you brought, I think.

Linda: I think stealing guitars should be a hanging crime. Hang them by their thumbs for four days.

Lowell: Linda is real pleasant.

Cerphe: I wanted to ask you, Lowell, where did you grow up?

Linda: He played the harmonica a lot. He listened to the "Harmonicats."

Lowell: I did.

Cerphe: You're sick.

Lowell: I know. It was rough. See, my mother didn't know. She took me to this guy who had two first names. It wasn't Louie, Louie, but something like William Williams. He told my mom that what I needed was harmonica lessons. "See I have one right here," he said. "How old's the boy? Five? Okay, this harmonica fits in his face." So I started playing the harmonica.

Linda: "Lady of Spain," right?

Lowell: No, it was "Peg O' My Heart." My brother, Hampton, who was five years older and two feet taller, got to play the huge chord harmonica, which he hated. He was older, and he should be playing lead. So there was already envy. And we played hospitals. But we also played *The Al Jarvis Show,* which was the Los Angeles version of the *Ted Mack Amateur Hour.*

Cerphe: Nice show.

Lowell: When that went defunct Jarvis started a teen dance show, which started some people into music like Johnny Otis. But before he had the talent show. As a matter of fact, Frank Zappa was a ventriloquist when he was young.

Cerphe: Frank's no dummy.

Lowell: Right, and Frank had a puppet. We both lost to tap dancers on *The Al Jarvis* show. Two girls from Anaheim.

Linda: So you and Frank Zappa were on the same show together?

Lowell: Yes. Same show.

Cerphe: Never mind, because you ended up writing a song called "Kiss It Off." Can you tell us about that song?

Lowell: Well, it's real political. It is about Nixon.

Cerphe: Let's give it a listen. Here's "Kiss It Off" by Little Feat. [Record plays.]

Cerphe: What do you say there? "Milquetoast Hitler?"

Lowell: Yes.

Linda: I thought it was milk-toast love. I've had a few of those.

Cerphe: Linda, I was listening last night to some Stone Pony songs.

Linda: How embarrassing. You're a brave soul.

Cerphe: You have gotten so good.

Lowell: That's a nice way to say you've come a long way.

Linda: I used to listen to those records when I ran out of sleeping pills. . . .

Cerphe: Your new albums sound really good. Lowell, have you and Van Dyke Parks been doing anything? You played on his last album, *Discover America.*

Lowell: Yes. I sang "Sailing Shoes" and another song "G-Man Hoover" on that. We're producing the next Little Feat album together.

Cerphe: What did Van Dyke Parks do with The Byrds? Was it on *Fifth Dimension?*

Lowell: He played piano. He was a studio musician. He played on Frank Zappa's first album, *Freak Out.* He sang on "Good Vibrations."

Cerphe: Didn't you do something with Frank Zappa?

Linda: Lowell was in the Mothers.

Lowell: Yes. I got to sing with Mother's bassist, Roy Estrada. We got to go way up high, and everybody else did the low stuff. If you remember Frank's song "Who Are the Brain Police?" The bass figure in that song is really Roy Estrada's invention. I've heard it used on other songs. He's a fun bass player.

[Note: In March 2008, Estrada was sentenced to twenty-five years for his third child-molestation conviction, and is ineligible for parole.]

Cerphe: I just got a tape of Zappa's new album, *Apostrophe,* that's coming out next month. It's outrageous. Real good. Have you heard the "Yellow Snow" song?

Lowell: [Laughing.] No I haven't heard "Yellow Snow."

Cerphe: You want to sing something now?

Linda: Why don't we sing that thing we did today?

Lowell: We don't have the harmonies.

Linda: Yes, today we recorded an a cappella song with Rickie Skaggs of the Country Gentlemen and John Starling of the Seldom Scene. I looked over at Lowell because I thought he was singing sharp, but it turned out he was the only one singing it right, and the rest of us were flat. I almost punched him out. He has Wonder Pitch.

Lowell: When you're producing a record or involved with making it, you listen to it ten million times. You start to hate it. But I still have to listen to my record completely from start to finish all the way through to see if there are any bumps or leaps in it.

Cerphe: I'll take this opportunity to say that Little Feat is probably one of the best bands in America. That's my humble opinion for what it's worth.

Linda: I agree.

Cerphe: Why don't you play something?

[Lowell and Linda harmonize on "Sailing Shoes."]

Lowell: I have some folks here.

Cerphe: Please introduce them.

Lowell: On my immediate right is Paul Craft, who is a songwriter and came up from Memphis to assist Linda and the Seldom Scene. And John

Starling from the Seldom Scene and Sue, his wife, who is a great singer. Sue is also playing on local dobro player Mike Auldridge's album.

Cerphe: Auldridge is not going to like being called a local dobro player.

[The group plays "Willin'."]

By the end of the year, Linda's album *Heart Like a Wheel* and Little Feat's *Feats Don't Fail Me Now* were big winners, gaining rave reviews and new fans.

I still play a lot of Little Feat on my *Music Planet Radio* show. Although it saddens me terribly, it also pisses me off that he's dead. I often wonder what he'd be doing today had he lived. This is true with all of the "27 Club" musicians who died at the age of twenty-seven, including Jimi Hendrix, Janis Joplin, Kurt Cobain, Brian Jones, Jim Morrison, Ron "Pigpen" McKernan, Robert Johnson, and, most recently, Amy Winehouse.

When Amy passed, I was so frustrated that I quit playing her music on Music Planet Radio for a long while. I thought Amy had it all, and I feel robbed and cheated. When the listening public looks back, they'll see a gap that will never be filled.

Lowell isn't a member of the 27 Club. He was thirty-four when he died. Eric Clapton, Robert Plant, Jimmy Page, and the Rolling Stones regarded Little Feat as their favorite band, as did their Washington, DC, fans during the eight years of Little Feat with Lowell.

Writer and producer Van Dyke Parks—the same artist that provided lyrics for Brian Wilson's *Smile* project—was working for Warner Brothers when Lowell was looking for a record deal. Parks told *Clash* magazine, "I think Lowell had the audacity of a schizophrenic, which I associate with great work, whether it's Van Gogh or Ravel. I think Lowell had a madness in his work that he wanted to explore, and he had the integrity to do it. [In songs like "Fat Man in the Bathtub"] You see the physical comedy in Lowell George that you get from Buster Keaton. It's the tragicomedy of man in crisis—that's what Lowell did for me."

Van Dyke collaborated with Lowell's musical daughter, Inara George, on the 2008 album *An Invitation,* and Jackson Browne wrote the song "Of Missing Persons" for Inara after her father's death. Inara was five years old when she lost her dad.

On the day this book was published Lowell would have been seventy-one years old had he lived. He once joked that he preferred to play for a live audience rather than a dead one. Much-admired early *Rolling Stone* journalist Ben Fong-Torres met with surviving band members and their friends and associates to author *Willin': The Story of Little Feat,* a definitive biography of our beloved Lowell. I was honored that Ben included me in his book. I told Ben, "This is revisionist history but if Lowell were alive, he'd be right up there with all the current Americana. He was so much into that. And his style of playing, his writing was so inventive. The musician community really responded to that, and there's no way to imagine the effect that he would have if he were still alive."

CHAPTER 11

Frank Zappa:
Them or Us?

"Frank Zappa was my Elvis."
—Matt Groening, creator of *The Simpsons*

In 1985, Tipper Gore, wife of Senator Al, and Susan Baker, wife of Treasury Secretary James, along with two other Washington wives, Pam Howard and Sally Nevius, joined forces to protect listeners against filthy rock lyrics.

Did anyone see this coming?

This "Washington Wives" consortium, monikers that reflected their prominent husbands' professions, started the Parents Music Resource Center (PMRC) a.k.a. "The Porn Wars" to propose and enforce a record labeling system that would identify records deemed to have "objectionable lyrics" with a "Parental Guidance: Explicit Lyrics" sticker

My friend, Frank Zappa.
Credit: © Big Al Sevilla/All Access Photography

slapped on the front cover and some kind of to-be-determined grading system.

The PMRC ladies had targeted a list of "Filthy Fifteen" songs they thought were the most offensive. Ironically, most of the heavy metal songs that they listed at the time were virtually unknown to the public. Heavy metal as a music format hadn't really blossomed. I believe that one of the reasons that metal took off in the 1980s as a successful format is that the PMRC brought attention to what they thought was unacceptable, and, of course, that put it very much in the spotlight.

Pop songs were targeted too. Here were their culprits: "Darling Nikki"/Prince, "Sugar Walls"/Sheena Easton, "Eat Me Alive"/Judas Priest, "Strap on Robbie Baby"/Vanity, "Bastard"/Motley Crew, "Let Me Put Love Into You"/AC/DC, "We're Not Gonna Take It"/Twisted Sister, "Dress You Up"/Madonna, "Animal: Fuck Like a Beast"/W.A.S.P., "High 'n' Dry/(Saturday Night)"/Def Leppard, "Into the Coven"/ Merciful Fate, "Trashed"/Black Sabbath, "In My House"/Mary Jane Girls, "Possessed"/Venom, and "She-Bop"/Cyndi Lauper.

By this time, I'd been Frank Zappa's DJ friend in DC for about twelve years. I had worn out his first record, *Freak Out,* back in Winchester, as a very early fan. It was the first double album I owned. *Freak Out* was so different. The music ranged from poetic rock to do-wop to comedic, psychedelic, and experimental. One song, "Trouble Coming Every Day," about the Los Angeles Watts riots, really stood out. It could have been written about the very recent racial issues in Baltimore of the mid-2010s. The saturated psychedelic cover art featuring Frank in a fur coat by Verve Records graphic artist Jack Anesh grabbed your attention.

I started promoting Frank's music on 'HFS the day I arrived there. Frank was one of the first musicians I interviewed in studio. He did this station ID for me: "Hey now, this is Frank Zappa and you're listening to Cerphe on radio WHFS in 'Ba-Tays-Da.'"

We talked about music censorship the first time we met. This was an evergreen hot topic with Frank. It wasn't just language but controversial topics, sexuality, and a general songwriting and life approach that many would consider depraved if not perverse—along with his unique musical talent—that ran through so many of his songs and helped make Frank's music so radical. Even the name of his band, the Mothers of Invention, was originally intended as "The Mothers" (as in motherfuckers). His MGM label insisted adding "of Invention" to soften the name.

Frank once told me, "Sex is good for you. The more you know about it, then the happier you will be. So don't be afraid about words that make you think about sex." I was in complete agreement with his position on censorship.

He'd usually call me when he was coming through DC. Sometimes, I would just hang with him when he did TV shows, and, of course, we'd always do interviews. His shows in DC were superior musical events and enthusiastically anticipated by his fans.

Early die-hard fans like me thought Frank was a genius. By 1985, his genius status was irrefutable according to his fans and most critics, although this esteem didn't always pack in a sell-out crowd. Although his fans were obsessed, his music was far from mainstream. Still, Frank's shows were very profitable.

Frank graduated from selling out two consecutive nights at Constitution Hall to headlining DC's Capital Centre. Cellar Door Productions owner Jack Boyle once said, "Look, I can get Elton John for the Cap Centre and it's an instant sell-out. But by the time I pay off Elton, I've made no money. I can get Frank Zappa for a more reasonable price, and even if he fills only half the Cap Centre, everybody makes money."

PMRC Testimony

My then-attorney, and years later, the best man at Susan's and my wedding, Alan Aronowitz (not the New York journalist) told me about the upcoming PMRC hearings. Two days later, I got a call from Frank, who said that he was testifying against the PMRC proposal before the United States Senate Commerce, Technology, and Transportation Committee. Someone in his circle said that the PMRC, which was part of a Senate select subcommittee, was looking for some music experts. I was sort of a go-to guy since at that point I'd been on radio in DC for sixteen years. Frank was nice enough to invite me to join him in testifying. I jumped at the chance.

The hearing was on September 19, 1985. I sat behind Frank in the New Senate Office building chamber. His son, Dweezil was there too. You could hear a pin drop. MTV and the music journalists were there. Flashbulbs going off. It was very unlike Washington. I saw Bill Holland there, and *Washington Post* music columnist Richard Harrington was also in the gallery that day.

In Frank's prepared statement, he said: "The PMRC proposal is an ill-conceived piece of nonsense which fails to deliver any real benefits to children, infringes the civil liberties of people who are not children, and promises to keep the courts busy for years dealing with the inter- pretational and enforcemental [sic] problems inherent in the proposal's design. In this context, the PMRC's demands are the equivalent of treat- ing dandruff by decapitation. . . . The establishment of a rating system, voluntary or otherwise, opens the door to an endless parade of moral quality control programs based on things 'others' do not like."

Twisted Sister's Dee Snider and John Denver also testified. Note that these musicians represented three distinct genres of music. How ironic that many people at the hearings thought Frank was wild and out of control, but in fact, Frank never took drugs, never smoked weed. His only vice was chain-smoking cigarettes—"Tobacco is a vegetable," he'd say—and the occasional crème de menthe.

Meanwhile, John Denver was stoned much of the time despite his wholesome image. Frank clearly owned the proceedings, but nobody knew what the testimonies would be beforehand. I gathered there was some concern about what Denver might say, but he was in agreement that these labels on records were not the way to go.

When my turn came to testify, I agreed with Frank that this was a freedom issue and that applying an edict could morph into something more stringent. My thought at the time—maybe naïve—was that the family structure should be aware of what their kids were listening to. You can't control that with a government organization and labels.

Frank mentioned me in his autobiography, *The Real Frank Zappa*, as an ally in this drama; I am very grateful for that recognition. When all the smoke settled, the Recording Industry of America settled on a sticker for records that simply said, "Explicit Lyrics." Just as Frank had predicted, many stores, including Walmart, stopped carrying these demonized records. But the proposed rating system, along with some of PMRC's other suggestions, like forcing retail stores to keep explicit albums under the counter, setting up an industry standards panel, and pressuring stations not to broadcast what these would-be watchdogs deemed to be explicit songs, never materialized.

In 2015, *Newsweek* magazine interviewed the survivors of those hearings to mark the thirtieth anniversary, including Barbara Baker; the late Gail Zappa; son Dweezil; Frank's lawyer, Jerry Stein; Dee Snider; me; and others. Tipper Gore declined to be interviewed. Dweezil said, "Oddly enough, during the Clinton administration, we did have several occasions to spend some time with the Gores and actually became friends with them. It was never a battle of, 'Oh, these people are terrible people.'"

Frank's next album after the hearings, *Jazz from Hell*, won a 1988 Grammy award. The Recording Industry put an "Explicit Lyrics" sticker on it.

It was an instrumental album.

Interview with Frank Zappa

In this 1985 interview, Frank talks with me about radio, his accomplishments, and his opinions.

Cerphe: Zappa and the Mothers of Invention took rock and roll through a whole lot of mutations. You were responsible for what was called the underground in the 1960s. Now, in the 1980s, it is very much above ground. It's changed, hasn't it?

Frank Zappa: It's changed, but I don't know what you mean. What commodities are we talking about that are above the ground and under the ground? Are you talking about explicit sexual lyrics in rock records?

Cerphe: This is what I'm asking. Now you see that radio has changed dramatically in the last ten years. There's not as much outlet for creativity.

Frank: Here's what happened. Here's radio history, okay? Rock and roll is forty years old, maybe. A few [broadcasters] played shows that were one or two hours long on certain days a week playing certain kinds of records. This grew and grew until entire station formats were dedicated to rock, but it was AM. It became incredibly corrupt, and people were handed cash to play certain records and some people became stars and others became busboys. It was irrelevant what the musical merits were. If you paid off, then you got to be a star. And then they had the "payola" scandals.

Somewhere in the 1960s, someone said "Let's put some of this music on FM," which was generally reserved for that mysterious signal that somehow enters the dentist's office when you're not looking. And on FM, you could do it in stereo.

So there weren't that many people listening, so not much pressure. The FM stations became very creative. You [Cerphe] were involved in some of that. You could play what you wanted and you could create an art form out of your own broadcast.

Every day you had the challenge of putting something together that was different and unusual, and the audiences would like it. Okay, so this turned into big business as more people bought FM receivers. So hey, this could be another AM but in stereo. FM stations were bought, and it became the new AM in stereo but with the same freeze-dried formula. Somewhere along the line, the hundred-dollar bill stuffed into the sleeve of the 45 rpm record was replaced by the syndrome of a bag of cocaine or a bigger bag of marijuana and somebody got the job done. Cash payola is back again. And that's the history of rock and roll radio.

Cerphe: When I knew we were going to be talking, I went back and listened to "Freak Out," and your early music, and surprisingly, it wears very well. You would think it would sound dated. Songs like "Trouble Coming Every Day" and "Who Are the Brain Police?" are very topical in what's going on out there.

Frank: Well, yesterday was the twentieth anniversary of the Watts riots in Los Angeles and people were making speeches from many of the same spots that I described in the song, "Trouble Coming Every Day." Like the woman getting machine-gunned from her seat. They're describing what that race riot was all about.

When *Freak Out* came out, it sold about forty thousand copies, tops. But over the years, it has sold volumes and volumes. Unfortunately, MGM lost all the sales receipts. They had a fire and a flood. They couldn't really tell me how many records sold. We had to take them to court to find out these things. That's the way it goes with record companies.

Cerphe: You've had a bad time with record companies between MGM and Warner Brothers.

Frank: And CBS, which I'm suing now.

Cerphe: Your first album, *Freak Out,* cost twenty-one thousand dollars, which was an enormous sum back then.

Frank: In those days, the average album cost about six to eight thousand dollars, because the typical rock album consisted of your hit single, plus nine or ten filler songs that you recorded as fast as possible, and you add a glossy photo on the cover and put some paisley crap around it, and stamp it out. That was a rock album.

Freak Out was a concept album, and things had to fit in different ways. But even at twenty-one thousand dollars, a startling budget at the time, the record company resisted spending it because nobody had ever spent that much on a record before and they didn't want to set a precedent.

So for our second album, *Absolutely Free,* they forced us to a budget to eleven thousand dollars, and literally threw us out of the studio at a certain point. Okay. Your vocals aren't done? Too bad. Zip, we were out. So that's one of the reasons I have my own record company now.

Cerphe: Barking Pumpkin Records is your new company. Can we clarify how many albums you have now?

Frank: It's about forty-five albums now. There are about a hundred bootlegs out there.

Cerphe: [Note: Zappa released sixty-two albums in his lifetime]. I saw you on the *Tom Snyder* TV show recently and you and conductor Arthur Fiedler were guests. I could see a lot of common ground between you and Fiedler.

Frank: Yes, but there's something else that happened on that show that I'd like to make a comment about. I had never met Tom Snyder before in my life as I walked out on the set. We shook hands. I sit in the chair. They strap on a microphone. Tom turns to me and here's the first thing he says to me: "You know, I made two million dollars last year in New York" and he starts scratching his neck and scratching around like he had the red spiders on him.

Okay, That's the first thing out of his mouth. I'll accept that. So we start the interview. He asks, "What about these groupies, Frank?" and this kind of crap.

So a few weeks later, I do an interview with this newspaper in Chicago, and I tell them this same story and they publish it. Tom opened his show a few days later with the newspaper with the story and tears it up. Hey, I'm sorry. I can't help it if Tom Snyder has red spiders and wants to tell me how much money he makes.

Cerphe: What about these groupies, Frank?

Frank: [Laughs.]

Cerphe: When you did *Freak Out,* it was the first concept album; the first rock opera album, if you will.

Frank: One of the reasons for the history of that album was the producer, Tom Wilson, unfortunately deceased now. He took the heat from the record company and was the one who actually spent the money that let us finish it.

Cerphe: With your film *200 Motels,* you did some things we might almost expect to see from The Beatles. Lots of surrealism.

Frank: Ringo played me. And as far as some of the things that were done, it was the first time they were done. It was the first feature-length

L-R: Frank, engineer Gary Kellgren, bassist Roy Estrada, producer Tom Wilson. Credit: © Charles Steiner

motion picture shot on videotape, and then transferred to film. The special effects in that movie were the precursors of about 70 percent of the technical effects you now see in videos on MTV or other video channels.

These effects were done with experimental hooking up of mundane equipment that was available at the time. The video editing itself had to be done manually. There were no computers. I had to stand up with a magic marker, mark my edits, back the tape up, push two buttons, and hope the editing locked. When the film opened, there were many technical guys present—not to see a rock story—but to examine how the movie looked on the screen. All of the film was shot on two-inch PAL, the best quality videotape available. We shot thirty reels.

The saddest thing about *200 Motels* is that the United Artists producer decided to be very frugal. He had the thirty original reels carted up, bulk-erased, and resold for scrap, thereby putting $3,000 back into the film budget. It was so stupid. Do you know what those original video reels would be worth today?

Cerphe: I know how much you like labels.

Frank: [Laughs.]

Cerphe: What kind of training did you have when you got started?

Frank: First of all, I am a middle-aged Italian father of four with a high school education. Everything else I've learned, I learned by doing it. I learned how to do video editing in one week, in a cold room with two English editors whose main goal in life was returning from the pub across the street with huge tumblers of Guinness, that dark, dangerous liquid. But, if you have a technical mind, you can learn the concepts of doing these things pretty easily.

Cerphe: Frank Zappa could be described as the All-American self-made man. I know you are a fundamentalist as far as the Constitution is concerned. You believe in the First Amendment.

Frank: I want to see someone who doesn't believe in the First Amendment. Where are these people?

Cerphe: They want to change it.

Frank: Yes, they want to make it the One Point Two Amendment.

Cerphe: I know you've been a prolific writer with your music, but you also produced many bands coming out of the underground

Frank: I produced the first Lowell George single, which never got released.

Cerphe: Lowell was in your band, the Mothers, for a while, and had a very big following here in DC with Little Feat.

Frank: There's still a tape somewhere in my vault with the songs "Lightning Man" and "Black Protruding Tongue" when Lowell had a band called the Factory.

Cerphe: How did you get started in music?

Frank:. When I started off, I was a consumer of rhythm and blues. I never thought I could play it. I liked to listen to it. And I collected rhythm and blues records.

While I was doing that, I was writing chamber music and orchestral music. I started doing this when I was fourteen. I didn't write a rock and roll song until I was in my twenties. I wrote all this classical music and sent it to orchestras, but nobody would play it. So I decided if I'm writing all this music I better write in a medium where someone would want to play it.

I presented my compositions to the conductor of the Baltimore Symphony. His name was Massimo Freccia. He looked at me like how can you be so young and writing this music? He started to quiz me, asking, "What's the lowest note on a bassoon?"

I said, "B flat." It's hard to convince someone you can write music if you don't look like you're from a university or something.

[Frank shrugs.] So I just went on and did something else. [Frank raises two middle fingers.] How many fingers am I holding up?

Cerphe: When you left Warner Brothers Records, it seems you got back into more of your satire and your creativity. It seems like it inspired you.

Frank: It would inspire you, too, if you had been with that company for eight years. The real thing that determines the character of an album is who is on it. For example, you couldn't take Mark and Howard ["Flo and Eddie"] from the *Live at the Fillmore Mothers* band, and put them in the Ruth Underwood/George Duke Mothers band. They are from different worlds.

So some people like some eras of the Mothers over the others, and some hate them all. That's all right.

Cerphe: With forty-five albums, it would seem there is something for all.

Frank: I hope so, but I still need to get the exposure on the radio. And today, you have to pay off. I refuse to do that. You also have to play the MTV ball game, and I've done that. I'll cooperate. I've been on MTV. But it's the whole ethic of selling your music with pictures when it is ultimately the pictures that become most important. You watch the girl's legs when she gets out of the car. Her butt going up and down like that. Can we really see her tits? And none of this has anything to do with the song. After you've watched the videos, the saturation point comes maybe after six viewings. If you are just listening to a record, you can listen a hundred times because the appreciation is on a different level. I'm interested in the music. The audience for what I do might be shriveling up like a prune, but tough tookus; this is what I do. I'm not going to change to do something else.

Dweezil: Son of Monster Magnet

Many thought Frank Zappa was a novelty act, one who only does parody. Maybe that's because his tune "Valley Girl," in which his daughter, Moon, parodies the teenage slang of 1970s Southern California, was his greatest commercial success. Slang expressions like "Fer sure, fer sure," "gag me with a spoon," and "grody to the max" went mainstream after that song hit big. Totally.

Ironically, Frank never performed that song in concert. His son, Dweezil, doesn't play it either in his current tribute band Zappa Plays Zappa, although the band is devoted to performing Frank's music very precisely and true to the art. Dweezil also skips some of Frank's other big hits.

Dweezil says, "I try to stay away from some songs that I feel *have* given some folks some misunderstanding about Frank. Songs like "Bobby Brown" or "Dancing Fool." They are great songs but they require Frank's sarcastic delivery to make them be what they are."

I caught up with Dweezil in 2012 and again in 2015 and spoke with him about Frank's music and how the Zappa Plays Zappa concerts honor his memory.

Cerphe: One of the great things you do to recreate your Dad's music these days is have a huge video image on stage and you play guitar with him.

Dweezil: We're doing more of that now. But we don't have many examples of Frank playing like that we can do overall because it requires certain footage of just Frank (alone) and also having the separated audio. We started with *Chunga's Revenge* last year but now we have seven songs we can do, and we change them up every night.

Cerphe: Frank was amazing in that he would incorporate everything from rock to jazz to classical to fusion, and even doo-wop.

Dweezil: Sometimes in the same song!

Cerphe: He would do that. Of the repertoire of over sixty-two albums, how do you choose what to play?

Dweezil: It's a combination of my own curiosity of certain pieces of music that I've always enjoyed, and I know that fans have enjoyed as well. I go by my own motivation for what music I want to learn and what secrets I want to uncover in certain compositions of his. But I also try to make it as broad as possible. Last year, we did a lot of stuff from one particular era. We did a lot from the middle seventies. We played almost the whole *Apostrophe* album, and most of *One Size Fits All.*

This year, we're featuring music from *The Yellow Shark,* his classical album, and the last thing he worked on before he died. And from earlier in his career like *Absolutely Free* and even some eighties songs to round out the music. But generally, I chose the songs that set him apart from others, that show off what makes him different as a composer, a guitarist, and songwriter.

Cerphe: You know I testified with your dad in the infamous "Porn Wars" hearings in the Senate. I was sitting behind him, and one of the first things he said was "Look ladies, this is like trying to cure dandruff. . . ."

Dweezil: [finishing the sentence] By decapitation.

Cerphe: His opening statement was essential Frank Zappa.

Dweezil: Yes, it was hilarious. I was at those hearings as well and watched the whole thing go down.

Cerphe: Did you see the VH-1 movie *Warning: Parental Advisory* they did on that?

Dweezil: Yes, that was a total travesty when VH-1 made that horrendous movie. They tried to show Dee Snider as the true savior of rock and roll.

Cerphe: They didn't exactly capture the moment, did they?

Dweezil: Not so good.

Cerphe: Looking at the amazing imprint of all the music Frank did, I'd like to point out one from his first album, *Freak Out,* one of the coolest albums ever, with the song, "Trouble Coming Every Day."

Dweezil: We do a version of "Trouble" he did around 1974, and we were closing with that song for a while.

Cerphe: Didn't you do a stint with MTV as a VJ in the late eighties?

Dweezil: Yes, I was on in 1986, but only for thirteen weeks. People think I was on a lot.

Cerphe: Frank was born in Baltimore and it is so cool that the city has acknowledged your dad.

Dweezil: We played in Baltimore on the day they proclaimed it "Frank Zappa Day." Someone came down from the mayor's office. I had my daughter with me, Zola, whose middle name is Frank, so she is a Frank Zappa also.

Cerphe: And you had John Smothers, who was Frank's bodyguard with you.

Dweezil: Yes, he was with my dad for a long time, and is from Baltimore. He came on stage with us. It was a lot of fun.

Cerphe: Your Dad raised the bar on cool.

Dweezil: I appreciate that. And I hope people will come out and support Frank's music. We're seeing parents with their kids coming to the shows. Maybe this exposure will be a good thing for the world.

Cerphe: Yes, we could use that help.

Another Mother

I interviewed Howard Kaylan when his memoir *Shell Shocked* came out in 2013. Howard was lead singer of the Turtles. Their 1967 hit song "Happy Together" has been played on the radio over five million times. The song penned by composers Garry Bonner and Alan Gordon, was rejected by so many performers that the demo was worn out. Bonner and Gordon also wrote "Celebrate" by Three Dog Night.

Howard and ex-Turtle and bandmate Mark Volman became "Flo and Eddie" following the Turtles breakup and then played in Frank Zappa's Mothers band from 1971 to 1973. Flo and Eddie still tour.

"'You're only as good as your last record' was the showbiz mantra that we heard coming up," Howard said. "But that's not true. It took Frank Zappa to teach us that you are the product of your entire career. Everything you've done makes up your body of work."

I told Howard I thought the song "Happy Together" had aged well. "It sounds as good today as it did when you recorded it."

Howard agreed, adding "There is a subtext going through that song that not everyone gets the first time or maybe even ever. It's not really a love song between two people but rather it's a guy wanting to be happy with the girl. [He is] imagining he is together with that lady. So it opens up a lot of possibilities.

"This song came out right in the middle of the Vietnam War, so there were a lot of soldiers imagining themselves with their girlfriends. In its own way, the song is very dark. The verses kind of throw you off because they seem very happy, but they are in such a minor key. By the time you get to the chorus, it bursts through with that line 'I can't see me loving nobody but you.' There is something very magical about that song."

On May 5, 2011, "Happy Together" was performed as a group performance by the top five contestants on the tenth season of the TV show *American Idol,* forty-seven years after it knocked The Beatles's "Eleanor Rigby" from Billboard's Number 1 spot for three weeks.

The Turtles played the song on the *Ed Sullivan Show* just three years after The Beatles debuted on that same stage. Howard was able to meet The Beatles but it was not that positive an experience.

Howard explained: "We went over to England and didn't know much except that we were in over our heads as far as our musical peers were concerned. It was like meeting the Queen of England, but John Lennon was merciless. He tore us a new one, so to speak. 'So you got yourself a Beatle haircut?' he asked our rhythm guitarist, Jim Tucker. "That brown suit gives rhythm guitarists a bad name, mate." Lennon told Tucker, and went on and on, relentlessly about Jim's name, his attitude. It was like John was trying to find Tucker's weakness, his chink in the armor, crack in the façade, and was getting great satisfaction breaking Jim down.

"Jim finally said, with tears in his eyes, 'Look, you guys were my idols. You're not what I thought you were. You aren't nice people.'

"Lennon shot back in his own sarcastic way, 'You never did, son. You never did [look up to us].'"

"Tucker freaked out. He was so upset. He left the club, left England, and disappeared. We never saw him again."

I said to Howard, "That's so sad, but you've got a screenplay there with a soundtrack."

Howard joked, "You can option it for a hundred grand."

CHAPTER 12

Tom Waits:
Glitter and Doom

*"They say that I have no hits and that I'm difficult to work with.
And they say that like it's a bad thing."*

—Tom Waits

It came as no surprise to me that David Letterman ended his thirty-three-year tenure as host of CBS's *The Late Show* by including musician, actor, and Rock and Roll Hall of Famer Tom Waits as one of his final guests. Tom sang his song "Take One Last Look" and had some advice for the retiring Letterman: "Do some hard work so it looks like you're busy. And be thankful you didn't work as a tire salesman." Waits told Dave, "It's very hard to retire from a tire job. It sounds like you're signing up again." Tom's always been a funny guy.

I first met Tom Waits when he joined me in studio after his 1973 debut album *Closing Time* came out. Out of the chute he was already

Smokin' Tom Waits.
Credit: © Elliot Gilbert

doing beautiful stuff. Nobody else sounded like him. Waits had that West Coast Southern California Beat style, and drew some of his influences from the Beat generation and rather obscure artists like Ken Nordine, a voiceover and jazz artist from the 1950s. Waits's hit songs are best known through cover versions by other artists: "Jersey Girl," a favorite number in many Bruce Springsteen sets, "Ol' '55," covered by the Eagles, and "Downtown Train," performed by Rod Stewart, Bob Seger, and others.

As he matured as an artist he took that folk singer/songwriter persona and threw it in a blender with jazz, rock, and even blues and hit "liquefy." He is brilliant both as a musician and performer.

He was always chain smoking during his studio visits, but it was Tom Waits. I wasn't going to ask him not to smoke. We'd play his music and he'd often play live on-air with his guitar. We even discussed that he might come back and do some broadcasting himself. We brainstormed that I'd engineer it and he could play some tunes he liked. Maybe we'd even do it from a diner. He seemed happy to dream up plans, but we never pulled it off.

Richard Harrington, writing in the *Evening Star* in 1973, observed Tom as having "the angular gait and thinness of a basketball player, but the prevailing notion in watching his actions is that he's moving in slow motion."

Tom launched his career playing Bob Dylan cover songs at "open mike" nights at Hollywood's famed Troubadour club in 1970. The Troubadour has a rich history. Comedian Lenny Bruce was first busted there for obscenity in the early 1960s. Other comedians, like Cheech and Chong and Steve Martin, were discovered there as well. The Byrds first met at a Monday open mike night. The Doors, James Taylor, Buffalo Springfield, Joni Mitchell, the Eagles, and many other musicians obtained notoriety there. Elton John made his US debut at the Troubadour. John Lennon and Harry Nilsson were kicked out of the club after their drunken behavior heckling the Smothers Brothers. John staggered out of the bathroom with a Kotex sanitary napkin on his head and asked a wait-ress "Do you know who I am?" She replied, "You are an asshole with a Kotex on your head."

Frank Zappa's manager, Herb Cohen, discovered Waits at the Troubadour and arranged an audition for him with David Geffen, then head of Asylum Records. Geffen was floored by Wait's songs. Former Lovin' Spoonful member Jerry Yester helped Tom produce *Closing Time* for Asylum. The cover art on *Closing Time* was done by Zappa's longtime artist/illustrator, Cal Schenkel.

Here is one of our interviews at 'HFS from 1975:

Cerphe: Tom Waits is with us, and he's down at the Cellar Door. Good to see you.

Tom Waits: It's good to be here.

Cerphe: In Bethesda.

Tom: In the womb of the nation. I love coming back here.

Cerphe: You've got a new album coming out.

Tom: It's called *Nighthawks at the Diner*. It's a live two-record set done in a studio with an audience.

Cerphe: You are really into diners.

Tom: I like to write about diners. I've spent a lot of time in diners. Yes, I can deal with grease.

Cerphe: There's a great diner in Silver Spring. It's about five miles from here.

Tom: The kind of places that I like is where the food is probably the worst I've ever had, but they give you so damned much of it that you really can't complain. And you've reached the end of an emotional cul-de-sac, and there's a Thunderbird moon and a Muscatel sky. And your emotional situation is starting to look like late night and early morn-ing low clouds with a chance of fog, and small craft warnings and swells from one to two feet. The extended outlook for an indefinite period of time is high tonight and low tomorrow. Precipitation is expected. So you drive down to Raphael's Silver Cloud lounge. So yeah, I enjoy grease very much.

Cerphe: And you let me do the weather report? With your new album do you have any poetry coming out?

Tom: Yes, it's half music and half spoken words.

Cerphe: You really get into the poetry.

Tom: I called them nocturnal emissions. So I have half inebriation travelogues and half songs. I think it will be a catastrophic album. I'm looking forward to it coming out. I hope it will be it a minor success.

Cerphe: Well, if we have anything to do with it, I think it will. Let's listen to something from [your previous album] *The Heart of Saturday Night.*

Tom: "Diamonds on My Windshield?" It's about a 1958 monkey-shit-brown Buick. It's kind of a midnight ride from San Diego to Los Angeles in the rain. I was drinking a bottle of something that said, "Please do not operate machinery" on the back of it. I had no spare. I had no jack. But under the circumstances, I wasn't coming back.

Cerphe: I'm surprised that you didn't put any of your verbal things on your first two albums. You do so many different things. You were doing the poetry early on.

Tom: I was, but I guess I was thinking of how palatable it would be. I was also in a quandary on how to do it. I had a lot of verse, spare parts, improvisational adventures I had written, and I really didn't know how to do them at that time. I have a better idea now. I've been working with a live jazz quartet now so I'll be exploring this.

Cerphe: That's great. Have you written any short stories?

Tom: Yes, I've written some stories.

Cerphe: Have they been published?

Tom: I'm having one published shortly in a music magazine, called "Putnam County."

Cerphe: Your work is so unique. I can't put my finger on its 'uniqueness.'

Tom: What I am most concerned about with the storytelling is it has to be done in an oral tradition. It can remain most prophylactic if it's not done in nightclubs in that fashion. Otherwise, it comes out on the Blues Soul Press, or something like that sold in Chatterton Books next to the Los Feliz theater. So as long as this stays in nightclubs then I have a better chance of continuing.

Cerphe: It can get lost in the big concert venues.

Tom: I've played the big concerts. I'm not particularly fascinated by big concerts. I find it's a bit grotesque when ten thousand people get together to watch anything. I prefer a nightclub where they have cleaning products. It seems when you get above five thousand people, especially for an afternoon concert, what you get are a lot of dogs, a lot of kids, patchouli oil, Frisbees, balloons, eating avocado and bean sprout sandwiches and drinking Boone's Farm. It gets a bit disjointed. I have played large concerts though. I played shows with Frank Zappa where I was his token opening act. That was a very strange and bizarre cultural phenomenon that I became a part of. But I've done clubs by myself for quite some time.

Cerphe: You're in a good one, the Cellar Door

Tom: Yes, this is the fourth time I've played there. I'm out on tour for the next four months and then I'll return home around Christmas.

Cerphe: Do you get a chance to listen to local music back in LA? At the Roxy or Troubadour?

Tom: Sure. If I'm not playing a nightclub then I'm looking for one to hang out in. I have a floating crap game going on at the Troubadour. So there are several reasons to be a part of that scene.

Cerphe: I understand you are really into dice. I've heard that but I could be wrong.

Tom: Well, do you have any cash on you?

Cerphe: You wouldn't be interested in how much cash I'm carrying.

Tom: I'll loan you some chump change. I'm not accepting pink slips or Bank America cards.

Cerphe: That was going to be my next question.

Tom: I'll roll you for your position at the radio station here.

Cerphe: You don't know what you might be getting into.

Tom: There will be a small, intimate crap game tonight at the Cellar Door after the club closes.

Cerphe: Getting away from gambling for a moment, I know the Eagles and Iain Matthews have recorded your songs. Would you be willing to record other people's work?

Tom: I'm doing Red Sovine's "Phantom 309" on my next album. If you are a merchandisable commodity and you are sticking your neck out as a writer, then when you hear something that you do enjoy then you think "Christ, I wish I had written that." Then I go and try to write something as good or better. I'm not against singing someone else's songs; it's just that I'm more interested in writing my own right now.

Cerphe: You've got your guitar. Will you play something for us?

Tom: [Picks up guitar and tunes.] Would you like to hear a story, Cerphe?

Cerphe: Yes, Tom.

Tom: [Sings "Putnam County."]

In 2008, the *Wall Street Journal* critic Jim Fusilli described Waits's music: "Mr. Waits has composed a body of work that's at least comparable to any songwriter's in pop today. A keen, sensitive, and sympathetic chronicler of the adrift and downtrodden, Mr. Waits creates three-dimensional characters who, even in their confusion and despair, are capable of insight and startling points of view. Their stories are accompanied by music that's unlike any other in pop history."

As a huge Tom Waits fan, I'm lucky that my wife Susan likes him just as much as I do. I get to play iconic albums like *Glitter & Doom,*

Small Change, Mule Variations, Rain Dogs, and his incredible box set, *Orphans: Brawlers, Bawlers, & Bastards* at full tilt. She especially loves the songs "Get Behind the Mule," "The Piano Has Been Drinking," and the extremely esoteric "Big in Japan." But we're the exception, not the rule. My dear friends Stilson and Tammy Greene have differing opinions on Waits. Stilson loves him. Tammy does not. Bottom line, no Waits will ever be heard growling through the windows of the Greene home. At least not when Tammy is there.

I've seen Tom Waits live four times now. He doesn't tour that much, so every January when we start getting snippets of who will be playing the DC area for the year, I look carefully to see if Tom is touring. One of my favorite shows I remember was at the Warner Theatre in the 1980s. He had one single streetlight on stage and the rear fender of a 1957 Cadillac, his piano, and guitarist, bass, and drummer. And a fog machine, which sometimes looked like it was pouring noxious gases into the theater. He is brilliant.

CHAPTER 13

CSNY and Richie Furay

To date, three members of America's supergroup Crosby, Stills, Nash & Young have penned autobiographies. Stephen Stills is still working on his.

David Crosby's *Long Time Gone* was first out the gate in 1998. *Publishers Weekly* called this book "a harrowing tale" as David, two years drug free, sharply chronicled his fourteen years of serious drug addiction. Neil Young includes a chapter in his 2012 book, *Waging Heavy Peace,* titled "Why I Wrote This Book." In this chapter, he admits that he wants to be the goose that laid the golden egg, and the egg . . . er, book, was going to make him a lot of money so he could take some time off from touring. I haven't thoroughly read either of these books yet.

However, Graham Nash's 2013 autobiography *Wild Tales* is wonderful. Now in his early seventies, Graham has been one of our best down-to-earth and most politically astute singer-songwriters. In 1972, Graham, then a phenomenal success as founding member of both the Hollies and CSNY, did a show at Ritchie Coliseum at the University of Maryland, playing some tunes on his acoustic guitar solo and telling stories, like how much he enjoyed seeing the "fine girls of Georgetown," how he writes songs, and performing great originals like "Immigration Man" and "Our House," the latter a song inspired by Joni Mitchell, an early love.

Graham and Joni were lunching at a favorite deli on Ventura Boulevard. While driving back to their home, they stopped at an antique store and Joni bought a flower vase. When they arrived home, Graham casually told Joni, "I'll light the fire, you place the flowers in the vase that you bought today." Joni said, "You better write that line down and write a song." Graham did.

"The secret about Joni, and me and all of CSNY, is that we want to write songs from our heart," Graham says. "And that gives us a chance to reach the listeners' hearts."

In *Wild Tales*, he also explains the origins of his fan-friendly attitude. He and childhood buddy Allan Clarke began a serious musical partnership when as teenagers they discovered the Everly Brothers. Their voices locked into Don and Phil's harmonies. When the Everlys appeared in their hometown in Manchester, they managed to locate their hotel and waited at the gates.

Graham greeted them with "Hi. We are Allan and Graham and we know all your songs and we sing like you."

This launched a long discussion among the four singers about how to perform and write songs. Phil told them, "Stick with your music. Something will happen."

It was exactly at that moment that Graham vowed to himself, "If I am ever successful in the music business, I will be as nice to my fans and as encouraging to young musicians as the Everly Brothers were to us."

Allan Clarke and Graham went on to form The Hollies a few years later. The Hollies would score with four Top Ten songs ("Bus Stop," "Stop Stop Stop," "On a Carousel," and "Carrie Anne") and had many other hits. By the way, the Hollies have never officially broken up and Graham has returned with them to record over the years.

Graham was one of my earliest favorite singer-songwriters in the Hollies. I loved their early music, for example, "King Midas in Reverse" and "Look Through Any Window," on which Nash primarily provided the verses and the beautiful high harmonies. It was when he left the Hollies and joined Crosby, Stills, and Nash that his original music was finally recorded and blossomed both artistically and commercially.

Creating CSN

Complicated legal constraints were obstacles when Graham decided to form a band with Stephen Stills and David Crosby. Graham was signed to Columbia Records, Stephen with Atlantic, and only "the Croz" (as they both refer to Crosby) was contractually free, as he had recently left the Byrds. Graham explained at the time to the press, "We hope to start a trio together to emphasize our individuality."

One year later, their eponymous album, *Crosby, Stills, and Nash*, reached Number 6 on Billboard's Top 100 albums, with two Top 40 hit singles, "Marrakesh Express," and "Suite: Judy Blue Eyes," the latter a romantic homage by Stills to his folksinger girlfriend at the time, Judy Collins.

According to Graham, the Hollies were thrown a party in Los Angeles in late 1966. A young fan invited Graham to meet his friends at a nearby recording studio. The friends were the Mamas and the Papas.

"So I was interested in meeting them," he told the Hudson Union Society in 2012. "When I got there Michelle, John Phillips, and Denny Doherty were recording tracks. So I talked with Cass Elliott." (By the way, Baltimore native Cass Elliott played the old Shadows club in DC with Denny Doherty and Zal Yanovsky as the Mugwumps. More about Cass in Chapter 15.)

Cass knew about the Hollies and everything else in the music scene. She introduced Graham to her friend David Crosby, who had just quit the Byrds, and they got along really well.

So well that when Graham moved to California, David Crosby gave him a an eighty-thousand-dollar check just to keep him solid. Adjusted for inflation, that's $1,190,000 in 2015 dollars. Indeed, "Croz" is a good friend to Graham.

CSN weren't Eric Clapton's Cream, but they were the cream of three very successful sixties bands. In the Byrds, David Crosby's harmony provided a distinctive element to lead singer Roger McGuinn's 12-string guitar and his Dylanesque snarl. Likewise, Stephen Stills provided a strong lead voice and driving guitar to the original Buffalo Springfield. Both had penned hits and more experimental material in their previous groups.

With Graham Nash at Lisner Auditorium with Smithsonian Associates, 2002.
Credit: © Cerphe Archive

In the Hollies, Graham, in his subtler way, provided a sonic presence on increasingly charming yet hooky music. He had balked when the Hollies wanted to record an album of Bob Dylan covers and then release a collection of past hits. Graham walked away from the band to keep "growing," he said. Musicians he was listening to as he quit the Hollies were The Beatles, Brian Wilson, Donovan, and Frank Zappa.

I met Graham in the 1970s. I'm very grateful that I can call him a friend today. Here are a few things we discussed in an interview in 2013:

Cerphe: I was reminiscing about the last time you were in DC for the "Pray for Peace" events at the National Cathedral with Jackson Browne, David Crosby, Keb Mo, and Emily Sailors. What a wonderful event.

Graham Nash: It was very, very special. To be able to sing and play that kind of acoustic music in that cathedral was wonderful.

Cerphe: And you know something about cathedrals. How did you happen to be able to do that?

Graham: The reason we did it was because of Bishop John Chane. The Bishop of Washington used to be a drummer in a rock and roll band in the sixties. He still plays today in his band, the Chane Gang.

Cerphe: Get out. Really?

Graham: Yes. Crosby and I went to see the Dalai Lama at the Cathedral. And the bishop's assistant came up to me and said the bishop would like to meet Croz and me. So we waited around. Bishop Chane came up and said, "Come, I want to show you something." So he takes us up to his bathroom and he opens the door. And his drum set is set up.

Cerphe: I love it.

Graham: And we immediately liked this guy.

Cerphe: On the subject of music in the 1960s, you created some amazing music with your band the Hollies, songs like "Bus Stop," "Carrie Anne," "King Midas in Reverse," "On a Carousel."

Graham: So tell me this: Why aren't we in the Rock and Roll Hall of Fame?

Cerphe: I don't have the answer to that.

Graham: Ah, I thought you might have the answer to that, Cerphe. The Hollies were great band. I spent many years not forgetting what I did with the Hollies, but it was on the second burner because I was so involved with working with David and Stephen. But in the last ten or so years, I've been listening to a lot of what I did with the Hollies. Quite a band, quite a band.

Cerphe: I love that song "King Midas in Reverse."

Graham: That was the beginning of the end.

Cerphe: By the way, I loved what you did with that box set of David Crosby's music.

Graham: Wait till you see mine.

Cerphe: I can't wait. With the body of your work, how do you decide what you would include in your box set?

Graham: It's an interesting dance. It always has been. As it was with Crosby's box collection, [coproducer] Joel Bernstein and I did not make that box set *for* David. We did it for history. If someone found this box set one hundred years from now, then would this music do him well? I've been able to take myself "out of myself" and decide if the music we choose is a fair representation of our music.

Cerphe: I've always been fascinated with how you choose music to put on a record, both collectively and individually, with your work both solo and with David, Stephen, and Neil.

Graham: It's been insane. [Laughs.]

Cerphe: It's funny. Whenever I get into a discussion with Stills, it always becomes political. He's such a history buff with the Civil War. You guys have always been involved with the politics of our day. I'm so proud of you. Never once have you lost that focus.

Graham: I think the young kids now are realizing that instead of this being a dry subject, politics is the essence of what runs their daily lives. I think they are beginning to get it. The Obama campaign registered so many young voters. If these voters would actually get off their backsides and vote, this would not even be a close election.

Cerphe: Have you attended any of the Obama campaign rallies?

Graham: I was there in Denver when he gave a beautiful speech. There was so much hope in the eyes and the spirit of the crowd. It was really astounding.

Cerphe: It has been awhile since we've seen that in politics, hasn't it?

Graham: We haven't seen that since Kennedy.

Cerphe: You wrote the song "Teach your Children" with CSNY and that song resonates today as much as it did back in 1971.

Graham: It was actually a little before then. I wrote that song when I was in the Hollies.

Cerphe: Really?

Graham: In my last week with the Hollies. I wrote three songs in one night. They were "Teach Your Children," "Right Between the Eyes," and "Lady of the Island."

Cerphe: That is amazing. It's the Hollies' loss that they didn't get to record those songs with you.

Graham: That was another reason I left the band. They didn't want to record those songs. And I started to doubt myself as a songwriter. But that's when the famous Croz stepped in and said, "No, it's them that's crazy."

Cerphe: During the Vietnam War CSNY created some of the best protest music of that era: "Ohio," "Teach Your Children," Stephen Stills's song "For What It's Worth" from the Buffalo Springfield, and as suggested by the title of your film *CSNY: Déjà Vu* all over again, you may well be stoked as well as provoked.

Graham: You know it's so crazy out there. People are looking for answers. But we've always said we don't have that many answers but maybe we can provide some more questions. But I was so proud of Neil as he always represented both the people who loved us but also the people who really hated us. I had never before been wanting to tour with bomb sniffing dogs.

Cerphe: Welcome to the new age.

Graham: Thank you.

Cerphe: When you were here at Lisner Auditorium with David Crosby recently we sat in the same room when your book came out [*Love, Graham Nash: A Portfolio of Prints*, 2009] and we had a Q&A with the audience. That was a great time.

Graham: That was a fun event. It was interesting just sitting up there, looking at the audience and asking, "Okay so what do you want to know?" But I am working on a new book and there's the possibility that we'll be sitting in those same chairs.

Cerphe: That would be an honor. I also know that you're an avid photographer and art collector. We have a wonderful art gallery here in the city called Govinda Gallery.

Graham: Yes, I know Chris.

Cerphe: Oh that makes sense because most everybody knows Chris Murray, who runs the Govinda Gallery, one of the legendary galleries in the country.

Graham: When I get the images finished for my new book, then I'll send them to Chris and see if he might want to exhibit them in Govinda Gallery.

Cerphe: You have a great eye.

Graham: Well it's the work that has to speak for itself, not just because it's me.

Cerphe: You're also humble. That's one of the reasons we love you.

Graham: Thanks, Cerphe.

David Crosby

I caught up with two-time Rock and Roll Hall of Fame inductee David Crosby at The Barns at Wolf Trap in 2012. We talked about David's time in the Byrds, Jerry Garcia, being part of the legendary CSN and sometimes Y, his wonderful new release *Croz* (his first in 20 years), letting his freak flag fly and much more! Here's my interview:

Cerphe: Congratulations on your sold-out tour.

David Crosby: [Laughs.] You mean my sold-out-got-so-sick-I-couldn't-stand-up tour?

Cerphe: It was interrupted but now you're back here in Washington, DC. With a little snow but you're here.

David: I didn't mean to bring the snow. I swear.

Cerphe: Thank you for making your new album, *Croz.*

150

David: I have to thank my son, James Raymond. We got together and got a writing streak going. After writing a few songs together, we knew we had to keep it going and make a record.

Cerphe: You have been part of some of the most forward music of our times, and I think you're making some the best music of your life right now.

David: Dude!

Cerphe: I'm serious.

David: Thanks.

Cerphe: You're welcome. I've been playing your music for a long, long time. And *Croz* is truly a masterpiece. I don't throw that term around a lot. Good on you.

David: I feel good about it. I think the songs are really good and for me that's what it's all about. If you have songs that make people feel something you've got the wherewithal, and from there it's just about crafting the music and having fun.

Cerphe: You've always written songs that mattered.

David: I certainly have tried.

Cerphe: Mission accomplished. This new one, *Croz,* reminds me of your first solo album in 1971, *If I Could Only Remember My Name.*

David: You know that you're not the only person who has said that. I'm trying to understand. Do you mean that the music quality level is very high because the songs are very different?

Cerphe: They are different but [they both have] the Croz mojo.

David: [Laughs.] We should bottle that and sell it.

Cerphe: For me on radio in 1971, it was your solo album and some of the early Steely Dan records [that had that vibe].

David: Steely Dan. My favorite band.

Cerphe: Yes, great band. Your passion for songwriting is as good as it was in 1965, and your voice is as strong and remains unaffected.

David: Isn't that weird? I sometimes think, "Is that me?" It's working and I'm not going to question it. Believe me, I'm grateful.

Cerphe: You recently went through a cardiac catheterization and angiogram. Are you okay?

David: That was a usual thing I do before I go out on tour. I get checked out. But they saw something when I did the stress test on the treadmill. I was here in The Barns and I got very sick. It was crazy and I had to fly back to California and go to UCLA hospital. They said I had something that was "just about to go." You know I'm a very lucky guy as I've been close to death many times. I guess I still have more things I need to do.

Cerphe: One thing I've noticed about your life is the people who are close to you just love you. They adore you. Look at Graham Nash.

David: Do you know how I like to think of him and I? We're like two old World War II fighter pilots in Spitfires, and we both know where our wingtips are. We can fly three feet away from each other at four hundred mph. And I don't know why. We just can. If Graham Nash isn't the best harmony singer in the world, then I don't know who is. Phil Everly is gone, so I think it's Graham. We do something fun.

Cerphe: Yes, you do. He's a good friend to have. And you have great guests on your debut solo album, and you also have good players on *Croz* like Mark Knopfler and Wynton Marsalis. How did that happen?

David: In the case of Mark Knopfler, it was because of a wonderful Italian friend of mine who's been working with me as promoter for over twenty-five years. He deals with Mark in Italy also, so he said to Mark's manager [affects an Italian accent]: "I ah tink dat Daveed Crosby and ah Mark Knopfler could do some-ting wonderful together." Mark's manager replied [in a British accent]: "Quite possibly." My Italian friend asks, "Do you a-tink they can write a song together?" Manager says, "Ah, no. Mark doesn't do that writing with others but he might play on something." Then I started talking and asked if I could sing him a song that my son had written called "What's Broken?" And he liked it. There has been a lot of this generosity where friends have come and played and they didn't have to do this. Playing on the cuff because we didn't have a lot of money. We made the album in James's house. Many friends came to the party and didn't ask for anything.

Cerphe: And Wynton?

David: My God, how that man can play. Holy yikes. When he comes in on the song it's the most beautiful sound I've ever heard. Tone for days.

Cerphe: Well, like I said: people love you.

David: I can't look at myself like that. I can't look at myself the way other people do. I know what a bozo I really am.

Cerphe: We were at a party a few years ago with Wavy Gravy, and everyone was given bozo noses. One of my prized possessions is a photo of myself with him and we're wearing the bozo noses.

David: Wavy loves to do that stuff. Not many people know that his name is Hugh Romney. I knew him when I was a kid playing coffee houses. He's a good man.

Cerphe: The man has heart. When I knew I was going to be talking with you, I went back to listen to some Byrds albums. They are some of my favorite albums. The first four Byrds albums: *Mr. Tambourine Man, Turn! Turn! Turn!, Fifth Dimension,* and *Younger Than Yesterday* have held up so well over the years. The passion still translates with them.

David: Yeah, I think they were good. The thing I love about them is that they were very musical, but also plainly willing to try new shit. To stretch the envelope. That willingness was a big part of the Byrds. I love them for that. I pushed it pretty hard. They all looked at me a little funny when I sang them "Mind Gardens." They asked, "Where's the track?" I said, "There isn't one." "*Dude?*" they said.

Cerphe: Before The Beatles and Bob Dylan, it was very unusual for performers to play their own material. With the Byrds, you did folk rock, country rock, jazz rock, and psychedelia. You threw it all in a blender. No one had done that cross-pollination in a band before. There were bands that did elements of it, but you guys did all of it. You created a totally original sound.

David: Well, that's the way you do it. You take disparate streams and things that are separate and you put them together. It's the same thing that Donald Fagan did. He took rock and put it together with jazz and created Steely Dan. The Beatles took the backbeat of rock and roll and put it together with folk song changes. More complicated changes than just four chords of rock and roll. They then put the whole world on fire and created a whole new music.

Cerphe: When you met The Beatles, you were already into world music. You listened to symphonies as a kid growing up in California. You were into folk music and West Coast jazz.

David: And Indian music.

Cerphe: Yes, you turned George Harrison on to Ravi Shankar.

David: That's what George said. Yes. I think maybe I did that. But I get a little nervous when I start thinking how significant I am. [Laughs.]

Cerphe: But you are, dammit.

David: But look at what George did with that. He was naturally always going for the higher ground. That is who he was. What he did with it and what it meant to his music is the important part. Incredible what he did.

Cerphe: You once said that whenever you had a lead vocal part in the Byrds, you choked up. But in Crosby, Stills, and Nash you found your voice. What was the change?

David: I grew more confident. I got better at it. Hopefully, you learn new stuff and expand your capabilities. At least I think that's what happened. But in the Byrds, it was never my job to be lead singer. We had very defined roles. I was supposed to be the harmony singer and the rhythm guitarist. The roles were correct. Roger McGuinn was one half of the Byrds. Fifty percent of what happened in the Byrds was Roger.

Credit where it's due. I liked what we were doing, but I wanted more. I was writing my own songs. It's natural. You grow.

Cerphe: The Byrds didn't want to sing "Triad"?

David: I think that's really not true.

Cerphe: It's a great urban legend.

David: We have a great version of "Triad" in the band I'm playing with now. It's killer. It rocks so hard you can't even believe it.

Cerphe: Jerry Garcia was on your first solo record. What was Jerry like for you?

David: He was a wonderful cat, man. If I had to pick one guy to speak for all musicians, it would be him. He was so bright. So articulate. And so fearless. He was willing to go wherever you could go, he could go.

Cerphe: I interviewed him three times. Once in the seventies, once in the eighties, and again in the nineties. That's my impression of him also.

David: I wrote a poem to him once. When I recorded "If I Could Only Remember My Name," Jerry was there every night we recorded. I miss him a lot.

Cerphe: Nobody sounds like you and Graham Nash when you two sing. How do you approach harmonies with him?

David: We were both raised on the same thing: the Everly Brothers. And nobody ever did harmonies better than the Everlys. Phil Everly was the greatest harmony singer ever. But the thing that's great about our harmonies in Crosby, Stills, and Nash is that they aren't just parallel. They don't go where Three Dog Night would go. They go to a different place. There are suspensions and tensions and little releases. Openings. And very interesting chords. I love that. It's our biggest strength.

Cerphe: In CSN, you're all songwriters. How do you decide what songs to use?

David: We use the reality rule. We sing them to each other. And we kind of know. We are competitive with each other. But we really treasure songs. If Stephen sings me a great song, then I can't deny it. It's the power of the song. The odd thing is that we have never gotten into a beef about what songs to play. We always pretty much know.

Cerphe: And with CS&N, you all seem to be fans of each other's. And Neil Young is on your list but he seems to be not as predictable as your other cohorts.

David: Neil is an unpredictable person. That's his nature. He's a brilliant writer. He sets the bar very high and he's a wonderful cat. I love working with him.

Cerphe: You also performed at rock's most legendary festivals: Monterey Pop, Woodstock, and Altamont. Do you enjoy being in front of an audience?

David: I love playing in front of an audience, but not like those audiences. When you play those blimp hangars and huge stadiums, the music kind of devolves. And it goes down to the level of waving scarves around. Setting off pyro. I like playing the smaller venues where you can do the more nuanced work.

Cerphe: You reconnected with your son James Raymond who was put up for adoption in the mid-sixties. You reunited with him in the nineties, and now he's the keyboardist in your band. I was adopted at birth, so this story is particularly close to my heart.

David: Yes, and you did a wonderful thing, too. He didn't bring any baggage to our relationship and allowed me to earn my way in. It was an incredibly kind thing for him to do.

Cerphe: I've had the opportunity to thank Stephen, Graham, and Bonnie Raitt and Jackson Browne for their political awareness and contributions. So I'd like to thank you too for your political awareness.

David: It's the most natural thing in the world. We all learned it from Pete Seeger. It's part of our ethic that came down from him, Woody Guthrie, Joan Baez, and many other brave people.

Cerphe: When you were twenty-two years old in the Byrds, did you ever think you'd be selling out solo concerts at the age of seventy-two?

David: No. I never thought I'd live to seventy-two.

Cerphe: When you were recording "Mr. Tambourine Man" with the Byrds, did you have any notion how successful that song would be?

David: Kinda. We thought it would be bizarre if it did become successful because no one had ever put such beautiful poetry to a rock song before. But we kind of did think it might be a hit. We didn't really know. We did sing it for Bob Dylan. He came to the studio where we were practicing it. He listened to it. And you could hear the gears working in his head. Shortly afterward, he was playing his music with The Band.

Cerphe: That's the Croz mojo. Thank you, David. It's been a pleasure talking with you.

David: Same here. We'll do more.

Stephen Stills

I was a huge fan of Buffalo Springfield. Stephen Stills's politically charged song "For What It's Worth" got my attention until I bought their second album and heard the Stills composition "Bluebird" and Young's brilliant "Expecting to Fly," "Mr. Soul," and "Broken Arrow." Both Stills and Young write with amazing passion, sometimes rage, and are such unique personalities that I believe they willed their success. Their creative playing and arrangements are innovative and hard to ignore. I still get chicken-skin when I hear "Mr. Soul"!

I loved Buffalo Springfield's music and was again delighted when Crosby, Stills & Nash (sometimes) toured and recorded with Young. Their reunion trek at the Capital Centre in 1974 was strong. Onstage, it became more compelling when Neil wore a Nils Lofgren T-shirt and a WHFS bumper sticker on his pants, given to him backstage by my fellow 'HFS alumnus Thom Grooms. Our listeners were so mesmerized seeing our call letters on Neil's left pant leg that they called us at the studio for many days reporting their "Home Grown Radio" sighting!

In 1966, a white van driven
by Stephen Stills and Richie
Furay and an old hearse driven
by Canadians Neil Young and
Bruce Palmer passed in a Los
Angeles traffic jam. They had
all met before, but this chance
encounter sparked the creation
of Buffalo Springfield. Thirty-
one years later, Stephen Stills
would become the first person
to be inducted into the Rock and
Roll Hall of Fame twice. And it
happened on the same night in
1997 for his work in with Buffalo
Springfield and Crosby, Stills,
and Nash. Really, you can't make this stuff up.

Stephen and Neil. Note Neil's 'HFS allegiance. Credit: © Paul Kasko / Rock Paper Photo

Stills is a prodigious songwriter and musician whom I've followed
ever since I brought a Buffalo Springfield album to my college drawing class. He's from Dallas, Texas, but his military upbringing took him
many places while he was growing up. Living in Florida gave him a love
for Latin rhythms. He graduated from high school in San Salvador. An
avid sailor, he's incorporated island rhythms to his compositions. He's
a Civil War buff. He's a long-time liberal. He's a multi-instrumentalist.
Here's an interview we did a few years ago:

Cerphe: Welcome back to the wicked town of Washington, DC, as my
guest on Music Planet Radio.

Stephen: It's wicked. You guys be careful.

Cerphe: I can talk politics with you all day long. But can we talk rock
and roll?

Stephen: Yes.

Cerphe: You, Crosby, Nash, and Young are all such great players and writers. I've always wanted to ask you how do you determine what songs are going to be recorded?

Stephen: Well, we all make solo recordings. I think we pick out the songs we want to do on our own and then the process is sort of inverse. We decide what songs we'll play and record together. These days, the records sell equally. It's apples and oranges but the solo records are also our escape valves so we don't drive each other crazy with our songs.

Cerphe: For my ears, to this day, the Buffalo Springfield is the most underrated group ever. You formed them in 1966 and then two years later started Crosby, Stills & Nash. Eric Clapton and Jimi Hendrix were close friends of yours who both appeared on your first solo album. You consistently make the list of the top one hundred guitarists of all time. You became the first person to be inducted twice on the same night into the Rock and Roll Hall of Fame with Buffalo Springfield and CSN. You performed at the Monterey Pop Festival and both Woodstock and Altamont, the three iconic music festivals of the 1960s. And you've been an outspoken liberal your whole life. You have been a part of the scene for a long, long time. Did you ever in your wildest dreams think that you'd still be doing this at this stage in your life?

Stephen: Well, I'm grateful. I'm grateful. I'm grateful that I have gotten to do my favorite thing all these years. A lot of people don't have careers this long so my dedication to my art demands I not be sloppy. If it takes me a little longer time to make sure I have a whole album that is right, then that's what I'm going to do. But I've already started on the next one.

Cerphe: Any moment of any day you can find one of your songs played on a classic rock station somewhere in America.

Stephen: Yes, I'm grateful to whatever higher power you want to name. Thank you. Basically, my church is sitting in the car listening to my radio.

Cerphe: Just outside of Washington, DC, is the city of Manassas, Virginia. I want you to settle an urban legend. A lot of people think that photograph of you with your band, Manassas, which also featured Chris Hillman, was not taken at the Manassas train station. True or false?

Stephen: It was.

Cerphe: Ha. I thought so.

Stephen: It was taken right there and that's the real sign. It shows how funky things were back then. Manassas was not the gentrified 'burb that it is today.

Cerphe: It's all grown up now.

Stephen: It was a country hick town with a Civil War battlefield close by.

Cerphe: The Battle of Bull Run.

Stephen: It was a dreary, stormy day when we took that photo. I was in my Civil War history period studying the Civil War and seeing how we could avoid another one. Obviously, I failed because we are in one right now. They just don't have guns. Politics.

Cerphe: I want to talk rock and roll with you, dammit, but you just keep going back to politics.

Stephen: [Laughs.]

Cerphe: You have written some of the most inspired music ever, and some of my personal favorites like "For What It's Worth," "49 Bye Byes," "Suite: Judy Blue Eyes," and "4+20." Thank you for the last forty-five years.

Stills: Thank you very much and I really appreciate your taking time with me.

Cerphe: And our mutual buddy, Thomas Grooms, says hello.

Stephen: Sure. He takes care of me whenever I come to town for fundraisers or little events. He is a great guy.

Cerphe: Yes, he is. We did radio together back on WHFS. Thanks, Stephen, for being on Music Planet Radio.

Stephen: Thanks and bye-bye.

Richie Furay

Although perhaps not a household name, even among music fans, Richie Furay, a Yellow Springs, Ohio, native and Rock and Roll Hall of Famer, has been in the epicenter of two of the most important bands in rock history: Buffalo Springfield and Poco. I got a chance to talk with him in October 2015. Our interview was in the Mansion on O Street near Dupont Circle and Georgetown.

Cerphe: You were just in your early twenties when you started the Buffalo Springfield. Did you know what you had at the time?

Richie Furay: I think we knew we had something special but I don't think to the degree that it really turned out. When we started as the house band at the Whisky a Go-Go, nobody knew who we were. And in six weeks, they were lined up around the block and up Clark Street.

Cerphe: Buffalo Springfield was a very short-lived band. 1966 to to 1968.

Richie: There were nine people in and out of the Buffalo Springfield in two years. It was one step forward and two steps back. It was sometimes hard to keep it together. At one point, not only did [our bass player] Bruce Palmer have immigration problems, getting deported a couple of times back to Canada, Neil Young couldn't decide whether he wanted to be in a band or be a solo artist. It was a difficult time. But as long as Stephen [Stills] was there, then I was there. Some people may argue with me on this, but in my mind, I believe Buffalo Springfield was Stephen's band. He was the heart and soul of Buffalo Springfield. Make no mistake.

Cerphe: It may have been Stephen's band. You're allowed to say that. But I want to give credit where credit's due. As a listener and a fan, the harmony parts you did with Stills and the guitar parts you worked out with him [demonstrate that you] were a huge part of this band.

Richie: When Stephen I put this band together, we were living in a little house on Fountain Boulevard. That's where we learned to sing together and work out the phrasing. Sitting together as close as you and I are.

Cerphe: And you and Stephen had been in Au Go Go Singers together before.

Richie: Yes, we had. [Laughs.] They needed a new name for that club. I had come back to New York with a couple buddies and we started a band playing at the Four Winds on West Third Street. We went back to school and returned the next summer and Stephen was playing there. That's where we first met. He passed the basket around. We passed the basket around. Charlie Chin, who played banjo on [the Springfield song] "Bluebird" was also there doing his sets.

Cerphe: I remember seeing the album credit on *Buffalo Springfield Again.*

Richie: That was really cool, that banjo part, and it was Charlie.

Cerphe: It was things like that—little nuances you'd add like the banjo and the harmonics on "For What It's Worth"—that no other bands were doing.

Richie: We were creative. We were an eclectic band. It was pretty cool.

Cerphe: In the mid-to-late sixties West Coast rock scene, Los Angeles clubs like the Whisky a Go Go and the Troubadour were making rock stars out of new bands like the Doors. You are on that list.

Richie: Those clubs were very significant in my career.

Cerphe: Atlantic Records had given your band a record deal. At twenty-three years old, did you think that was going to last forever? That was a huge label back then.

Richie: Well, I certainly thought that we'd go longer than the two years that it did. It came to an end. I was still on Atlantic and Graham Nash was on Epic. They switched us around so I got to become part of the first baseball trade in rock and roll.

Cerphe: Yes, after Buffalo Springfield, you formed Poco with Rusty Young, George Grantham, Randy Meisner, and Jim Messina. It always seemed to me that there was less drama with you and Jim Messina in Poco than in the first band.

Richie: Gosh, I don't how to say it. There was more drama put on the Springfield than was actually really there. Yes, we had conflicts. In any relationship you have those. In Poco, I was hoping that some of the old drama wouldn't resurface but it did. Randy was gone before we even got the first record out. Jim and I were pretty focused on mixing the record and Randy wanted to come in and I still don't know what happened. We were spending a lot of money on trying to get the record mixed but it wasn't like we didn't want Randy's input. Sometimes, when you get too many people in the studio, it becomes a party and not a business. It was sad but it happened.

Cerphe: But your debut Poco album, *Pickin' up the Pieces,* in 1969, set the blueprint for country rock and Americana. And today I hear influences in many bands and music going back to that album.

Richie: Thank you for that observation. We certainly did pave the way and created a sound. I tell that story on my new CD. It was something that Jim Messina and I wanted to do. It wasn't haphazard. Rusty Young had played on "Kind Woman" on the Springfield album. As soon as we heard him play, we [later] said, "Rusty, you got to be in Poco." And Rusty brought in [drummer] George Grantham.

Cerphe: "Kind Woman," the song you wrote in the Buffalo Springfield, is about your wife?

Richie: Absolutely.

Cerphe: How did I know that?

Richie: I don't know. Forty-eight years later [my wife] and I are here, hand in hand.

Cerphe: Your new album, *Hand in Hand,* is your first solo effort in eight years. I love the cover art on this. It's a beautiful portrait of you and your wife.

Richie: The photo of Nancy and I was taken during a Springfield shoot when we first got married in 1967. It wasn't a wedding photo but it could have been.

Cerphe: Your song on the new album, "We Were the Dreamers," is a fascinating music history lesson about Southern California country rock. Young listeners should listen to this because it's like a family tree that you can trace everything from the seventies to today back to Poco.

Richie: I had the lick and the chorus but I was having a hard time with the lyrics. My manager said he'd call Dickie Betts or someone like that to help me finish it. When I heard that, I sat down and wrote the lyrics just like that. The song tells the story of Poco. We were the house band for the Troubadour. We worked there at night and they let us rehearse during the afternoon.

Cerphe: Politics and music. You made the great "For What It's Worth" and forty-nine years later, you've written a song called "Don't Tread on Me." Politics and music.

Richie: Yes. I love this country. I'm known as a love-song writer, and this is a different kind of love song. Nancy and I have been married many years and we would not be together now unless we talked and communicated. I don't care if it's a rock and roll band or a business or our nation. We are so polarized. And it breaks my heart. We are the greatest country in the world, yet we aren't talking [with one another]. We are drifting further and further apart. So we have to talk with one another to know what we are all about. It is a patriotic song. And it definitely has political overtones.

Cerphe: You know we're not that far from Capitol Hill. We could take a ride up there and talk to some of the lawmakers. Do you see any of your former bandmates?

Richie: The last time I saw Neil was when we walked off the stage at Bonnaroo at our [Buffalo Springfield] reunion. I was invited to Nashville to give Stephen Stills an award that he received from the Americana group. I do see Stephen and talk with him through text. I stay in touch with Rusty, Paul, Jimmy, and Timothy.

Cerphe: After the Springfield reunion in 2012, I would've loved to have seen an album come out of that. It left me wanting more.

Richie: That's where the songs from *Hand in Hand* come in. After the reunion, I started putting riffs and lyrics together and I ended up with some songs I had to record.

Cerphe: You have made a lot of people happy with your music for a long time. Thank you.

CHAPTER 14

Nils Lofgren: Believe

Washington, DC, rocker Nils Lofgren joined me in studio in 1975 at 'HFS. After four promising records, disappointing sales, and a farewell concert at the Kennedy Center, Nils had broken up his popular band, Grin, and gone solo. The then-twenty-two-year-old Nils returned to my radio show to share his first solo album on A&M records, *Nils*

With Nils at the Hard Rock Cafe, DC, 2004.
Credit: © Cerphe Archive.

Lofgren, with listeners. It is also known as the "Fat Man" album because of the circus-style cover art showing Nils drinking a Coke in front of a painting of a freakish sideshow-type fat guy. *Nils Lofgren* had Nils on guitars, piano, and vocals, DC native Wornell Jones on bass, Stu Gardner (who went on to write the *Cosby Show* theme song) on backing vocals, and ex-Zappa band drummer, Aynsley Dunbar. Nils penned eleven out of the twelve tracks, including "Back It Up," "Keith Don't Go," and the prophetic "The Sun Hasn't Set on This Boy Yet." The album's sole cover song is "Going Back," written by Carole King and Gerry Goffin.

Nils brought his guitar with him and played on-air his brilliant version of "Little Wing" by Jimi Hendrix. I play a little guitar but I instantly recognized that my "Louie Louie" was never going to come close to Nils's "Little Wing" rendition.

Nils remembers it well, "As great as Jimi Hendrix was and all the things he did for us, Jimi rewrote the whole book on rock music with that sixty-second intro to "Little Wing," one of the most stunning pieces of music ever created."

I thought Nils's first solo album was simply great. Honest lyrics. Beautiful melodies. Original guitar solos. *Rolling Stone*'s Jon Landau agreed, calling it "a tour de force of unquenchable vitality and disarming subtlety." Landau had one year earlier proclaimed, "I saw rock and roll future and its name is Bruce Springsteen." Bruce subsequently hired Jon to become his coproducer on studio records from 1975's *Born to Run* through 1992's dual-released *Human Touch* and *Lucky Town*. Landau would also become Bruce's manager, helping him both artistically and personally.

Little did Nils know in 1975 that both Landau and Springsteen were carefully listening to his solo record. Nils told me in 2012: "It was kind of a pleasant shock to learn this. Over the years, Bruce and Jon let me know that they had taken notes on my solo record, and there were some elements on arranging, my approach, and the way it was put together that was meaningful to them. That was a great bit of news for me, as I have been an early and great fan of Bruce up to this day, of course."

Nils Lofgren was born in 1951 in Chicago of Italian and Swedish heritage. He was raised in Garrett Park, Maryland, a few miles from Washington, DC's northern border. He became a serious classical accordion student at the age of five. "I first took the stage playing my accordion at a ninth-grade talent contest," Nils recalls.

I remember a 1979 dinner with Nils, his brothers, and parents at the Pines of Rome restaurant in Bethesda, Maryland. It was wonderful to see how proud they were of Nils.

Although his parents were not musicians, Nils said, "My brothers and I got to grow up listening to the Big Swing music of their era (for example, the Benny Goodman and Woody Herman bands) and watching my parents dance and love music. They were very tuned into the therapeutic and spiritual healing properties of music. So at the age of five, I said to them, "I want accordion lessons," and they said, "Of course, you want accordion lessons. Music is a beautiful thing, so here you go." A more traditional or cautious or even adversarial approach from my parents would've really slowed down my career and my spiritual growth. So I've been very blessed to have parents and my brothers, who were supportive of my music. And for good reason. They love music."

Nils had his rock and roll epiphany at age sixteen watching then-unknown Jimi Hendrix play at the Ambassador Theatre in Washington's Adam's Morgan neighborhood in 1967. This show took place the day after the Jimi Hendrix Experience got everyone's attention at the Monterey Pop Festival, but we wouldn't see that movie until a year later.

Nils remembers Jimi's Ambassador show. "Before that show, I was just a fanatical guitarist, playing for a hobby. I never thought I could make a living in Bethesda, Maryland, playing rock music. Nobody thought you could do that in Middle America that I knew. But seeing Jimi play with the Experience, I became possessed with the idea that I could be a professional and make music a career. Jimi, accompanied by drummer Mitch Mitchell and bassist Noel Redding, did that to me with their brilliance and passion, raw talent, and guts."

Soon afterward, in 1968, Nils formed his band, Grin, with bassist George Daly (later replaced by Bob Gordon), and drummer Bob Berberich, former members of the DC band the Hangmen. Nils's brother, Tom, would graduate from high school to join Grin on rhythm guitar a little later. The Grin shows would be punctuated by the occasional back flip Nils would do from a minitrampoline on stage.

"And two years later, after Jimi's Ambassador Theatre show, on my nineteenth birthday, my band Grin got to be Jimi's opening act for three shows in California," beamed Nils. "On my birthday were Ventura, and then San Bernardino and Sacramento gigs. And man, opening for Hendrix and then sitting on the side of the stage. Just powerful and inspirational visceral moments watching him. I got to go back and knock on his Winnebago door, shake his hand, and tell him how much I loved him and his music, thank him, and leave before I became a bother."

Some DC-area readers may remember an early seventies show at the University of Maryland, where Grin opened for the James Gang, riding high on the popularity of their second album *The James Gang Rides Again*. This record included the hit "Funk #49" and the fresh guitar of a young Joe Walsh. Grin's show was superb and greatly received. But the James Gang had to stop their show twice as sound problems occurred. It seemed the crowd was feeling "bring back Grin," as the headliners failed miserably.

A few years later, in 1975, Joe Walsh joined the Eagles. Twenty years later Nils would share the stage once again with Walsh as part of Ringo Starr's first All-Starr Band, also featuring Clarence Clemons, Billy Preston, Dr. John, Rick Danko, Levon Helm, and drummer Jim Keltner. At Ringo's Merriweather Post Pavilion show in Columbia, Maryland, on

August 28, 1989, Nils would bring his brother, Tom, on stage to join the band.

Meeting Neil Young

In 1969, Nils, only seventeen years old and poised to go to Los Angeles on tour with Grin, met Neil Young between sets at the Cellar Door in Georgetown. Nils played him a dozen original songs.

Neil was taken by his talent, asking him to come over to Neil's Arlington, Virginia, motel room to hang around the following afternoon. A long creative association between the two musicians started. A year after their first meeting, Neil invited Nils to stay at his Laurel Canyon, California, home and contribute vocals, piano, and guitar on Young's acclaimed 1970 album, *After the Gold Rush.* He briefly joined Neil's band Crazy Horse in 1971 and played on Neil's *Tonight's the Night,* touring worldwide promoting that record. That same year, with Neil's support, Grin landed a record deal and became a local DC favorite, releasing four excellent albums, *Grin, 1+1, All Out,* and *Gone Crazy.*

Unfortunately, with only one song, "White Lies," getting heavy air-play on local DC radio stations to show for all their work, Grin's record label, Epic, released them from their contract, and Grin disbanded in 1974. Nils and Grin inspired many local garage bands to believe in one of the great American dreams: becoming a successful rock band. Their songs were innovative and adventurous. It became obvious to me early on that Nils had paid close attention to the amazing guitar techniques of Jimi Hendrix and local favorite Roy Buchanan.

The late Roy Buchanan played in DC bands, including the British Walkers, before he gained recognition as a virtuoso blues guitarist. Many fans, including Nils, would trek to edge-of-town Bladensburg, Maryland, to see Roy playing sideman with Danny Denver's band at a club called the Crossroads, adjacent to the Peace Cross. Nils proclaimed Roy as the greatest guitarist in the world in 1970. Sageworth and Drums founder

Walter Egan remembers being impressed when Roy played the Cuban instrumental tune, "Malagueña," with one hand—while holding a beer bottle in the other—at Georgetown's Silver Dollar nightclub.

Nils's band, Grin, attained prestige in the music industry as well as with local audiences. The four albums the band produced deserve a more prominent place in rock music history. Although Nils's 1975 solo album followed his band's breakup, it also fueled optimism among his wide fan base that it was still his turn to make it big. "Nils is Next" was a popular pin-back button I used to see at his shows.

Another nine years would be needed, but when Steven Van Zandt left the E Street Band in 1984, Nils got his break and Steve's job as lead guitarist in Bruce's band, just in time for the *Born in the USA* world tour. Nils played 150 shows on that tour.

"I was very surprised that Steve left the E Street Band," Nils told me in 2013, "but as I got to understand some of Steve's solo work, it kind of made sense. I had been fortunate to be doing my own original music. Gosh, I had started writing rock songs on my accordion when I was fourteen. I had always been able to get that out with demos, recording, and so forth since I was sixteen. And Steve had written songs and was a great singer and he needed to get that out for himself. Otherwise, it starts to build up. And being a bandleader is a fulltime job. For Steve to make a record and be the bandleader, and also be true to the E Street Band, which is a huge job, was kind of rough on him. So Steve decided to go, and this was a great opportunity for me. I was certainly honored to get the seat.

"And it was even better—a kind of old homecoming—when we got Steve back in the band in 1999 for these last fourteen years. It's been great to hear that rough duet rock voice every night. Really, Bruce and Steve are the only guys that still have that going on except for Mick and Keith."

For a very long time, Bruce and the E Street Band have set the standard for a first-class world touring rock band. For me, the E Street Band has been the greatest band there ever has been. I just don't think it gets any better. I noted to Nils that on the last few tours, the band hadn't followed a set list. Bruce is taking requests. That has changed the dynamic of the band, too.

"Yes," Nils agreed. "Doing audibles is one thing, but doing audibles you've never done before, and coming up with an arrangement, and then have Bruce count it off—all in thirty seconds—is quite the challenge. The offshoot of this is maybe we've never played a song together, but we each know the song. We know how to be a live band. We know what works, where to cut corners, and where to take chances. Where to use hand signals, and how, as an ensemble, to present something without rehearsal or even any idea that we were going to do it that night. It's exciting.

"We often talk about how we feel our generation was the last to have to learn how to play music in front of people. There was no Internet or 'how-to' videos, no choreography. Almost anything you wanted to learn from music required you to play for people, sometimes for thousands of hours in a club playing the same things."

The Wack Brothers

I asked Nils who the Wack Brothers were. What a great name for a band.

"I have been working a lot with Patti Scialfa, Bruce's wife, on her last two records," Nils explained. "She's a great writer. We got this core of musicians. Steve Jordan on drums, who produced it as well. Of course, Patti singing and playing guitar. Cliff Carter on keyboards and either Willy Weeks or Bruce on bass. I'm the swingman, playing different guitars, the dobro, and whatever. Because it is their home studio, it is a very relaxed atmosphere.

"When you do session work, even with great players and a producer cracking the whip and saying we got to get eight good tracks here, you sometimes don't take chances. You have to play it safe. You are professional. You don't take a lot of chances. You stick with the format. Like here's a good verse, here's a good chorus, now we're going to repeat it. Okay, here's a good track. That's a good song. Okay, I'm going to repeat it. This session process doesn't necessarily let their musicians express themselves.

"With Patti, we will just take the liberty of not rolling tape and just jam and explore without the pressure of, 'Hey, we got to get the track done in two hours.' There was one day in particular, I think it was on the *23rd Street Lullaby* sessions, I just started going off on some crazy riff that I felt because I had this freedom and there was no pressure. At the end of the take, everyone was just sort of smiling at me and laughing a little bit. I asked, 'What?' and Bruce said, 'That was pretty wacked out, Nils' and he was laughing. We realized that every time we go off on crazy, wacky ideas, then one or two might have some real powerful significance for a song. So we all started doing this, including Bruce. He's such an underrated musician, by the way. No matter what instrument he picks up, whether it's guitar, the bass, the organ, the piano—he really has the sensibility of being able to pick five or six notes and just creating a brilliant part. So after a dozen of these wacky ideas over a couple of days, we affectionately decided to call ourselves the Wack Brothers."

Nils was a bandleader for many years, both with Grin and his solo work. I suggested to him it must be refreshing, just playing in the E Street Band.

"Yes, that's right. I learned when I was eighteen and working on *After the Gold Rush* with Neil Young that if you love the people and the music, then it's really nice not to be the boss, just to be in the band. You can play more subtle parts and it's a very different perspective. I am known as a soloist and I'm quite happy to go in front of my own band or during Bruce's shows after "Youngstown" or "Because the Night" and rip off a couple minutes of a solo that stands out. But many people might not know that if someone gives me a choice between solo turns, or just playing acoustic rhythm to "Prove It All Night," I'd rather play rhythm. You get to be a giant shaker. It's a kind of a hypnotic thing that goes through your entire body. That's why playing in Ringo's bands and with Patti and others, I've really embraced this nonleader role."

On the other side of that, I've noticed while watching Nils, especially on recent tours with the E Street Band, that he'll step out and play, for example, the lead solo of the song "Tunnel of Love" two or three times longer than it's on the record. The audience loves that, and I love watching Bruce and the band just enjoying Nils and his spectacular guitar work.

Old School

Cerphe: You released a new solo album, *Old School,* in 2014. Tell us about it.

Nils: After the last two years with two tours and back-to-back Bruce albums, I wanted to do something that was authentic for me. I was coming

Nils sits in with Bruce at the Count Basie Theatre in Red Bank, New Jersey, 1983, one year before Nils joined the E Street Band.
Credit: © Laura Balducci

up on the big six-oh. I wanted to put something together that said what is right and what is wrong with where I'm at. Things that I would never think of as a teenager.

Cerphe: Yes, I see you have songs like "60 Is the New 18" and "Ain't Many of Us Left."

Nils: I had a double hip replacement three years ago and I was recuperating. My wife, Amy, brought the phone to me. It was Neil Young calling to check up on me and see how I was doing after the surgery. We talked for a while and he said, "Okay, get better because we need you around. There ain't many of us left." So I knew I had to turn that into a song, and it's on *Old School.*

Cerphe: You are more reflective than I've seen you before, not that I expect to see the trampoline on stage or you jumping off the stage risers. This is a very personal album.

Nils: I needed to be serious because I've been doing music for so long. You want to be excited [about these projects]. I wanted to do something that was very honest. You mentioned the song "Sixty Is the New Eighteen." Of course, I've been blessed with a fabulous wife of fifteen years, Amy. My mom and my three brothers are alive, so I'm doing pretty well, but the guy in the song is not. He's kind of abusing everything in sight. But he feels there has to be some hope and redemption for him. He just can't find it. It gets a little bit startling when things aren't right, as you get older. More alarming. Personally, things are pretty much going right. But I got a great problem now. I get homesick and I got a great home. I'm a performer and I've got to leave home to do it. When I pull out my suitcase and start packing, the dogs start getting sulky and give me dirty looks. Amy calls this my champagne problem.

Cerphe: Speaking of performing, I see the credits on your album. You're listed as singer, guitarist, and producer. You are wearing a lot of hats. How do you balance these roles?

Nils: I've been away from home for so long [on tours]. Amy has created this beautiful home for us, a 1935 adobe home in the Old Town section of Scottsdale, Arizona. We have a couple acres for our six dogs to roam around. It's kind of a dog park. I have a garage recording studio across the yard and I leave the doors open. The dogs come and visit me. So I started demoing and recording songs. It's not a public studio so I can shut things down when I want. But if I want to go in at 5:00 a.m., turn everything on, and keep working, I can. Next thing I knew was that I just liked the peace. And [the ability] to run errands and go to the grocery store and being part of my family. I encouraged everyone to interrupt me if they wanted to. Amy is a professional cook. She's brilliant. She's a great host, and she loves music. So if I invite my friends over, she helps me take care of them.

So I started making great progress on my solo record and I just stuck with it. I went across town to a professional studio and with a great engineer, Jamison Weddle, which was useful because I'm not an engineer but can get things on tape that sound and feel right. Luckily, some dear friends, Paul Rodgers [Free and Bad Company], Sam Moore [Sam and Dave], and Lou Gramm [Foreigner] were kind enough to sing with me, which was the icing on the cake.

Cerphe: For me, Paul Rodgers is on a pretty short list of great rock singers. He even sat in with the band Queen for a while. He's amazing.

Nils: Yes, and Paul didn't "replace" [the late] Freddie Mercury in Queen. Paul did his own thing with respect and honor. Something that very few singers could do. I've been a big fan of his for a long time. I don't know if you have a copy of the old *Gone Crazy*, our fourth Grin record. On the back of it is all these Salvador Dali-esque drawings by our friend Lanny Tupper, a local Maryland artist back then, now living in Japan. There's a drawing of a stairway going down into another dimension. If you hold the album up to a mirror, you'll see it says "Number One: Paul Rodgers" at the bottom of the stairway. So

I've always been a fan of his and yeah, you can't go wrong with great singers like Paul Rodgers.

And of course Sam Moore just standing there in front of me in the studio was a big thrill and also a little intimidating. Sam's a sweet man and there aren't many singers like Sam left.

Root Boy Slim

Cerphe: You have another song, "Let Her Get Away," on *Old School* that you cowrote with the late Root Boy Slim. He was a very unique singer and writer. Some of his work was so outrageous.

Nils: I used to go see Root Boy in clubs. He had great musicians like Steuart Smith, who was in my band for a while and is now with The Eagles. Root Boy was fascinating, unusual, articulate, brilliant—kind of like the Hunter Thompson of songs.

It was one day in the backyard at my Bethesda house. Root Boy and I were sitting around talking and thinking about writing a song together. Root Boy wrote this very beautiful and haunting lyric, which was not typical of the sarcasm and wit of what he was usually writing back then. I don't know if you've ever heard Root Boy write lyrics like this. His lyrics usually either made you feel uncomfortable or you just laugh your ass off.

I had a demo of it but the demo is so scratchy. I just said get over it; let me do it right. It's a song I've always wanted to share and this was the album for it.

Cerphe: You stood next to the Big Man, Clarence Clemons, for so many years. How do you fill that void?

Nils: It was an awful loss. Clarence and I spoke every week off the road, and every day on the road. He was a very dear friend. We stood next to each other on stage for over twenty-seven years.

It's strange, because it was getting near my birthday, just before Clarence got ill, when I wrote this song, "Miss You Ray," about the loss of Ray Charles. The concept was if you live long enough, then when people get old, you start saying goodbye to them, to family and friends. You have to focus on the people you have left or it can take you under. Clarence's death was an awful hit. But we are focusing on the new music. And we have to figure out how we're going to present them live. Of course, there're lots of options but none of them include Clarence. I don't think we know what we're going to do. Bruce is going to have to try to figure out what he wants. But I am grateful that Bruce is continuing to see what kind of band we can be. We can't be the band that we were because Clarence is gone. There is no replacing him. But I know Clarence is up there wishing us well and telling us: "In addition to sitting around and being sad because of his loss, get up off your ass and play some music." That's what I've been trying to do with my buddy Greg Vurlata for the last six months. On "Miss You Ray," I've been singing it "Miss You C," and of course I dedicated the record to him."

Cerphe: I noticed the Nils Lofgren Guitar School on your website, http://www.nilslofgren.com. Tell us about that.

Nils: For decades, kids have come up to me to say, "I want to learn how to play rock guitar for fun but I'm not allowed because I have no talent or rhythm." And I would ask them, "Who's telling you that?" And they never seem to know, so I began to offer both beginner and intermediate guitar lessons on my website. Calisthenics for the hands. The goal is to get folks engaged and make music. And get excited about it. Then if you can add ten or twenty minutes of frustrating practice into the equation, I'll back you up. Hopefully, you'll get inspired. You'll see the light at the end of the tunnel on the hard stuff.

I'm still coming up with guitar parts that I can't play. I think if I can stick with practicing a hard lick on the road for a month, then maybe I can add it to a solo. But most people aren't as crazy as me to work for hours on music and still suck. So the guitar lessons are more for "let's make music now." But if you work for twenty minutes on some of the harder stuff, you can go back to some easy lesson and then walk away happy.

Cerphe: And you've been playing many different instruments in the past years.

Nils: When Steve Van Zandt came back in the band we had four guitarists—Steve, Patti, Bruce, and me—so I became the swing man and started to learn some new instruments, including the lap and pedal steels, six-string banjo, and bottle-neck dobro. I can't become a virtuoso on any of these instruments because I'm too far down the road and have too many responsibilities. But Bruce is such an authentic writer he can give me parts that sound right so I don't have to be a virtuoso. So it's exciting to be a beginner on these instruments.

I spent five months on Bruce's *Rising* tour teaching myself the bottle-neck dobro and wrote a song, "Into Your Hands," for the dobro. The next thing I know, it's on a record, with me singing a duet with Willie Nelson.

Cerphe: You've always been a quick study. I remember when Neil Young asked you to play piano on *After The Gold Rush* you really weren't a piano player but you rose to the occasion.

Nils: God bless Neil Young and [coproducer] David Briggs. I was the one with the bad news. I told them, "I'm not a piano player." They asked, "But aren't you the guy who's been winning accordion contests and playing since you were five years old? The piano is kind of like the accordion. We just need simple parts. You'll figure it out."

It was so bizarre. I wasn't going to say no to Neil Young. But I had to be honest. After I tell them I'm not a professional pianist, they tell me they don't care. "Just do your best," they said. I said, "Okay," and luckily my best was good enough.

Cerphe: You passed the audition.

Nils: I passed the audition. Thank God!

CHAPTER 15

Little Steven: Wicked Cool

Steve Van Zandt is Bruce Springsteen's E Street bandmate *and* creator and host of the amazing *Underground Garage* radio show, now syndicated to two hundred-plus terrestrial outlets and Sirius satellite

With Steven Van Zandt and my wife, Susan, at the Verizon Centre, DC, at the Bruce Springsteen concert, 2006.
Credit: © Renegade Nation-Wicked Cool/Cerphe Archive

radio. He has been political activist, bandleader to his own Little Steven and the Disciples of Soul band, and Tony Soprano's loyal guard, Silvio Dante, owner of the Bada Bing ... strip club on the HBO series *The Sopranos*. Most recently he cocreated and starred for two seasons in the Netflix gangster comedy/drama *Lilyhammer*.

Bruce Springsteen made a beautiful confession at an October 2012 tribute for his longtime friend. Bruce revealed that Van Zandt is the first person he plays his songs to after he writes them: "I always ask, 'What's Stevie going to think?' Bruce admitted. "I may not always take his advice, but I am always wondering what his opinion is. Whether he was alongside me in the band, or whether he wasn't, that part of our friendship always endured."

Steven Van Zandt was born on November 22, 1950, in Winthrop, Massachusetts as Steven Lento, with Italian heritage on both sides, Calabrian and Neapolitan. His mother Mary remarried when Steve was young. He took the name of his stepfather, William Van Zandt, and his family moved to the New Jersey Shore in the mid-1960s. There he met another teen, Bruce Springsteen, who shared a mutual obsession with rock and roll. They both concluded that The Beatles's TV debut on the *Ed Sullivan Show* changed their lives. Steve said, "I had seen Elvis before and I got nothing, but these Beatles were in a band!"

In 2003, Kirk Sillsbee, a Santa Monica, California, rock writer, asked Steve about those early days: "What was it about Middletown, New Jersey, that prepared you for a life in rock and roll?"

Steve replied, "After World War II, everybody moved to the suburbs. In the late fifties, for the first time, teenagers became a demographic with money to spend. Rock and roll captured the imagination in a way that took your mind away from the goal of getting a job and a career. Momentarily, anyway. Rock and roll suggested the possibility of getting a job in rock and roll. Before The Beatles, there were no bands, except the

(L-R) Southside Johnny, Ronnie Spector, me, Steven Van Zandt, and Richie "La Bamba" Rosenberg at WHFS, 1977.
Credit: © Big Al Sevilla/All Access Photography

Crickets, Buddy Holly's band. On February 14th, everybody wanted to start a band.

"For me, it all stemmed from the British Invasion. It started with George Harrison and Keith Richards, and then the three Yardbirds' guitarists: Eric Clapton, Jeff Beck, and Jimmy Page. Through George, I learned about rockabilly guitarists like Scotty Moore, Carl Perkins, and Don Rich with Buck Owens's band. Through Keith, I learned about all the blues guys."

Steve helped define the "Jersey Shore" sound by founding, writing for, and producing the bar band Southside Johnny and the Asbury Jukes. Steve gained true cred when he created the iconic horn arrangements, on the spot, for "Tenth Avenue Freeze-Out" during the *Born to*

Run recording sessions. Bruce has also credited Steve with contributing to the main riff for the album title song. Steve would officially join the live band on July 20, 1975, at the Palace Concert Theatre in Providence, Rhode Island, for the start of the *Born to Run* tour, just in time for the explosive worldwide popularity predicted by critics and fans.

His cool suits, hats, and dapper style would sparkle on stage. Later he switched from hats to his now trademark babushka head scarfs. The reason you never see him without a headdress is because his scalp was disfigured when he was thrown though the windshield in a car accident. I've never seen his scalp, but I've been told that there are patches where hair won't grow.

On bootleg tapes of the Palace Concert show, Bruce can be heard introducing Steve, with the band premiering both "Tenth Avenue Freeze-Out" and "Thunder Road." Also notable is a slice of Isaac Hayes's "Theme from Shaft" that emerges surprisingly in "Rosalita." Cover songs "Shout," "Sha La La," and "Quarter to Three" closed the show. This tour would end in May 1976 after 116 shows. I was lucky enough to bring the band onstage on December 5, 1975, at Georgetown University's McDonough Gymnasium and again when they returned there on October 17, 1976. I also emceed their show at Carter Barron Amphitheatre in Washington, DC, on July 28, 1975, and at the Capital Centre in Landover, Maryland, on November 23, 1980.

Chimes of Freedom

Little Steven left the E Street Band in 1984 to pursue his own musical and political projects. His first master move was to organize over fifty artists to help him record "Sun City," an in-your-face musical protest against apartheid in South Africa. Then, Sun City was a ritzy "whites only" resort. The song's refrain, "I ain't gonna play Sun City," affirmed the singers' opposition to the white minority government's policy of apartheid, established in 1948.

The song became an anthem to the freedom message of Nelson Mandela, incarcerated in jail. Mandela fought for and cherished the ideal of a democratic and free society in which all persons live together in harmony and with equal opportunities.

Initially, Steven wasn't going to invite Miles Davis because of the jazz man's legend status, or Bruce, so as not to take advantage of their friendship, to participate in "Sun City." But they both came on board. The resulting video—aired heavily on MTV—was triumphant. Many artists joined in on "Sun City," including Bob Dylan, Bobby Womack, Bonnie Raitt, Clarence Clemons, Darlene Love, David Ruffin, Eddie Kendricks, George Clinton, Gil Scott-Heron, Hall and Oates, Herbie Hancock, Jackson Browne, Jimmy Cliff, Joey Ramone, Keith Richards, Lou Reed, Pat Benatar, Pete Townshend, Peter Gabriel, Peter Garrett, Peter Wolf, Ringo Starr, Ron Carter, Ronnie Wood, Rubén Blades, Run DMC, the Fat Boys, U2, and Zak Starkey.

"Sun City" was an intense song that raised the world's consciousness on racism. It also made you want to dance.

Acting

I loved Silvio Dante in *The Sopranos*. I talked with Steven the day after the final, controversial episode aired on June 10, 2007, at my former CBS radio show on 94.7, The Globe:

Steven: Cerphe. How are you, baby?

Cerphe: Steven, I'm great. The question is, how are you?

Steven: I'm nuts.

Cerphe: You're still among the living.

Steven: I'm still breathing. I got to tell you that I've seen a lot of things. I've done a lot of things but this finale down here. I wish you were here, Cerphe, so you could see what happened at the Seminole Casino.

Cerphe: Down in Hollywood, Florida.

Steven: It's only been rivaled by maybe three or four things in my rock and roll life.

Cerphe: Everyone had different ideas about how *The Sopranos* series would wrap. Not since the Kennedy assassination have there been so many theories flying around.

Steven: [Laughing].

Cerphe: Am I right?

Steven: You're so right. I stopped counting at 200. Every interviewer, every pundit on TV, they all had a different ending. The genius of [series creator] David Chase is that everyone was wrong.

Cerphe: I absolutely loved it.

Steven: Me too.

Cerphe: The greatest double-take in television history.

Steven: Yesterday, everyone was in shock. They couldn't quite figure out what had happened. But today, everyone I think is figuring out what happened and how brilliant it was, and how David Chase is a genius.

[Note: David Chase directed *The Sopranos*' final episode, "Made in America." He has said he was going for an ending that had a similar effect as the final scene of *2001: A Space Odyssey*. The song "Don't Stop Believin'" by Journey is used to full effect, with its refrain "on and on, and on, and on." The last episode finds Silvio Dante comatose. In the final scene, Tony Soprano is in a diner with his wife and son, and other characters nearby. His daughter, Meadow, arrives late. As the diner's doorbell rings, Tony looks up. Cut to black. It's an unexpected, unresolved ending.]

Cerphe: The cool thing about *The Sopranos* is that there's a lot of humor, but it's really a tragedy, don't you think?

Steven: The tragedy is much disguised. But yes, there are some very funny moments.

Cerphe: Like when [Silvio Dante] is sitting in the office of the Bada Bing bar reading books on hobbies.

Steven: Yes, once in a while you have to be reminded that this is not your typical daytime soap opera.

Cerphe: The way it ended, with the lyric "Don't Stop" and Tony's face, let me ask you if there is a film in the future?

Steven: The rumor [of a future film] actually started about a month into the first season. Now that the TV show is over, you can figure that a film is possible one, two, three years down the road.

Cerphe: But a movie's has never been discussed?

Steven: Never, ever been discussed.

Cerphe: So you didn't shoot multiple endings?

Steven: I've seen that we shot three different endings stated as a fact on many news programs. But it never happened.

Cerphe: You can imagine there might be many different interpretations of the ending.

Steven: Yes, you saw the only ending that David Chase intended. It accentuated that we flew in to meet these people [eight seasons] ago, and now we are flying out. We checked them out for an hour each week. The song says, "Life goes on."

Cerphe: And when your character, Silvio, got shot, there were millions of us saying, "No. No. Not Silvio!" But Silvio lives.

Steven: [Laughs.] Yes, Silvio lives. That's the main thing. The rest is superfluous.

Cerphe: Thanks for being in a cast of characters that has literally changed television forever.

Steven: Thanks. It has been an honor and a pleasure. What a thrill it's been to have a whole new craft, a whole new art form to jump in and learn about. And a whole new set of friends. And on top of that to have it be such high quality. It's really wonderful.

Cerphe: And on top of that you're not such a bad guitar player either. We love you buddy. We'll see you this summer.

Steven: [Laughs.] Thanks.

Cerphe: I can't think of a better song to play than "Murder, Inc." by Bruce Springsteen and the E Street Band on 94.7, The Globe.

Lilyhammer

Van Zandt married the former Maureen Santoro—who also portrayed Silvio's wife on *The Sopranos*—on New Year's Eve 1982, with Springsteen serving as best man and Percy Sledge singing "When a Man Loves a Woman." Little Richard officiated the wedding.

Lots of us believed that his acting career might be over when we heard "Don't Stop Believin'" at the end of the series. Fortunately, *Lilyhammer* was a Norwegian television series that Little Steven engaged in after *The Sopranos* ended. He played a fictional New York gangster, Frank "The Fixer" Tagliano (styled closely on his previous Silvio Dante character), who starts a new life in the witness protection program in isolated Lillehammer, Norway. The show debuted on Norwegian NRK1 TV with a record audience of 998,000 viewers (one fifth of Norway's population) in January 2012 and in North America in February 2012. *Lilyhammer* was promoted as "the first time Netflix offered exclusive content." It ran for three seasons.

Little Steven was very excited to talk with me about this project in 2012:

"I am very proud of *Lilyhammer*. You take a shot now and then and this is a crazy, risky business. The fact that Netflix chose this to be their first original show is a validation and a compliment. I had very serious doubts that America would ever see it because it is a show for Norwegian TV.

I told Steve that I was surprised he was playing another gangster. He replied: "It was a surprise to me, too. I didn't think I'd be playing a gangster so soon, unless Marty Scorsese called. But the story was too good. Plus it's such a monoculture. Nobody locks his or her doors outside Oslo. They make rules and follow the rules. Here we make them and break them.

"And nobody in America knows much about Norway. You can't name a Norwegian celebrity. You can't name a Norwegian product. So it was fun to make Norway one of the characters of the show. And I knew everything we revealed about Norway to our American audience would be new."

Asbury Park's Stone Pony

It's been forty-plus years since Van Zandt and Springsteen, with Southside Johnny and others, wrote songs, formed bands, and played Asbury Park's boardwalk bar the Stone Pony, one of most famous rock and roll clubs in the world, although Bruce didn't get his start there as many believe. His Asbury Park music career began in 1969 at the Upstage Club on Cookman Avenue. But he has played at the Pony about a hundred times, more than any other venue. According to the excellent website Brucebase, Bruce's first performance at the Stone Pony was on September 8, 1974, when he jammed with the Blackberry Booze band, headed by Steve Van Zandt and Southside Johnny. That band would later become Southside Johnny and the Asbury Jukes, who did get their start at the Pony.

In the last ten years, Bruce Springsteen has played the bar at private fundraisers for area schools with expensive tickets going to parents and guests. Before that, he jammed with many artists, including Levon Helm, Lord Gunner Group, La Bamba and the Hubcaps, Cats on a Smooth Surface, Marshall Crenshaw, Killer Joe, Nils Lofgren, Little Steven, Jimmy Cliff, and Clarence Clemons.

Today, the bar is alive and well.

CHAPTER 16

Cellar Door Acts

"Jack Boyle began investing his poker winnings into DC clubs and ended up creating and selling Cellar Door Productions for 135 million dollars. You got to love a guy like that."

—Michael Oberman

I was fortunate to have spent hundreds of nights in the old Cellar Door club in Georgetown. It was the best place to see superb music. Some memories include the late singer-songwriter Steve Goodman, who first played the Cellar Door in 1972 and returned seven times.

I remember Steve's three-night run in 1975. By this time, Goodman was best known for writing Arlo Guthrie's hit song, "The City of New Orleans." In person, he was always having fun on stage with different styles of music and had a loyal following due to his winning personality and eclectic repertoire of storytelling songs.

The intimacy of the Cellar Door was something I remember that was a big part of its appeal. That intimacy of the room leads to a Steve Goodman story from our editor, Patty Johnson Cooper, that illustrates how fun his shows were: once he asked the audience for requests. Some wiseguy yelled out, "Eat my shorts." Steve grinned that impish grin and launched into a totally improvised-on-the-spot blues song that began

"Eat my shorts, that's what he said. Now he wishes he were dead" and ended with "And someday I will go to court and copyright 'Eat My Shorts'." The audience was in convulsions.

Steve's close friend Kris Kristofferson was accompanying him on selected gigs on the 1975 tour, and I was hanging with Kris. During a set break, Kris and I walked across the street to the Apple Pie bar. After Kris downed a few vodka shots, he started getting weepy on me.

"It's such a shame," Kris said.

"What is?" I asked.

"Steve," Kris said. "He's dying from leukemia."

I didn't know what to say.

In the final years that he battled leukemia, in keeping with his droll sense of humor, Steve called himself "Cool Hand Leuk." The title of his 1983 album *Artistic Hair* referred to his chemo-induced hair loss. Gone too soon, Steve Goodman's memory and music are still treasured by his many fans.

Biff Rose

Biff Rose first played the Cellar Door in 1965, the year the club began to truly take off. Biff would return ten more times over the years. The New Orleans native found an early outlet for his comedy talents in Hollywood when George Carlin hired him to write jokes and sketches. George, by the way, began as a fairly conventional comedian but increasingly adopted and perfected his hip, inventive humor. Jack Boyle booked him at the Cellar Door, where he recorded his 1971 transitional album, *FM and AM*. This was his only Door appearance, but that album broke him into stardom. It earned him a 1972 Grammy award for Best Comedy Record.

Biff became a standup comic who morphed into a piano-playing humorist and composer. His first record, *The Thorn in Mrs. Rose's Side* (1968), led to appearances on TV's *The Tonight Show, The Smothers*

Brothers Comedy Hour, and others. He emceed both the Atlantic City Pop Festival (1969) and the Atlanta Pop Festival (1970).

We contacted him at his Oakland, California, home to share his Cellar Door memories: "My first gig at the Cellar Door was March 1965. I opened for Glenn Yarbrough of the folk group the Limelighters. Glenn was riding the crest of his big, hot hit "Baby the Rain Must Fall." I played the long-neck banjo and did politically tinged songs that found a ready audience in DC. But I had to be careful or you were bound to step on somebody's toes. Glenn heard my act when I opened for him. He said, 'Put down the banjo. You'll never be a singer.'

"So he took me on the road for two years opening for him. So I credit the Cellar Door for springing me from the Village coffeehouse circuit to Big Time Hollywood and the Smothers Brothers Show, which you can see me on through YouTube."

Biff remembers: "Drinks were free at the Cellar Door for the acts. I picked up a guitar player, Wall Matthews, and dove deeper in pure music improv without the showiness of performance. I remember playing the Cellar Door later with all this improv going on and the crowd accepted me because they liked me from before.

"It was like exploring new ground, and that's always shaky. Civil rights was raging all over America back then and every room in every big city had its black folksinger. Philadelphia had Don Crawford. Boston had Jackie Washington. Cincinnati had Billy Cox. The Blue Dog Cellar in Baltimore had Levi the Cook. The Cellar Door had Donal Leace. I was movin' on up to play the Cellar Door. I was coming direct from Greenwich Village, which was stinky, funky, and real. You had to bathe to get into the Cellar Door. But I can't exaggerate the importance of Donal Leace in the forming of the Cellar Door. He made the room the place to go."

Donal Leace

A West Virginia native, singer/songwriter Donal Leace began singing folk songs in local coffee shops while a freshman at Howard University in 1960. "On a good night, I could make $60 and on bad nights, I was guaranteed $10," he recalls.

Soon he was pals with folkies like Paul Clayton, Carolyn Hester, Mike Seeger, and Dave Van Ronk. They helped him get a gig at the Showboat Lounge, a preeminent jazz nightclub in the Adams Morgan neighborhood that featured folk music on Sundays. Otherwise, the Charlie Byrd Trio (with Keeter Betts on bass and Bertel Knox, and later Bill Reichenbach, on drums) played the other six nights. Keeter Betts went on to become bass player for Ella Fitzgerald.

Donal remembers, "In 1961, Van Ronk invited me to Gerde's Folk City in New York City to meet the new folksinger, Bob Dylan. I was most interested in Bob's arranging then, on songs like 'House of the Rising Sun.' It was interesting when Bob later came down to do the Showboat Club. Some guy kept giving Bob the Nazi salute during his set until he was thrown out. Bob's new original songs were a little off-putting because most of us were trying to perfect the traditional folk songs."

Leace was offered the opening spot at Georgetown's Shadows Club in 1962 by then-owners Jack Weiss and Bob Covallo. Donal says, "I gave up a sure thing—one night a week at the Showboat—for six nights a week at a club that might not work out. It was a Georgetown University hangout. Lots of students. I moved into the upstairs apartment and went to work. The Showboat was known as the 'Home of Charlie Byrd,' so they hung a sign outside the Shadows, 'The Home of Donal Leace,' which was an ego boost and also literally true. The first acts that came in were the Journeymen (Scott McKenzie, John Phillips, and Dick Weissman), Josh White Jr., and someone I had lobbied for, Judy Collins.

Jack Boyle

World-renowned printmaker and artist Lou Stovall got his start in DC while he was a student at Howard. Lou was responsible for creating the large black and white signs that hung in the front window of the Cellar Door displaying the names of the acts appearing nightly. Jack Boyle had a sign that Lou made for him that hung behind his upstairs office desk. It read, "If You Fuck with the Hawk, You Get Clawed."

Jack Boyle was born in Youngstown, Ohio, in 1934. His dad graduated from Georgetown University and successfully practiced law until he became very ill. Jack was eleven when he lost his dad at age thirty-four. By seventh grade, Jack was running a gas station after school. At age fourteen, a golf caddy master slapped him, and Jack picked up a club and beat the hell out of him. Jack got his job.

At sixteen, he made a fake birth certificate so he could get an adult factory job. He'd catch the bus downtown and work from 6:00 p.m. to 4:00 a.m., walk two miles home, be in school by 8:30 a.m., sleep for three hours after school, and start all over. Jack was able to graduate from both high school and college without studying. Now in his eighties, he says he has a good memory.

Jack graduated from Georgetown with a degree in Foreign Service on a Sunday in 1959 at the age of twenty-five. He graduated from Youngstown College the very next day. I've heard Jack try to explain how this was achieved and it still confuses me. Evidently, he was a longer-term student at Youngstown and needed just a few credits for a degree. Before he finished that, he flew through his courses at Georgetown, and then completed both degrees at the same time.

Jack has admitted in interviews that he was a heavy drinker and a rather wild character in those early days before he married his second wife, Janet.

While at Georgetown, Jack began as a cleanup boy, then dishwasher, then bartender at the Shadows bar. He won some money in a poker game and invested in some area nightclubs. In 1964, he bought Shadows and renamed it the Cellar Door. Boyle booked a local jazz group, the Eddie Phyfe Trio, for several months as entertainment. He really didn't know or care much about music then. He tells interviewers that he is "tone deaf." Boyle soon sold the Cellar Door to his Crazy Horse club partner, Tom Lyons, for a nice profit.

Meanwhile, the name "Shadows club" migrated a few blocks up the street to a new, plusher location at 3125 M Street. Donal followed. The new Shadows began attracting some very big acts like Bill Cosby, Nina Simone, and Woody Allen. Today, the building houses the Ri Ra Irish Pub.

Next Tom hired Leace to return to the 34th and M Street Cellar Door. Donal confirms, "I played there for the next six years, more than any other person."

His small apartment became the local hangout for acts and visitors to both the Cellar Door and Shadows. Donal was so well known that even his dog Bourbon would get Christmas cards.

One visitor was Baltimore native Ellen Naomi Cohen. She had previously attended George Washington High in Alexandria, Virginia, where she adopted the name Cass and added "Elliot" later. Upon graduation, she pursued a musical comedy career in New York City. She toured with a production of *The Music Man*, but lost an important Broadway audition to Barbra Streisand for the role of Miss Marmelstein in *I Can Get It for You Wholesale*.

Cass returned from New York City to attend my alma mater, American University. She called herself a radical at AU but this is when she began her popular singing career, first playing with Tim Rose and James Hendricks in the Big Three, and then joining the Mugwumps with Canadians Zal Yanovsky and Denny Doherty. The Mugwumps lasted eight months and primarily headlined at the Shadows club. Cass and Denny would next join former Journeymen guitarist John Phillips and his wife, Michelle, to form the Mamas and the Papas. John Phillips also grew up in Alexandria, Virginia, and even played basketball for George Washington High. Other notable GW High alums include former *Today Show* weatherman Willard Scott and The Doors' Jim Morrison.

After a strong string of harmonious hit songs, including "California Dreaming" and "Monday, Monday," the Mamas and the Papas broke up in 1968, mainly because Cass wanted a solo career. She recorded, performed, and appeared on an array of TV shows, including subbing for Johnny Carson on *The Tonight Show*, a serious TV role about obesity on *Young Dr. Kildare*, guesting on *The Carol Burnett Show*, and her own variety specials. Sadly, Cass died of heart failure at age thirty-three in 1974. The group was inducted into the Rock and Roll Hall of Fame in 1998.

Charlie Fishman, a George Washington University student, moved up through the ranks from waiting tables to take full ownership of the Cellar Door from Lyons. In 1969, Fishman sold it back to Jack Boyle and new partner, attorney Sam L'Hommedieu. Jack, with Sam, moved back into the upstairs offices, adjacent to Donal's apartment.

Leace graduated from Howard while still performing at the Cellar Door and began teaching English at Western High School. One of his students was Richard Harrington, who became music writer for the *Washington Post*. Today, Western High is the Duke Ellington School of the Arts.

Donal says he never understood why Harrington, in all the many articles he wrote about the Cellar Door, never mentioned him. Today, Donal wonders, "Maybe I flunked him in something."

By the way, Donal Leace started life as *Donald* Leace. An early newspaper typo mention of him left off the "d" in his first name and he rolled with it. And when asked about the best experience of his life, he answers, "The 1963 March on Washington For Jobs and Freedom. My family came from all over. We had seats near Harry Belafonte and Josephine Baker."

Enterprise Level

Michael Oberman became Boyle's assistant in 1975 and has many stories: "I sat in an office between the owners and sometimes Jack would tell me to do one thing, while Sam would tell me the opposite. Also, Sam would be calling me at 6:00 a.m. asking how things went the night before. One night, when Rita Coolidge was headlining, Jack and Kris Kristofferson sat in the balcony having a contest, drinking shots that led to a fistfight with tables flying. And Jack's pants fell down."

Boyle extended his enterprise by booking Gordon Lightfoot and subsequent artists into DAR Constitution Hall. He next bought the Stardust Lounge in Waldorf, Maryland. Oberman tells a charming story about meeting Jerry Lee Lewis at a Stardust motel room for an interview. "Jerry Lee greeted me by letting me know there was a keg of beer in the bathtub, and help yourself. When I went in the bathroom, I discovered that Jerry Lee had taken a big shit in the bathtub. It was his joke."

Jack took a liking to the Stardust bouncer, Dave Williams. Dave did very well working with Jack as he ended up in charge of Cellar Door Enterprises when Jack moved to Florida. I heard he invested six million of his own money into the Nissan Pavilion when Jack bought it. Now named Jiffy Lube Live, its address is 7800 Cellar Door Drive, Bristow, Virginia.

The moment that Jack Boyle's future went supernova occurred when Jack flipped his car keys to Oberman and asked him to drive a contract he had signed with Capital Centre owner Abe Pollin in Landover, Maryland. The contract spelled out an agreement stating that Boyle would handle all music acts booked into the Cap Centre. This was the moment when there would be no looking back for Cellar Door Productions. Today, Jack Boyle is retired in Florida, with a second home in Kennebunkport, Maine.

Tracy Nelson

On reflection, it feels like I played blues and country singer Tracy Nelson's signature song "Down So Low" about a million times at 'HFS.

Tracy played the Cellar Door at least ten times beginning in 1975. She remembers it well. "I loved playing there. It was one of the best gigs we did," Tracy told us for this chapter. "The first time I requested a fifth of Jack Daniel's in my upstairs dressing room and every time I came back, they remembered to have a bottle waiting for me."

Born in California and raised in Madison, Wisconsin, Tracy moved to San Francisco in the early sixties to begin her music career. Her resume includes playing Bill Graham's Fillmore Auditorium with her band, Mother Earth. She was on bills with the likes of Jefferson Airplane, the Grateful Dead, and Jimi Hendrix.

It was the Jefferson Airplane's success that convinced her that she could also be successful. Tracy worked at a record store in Berkeley that had an in-store promotion for the Airplane's first album, *Jefferson Airplane Takes Off*. Original singer Signe Anderson was a no-show. "We're both Scandinavian. I looked enough like Signe for the band to ask me to pretend I was her. So I signed her name on albums for a while but soon just signed random signatures," Tracy says.

As a local side note, both Airplane guitarist Jorma Kakounen and bassist Jack Casady are Washington, DC, natives, were friends as teenagers, and played in their first band, the Triumphs, in the DC area before heading to San Francisco. Weird and cool fact: the Triumphs' first paid gig was at the infamous Chestnut Lodge in Rockville, Maryland, a home for the mentally ill, on New Year's Eve in 1958.

Tracy wrote and recorded "Down So Low" in 1969, her most requested song. "First and foremost, that song is most important to me. People to this day tell me how powerfully and positively that song affected their lives. It's mind-blowing to me because I didn't really think it was that good when I wrote it. It was the first song I wrote."

Today, she calls that song one of her "Mailbox Money" tunes because she's been receiving great royalties from artists who have covered it over the years, including Maria Muldaur, Etta James, Diamonda Galas, Cyndi

Lauper, and Linda Ronstadt. When the royalties came in from Linda's cover on her *Hasten Down the Wind* album, Tracy bought a farm.

Her Cellar Door opening acts were often comedians. She recalls, "Rich Hall [an Alexandria, Virginia, native who later joined the 1984–1985 cast of *Saturday Night Live*] had a great joke about that far back table stuck behind a big square pillar at the Cellar Door. Rich called it the 'Dental Chart' section because he was sure if there was a fire in the place, the people sitting at that table would be identified only through their dental records."

For younger readers here who may not be familiar with her work, she points to both her early album, *Living with the Animals,* and also her current collaborative group live album, *The Blues Broads,* which features Tracy joining three other highly regarded vocalists, Dorothy Morrison, Annie Sampson, and Angela Strehli.

She also asked us to dispel a myth. It's been written that she was mentored in her early career by blues greats Muddy Waters and Howlin' Wolf. The truth is that she was the girlfriend of Charlie Musselwhite, one of the great blues harmonica players, after whom Dan Ackroyd modeled his "Jake Elwood" character in *The Blues Brothers.* Charlie played on her 1964 album, *Deep Are the Roots.*

"Charlie knew everybody, so one night in the Chicago club Peppers, Muddy Waters dedicated his song "She's 19 Years Old" to "Charlie's Woman," which was me. I was underage at the time. The only thing Howlin' Wolf ever said to me was, 'Can you bring me some beef jerky?'"

At the Door

In researching this book, we identified over 2,830 acts that played the Cellar Door between 1965 and when it closed in 1982. In addition to Donal Leace, Biff Rose, and Tracy Nelson, other headlining acts who returned for ten or more engagements include Ian and Sylvia, Tom Paxton, Tom Rush, Livingston Taylor, Jonathan Edwards, Tim Eyerman,

Brewer and Shipley, John Hartford, Odetta, Bill and Taffy Danoff, the Persuasions, Muddy Waters, Larry Coryell, Happy The Man, Mary Travers, the Dillards, Bill Holland, Aztec Two-Step, and comedians Patchett and Tarses (Jay Tarses went on to create *The Bob Newhart Show*).

And then there were famous acts that played only once. Pop singer Anne Murray's single 1973 week holds the record for sold-out shows and highest bar tab profits. Owner Jack Boyle earnestly tried to rebook Murray but she declined.

Other one-gig notables include Les Paul, Marvin Gaye, Rod McKuen, Chubby Checker, Melanie, Bill Haley and the Comets, Count Basie, Art Blakey, the Staple Singers, Lauro Nyro, Paul Butterfield, Henny Youngman, Theodore Bikel, Dizzy Gillespie, George Shearing, Johnny Rivers, Spencer Davis, Carly Simon, Michael Nesmith, Al Kooper, Lily Tomlin, Jim Croce, Minnie Riperton, Gabe Kaplan, Janis Ian, Gil Scott-Heron, Patti Smith, the Alpha Band with T-Bone Burnette, Willie Dixon, Jean-Luc Ponty (with Zappa's bass player, Tom Fowler), George Duke, Barbara Cook, Charles Mingus, Carl Perkins, Jan and Dean, Spirit (with Randy California), Jimmy Webb, Billy Crystal, Jesse Winchester, Joni Mitchell, and James Taylor.

Joni Mitchell's much-anticipated show at the Door was initially canceled because of a bout with hepatitis, but she came months later for five nights, making an astonishing Washington, DC, debut in November 1968. The *Washington Post* noted, "The Cellar Door is an ideal showcase for Miss Mitchell. Her voice carries well, even when she is talking half to herself between songs, and the lighting engineer has come up with a bonus for balcony viewers in a surrealistic blob of blue light that dances in her hair."

James Taylor was originally booked into the Cellar Door in early 1969, but his tour was canceled when he broke several bones in a motorcycle accident. His Cellar Door debut was later that year. Some disappointing cancellations—never to appear—include guitar legend Wes

Montgomery, who died shortly before his 1968 booking, Van Morrison, Helen Reddy, and The Band's Rick Danko. Rick hopped on Boz Scagg's national tour instead and skipped the Cellar Door.

When Long John Baldry canceled a gig, Jack Boyle booked the subversive Captain Beefheart as replacement. The good Captain arrived with band instruments on the afternoon of the gig, checked into his Georgetown hotel, and abruptly and mysteriously caught a plane back to Los Angeles. Boyle held the instruments captive until Beefheart returned Boyle's advance money. Claude Jones filled in that night.

Many other local bands got their chance to shine at the Cellar Door. The club launched a Sunday Hootenanny contest series hosted by WMUC DJ Rick Gordon. Winners won a week-long spot opening for a headliner. "Best of the Hoots" winners include Emmylou Harris, Mary Ann Chin, Meg Christian, Evernow, Breakfast Again, Patti Scholl, Lazy River, Bryan Bowers, comedian Ron Maranian, and many others. Bryan Bowers, the gifted Yorktown, Virginia, autoharpist, once leveraged an unexpected hum in the house PA system. He grabbed the key of the hum and led the audience in an impromptu gospel singalong.

Dave Nuttycombe, DC writer, filmmaker, musician, and one of the 1970s spoofy movie makers, the "Langley Punks," remembers Ron Maranian: "He called himself the Armenian Comedian. He had long hair and full beard on one side of his head, cleanshaven on the other, and did hippie versus straight material. In 1978, I was sitting in the Improv in Los Angeles, waiting for the show, 3,000 miles away from anyone I know. I hear, 'Dave? Dave Nuttycombe?' It was Ron. The MC that night was a guy named Jay Leno. No idea what happened to him."

Repeat Offenders

The next category of Cellar Door acts might be the fan favorites who played at least two engagements for audiences lucky enough to have been there. What follows is a selective listing.

Neil Young tops this category. His first 1969 show was in such demand that it became the first to require hard ticket sales at the club. Up to that point, phone reservations were fine. Neil returned a year later and recorded that show. Released in 2013, *Live at the Cellar Door* features songs from his six shows and contains the only known recording of his classic "Cinnamon Girl" performed on piano.

When Roger McGuinn's career stalled in the late 1970s—Columbia Records dropped him because he wasn't selling records—he refocused on performing, including several strong Cellar Door shows. I'm a major Byrds fan, saw his shows, and got to know him.

Back then I was drinking a lot of carrot juice and, over time, this gave my skin an orange hue. The last time I ran into Roger at a show at Wolf Trap, he grabbed and examined my hands. "I was just checking to see if you were still orange," he joked.

Former teen star Rick Nelson brought his Stone Canyon Band to the club for several shows between 1968 and 1970. I remember sitting upstairs watching his brother David filming Rick. Rick was the first "teen idol" lucky enough to use TV to routinely promote his career, week after week on his parents' 1950s TV show, *The Adventures of Ozzie and Harriet.*

A few years later, Michael Oberman was outside the office of the vice president of Epic Records in Los Angeles waiting to pitch a demo recording of the Rossyln Mountain Boys, who he was then managing. Rick Nelson walked out, recognized Michael, and said, "I hope your demo doesn't have any pedal steel guitar on it." Michael asked why, and Rick said, "Because Epic just dropped our band because we are too country." Michel laughed and replied, "Every cut on this demo has pedal steel." *Saturday Night Fever* had just hit, so everything became disco overnight.

Rick died in a plane crash in 1985 at the age of forty-five. He was inducted into the Rock and Roll Hall of Fame posthumously in 1987.

Other well-known Cellar Door acts include John Denver, Ramsey Lewis Trio, the Everly Brothers, Linda Ronstadt, Peaches and Herb, David Bromberg, Richard Pryor, Jimmy "J. J." Walker, Seals and Crofts, John Prine, Loudon Wainwright III, Nighthawks, Billy Joel, Tom Waits, Proctor and Bergman, Starland Vocal Band, Rosslyn Mountain Boys, John Lee Hooker, Sageworth and Drums (featuring singer-songwriter Walter Egan), B. B. King, Dick Gregory, Mort Sahl, Catfish Hodge, Root Boy Slim, Don McLean, Mose Allison, Townes Van Zandt, Robert Hunter, Holly Near, and Riders in the Sky.

Miles Davis played the Door three times. His *Cellar Door Sessions* was recorded over several nights in 1970 and released in 2005. It features the only recorded live tracks with guitarist John McLaughlin. Although Michael Oberman nominates Sly and the Family Stone as the "chief act that canceled" during Jack Boyle's tenure as owner, he adds that "Miles Davis was the act I hated seeing booked, because he would not only cancel but when he did show up he wouldn't talk to anyone, and he played with his back to the audience."

Another fantastic live Cellar Door recording is *Seldom Scene: Live at the Cellar Door,* released in 1975. The album cover is a beautiful portrait of the exterior of the club by night.

This progressive bluegrass band's name came about because they all had day jobs. The classic line up was John Starling, lead singer (his day job: US Army surgeon), banjo player Ben Eldridge (cartographer), Mike Auldridge on dobro (commercial artist, but considered then the best dobro player in the country), and John Duffey on mandolin and high lonesome tenor. Duffey was a founding member of the Country Gentlemen. He ran an instrument repair shop in his Arlington, Virginia, home.

Duffey, who passed away in 1996 at age sixty-two, befriended my coauthor, Steve. He once told Steve that he had quit the Country Gentlemen and its leader, Charlie Waller, because he got tired of "Charlie wanting to drive 150 miles each weekend to play anywhere, even on the roof of a drive-in movie concession stand."

Duffey told Steve, "Record store owners tell me we have strange fans. They'll buy the new Led Zeppelin album and ours at the same time." He asked Steve how many Seldom Scene records he had, and when Steve said, "None," Duffey walked him to where he kept different boxes of the band's albums and took one from each box and handed the stack to Steve. "Now you have them all," Duffey said.

John Starling once described the group: "Left to our own devices, the Seldom Scene would have cleared a room in ten minutes without John Duffey. He was the entertainer, the rest of us were players and singers. He did it all."

When *Live at the Cellar Door* was recorded, the Washington area was considered the "Bluegrass Capital of the World," with more bluegrass and "newgrass" music and musicians than anywhere else. Indeed, bluegrass was featured at scores of local clubs like the Red Fox Inn (the Scene's home base in Bethesda), Childe Harold, Annandale Grill, Chancery, Reading Gaol Pub, the Williams restaurant, Beltsville Tavern, the Italian Gardens, Village Green Tavern, the Corsican, and the Shamrock, with concerts and festivals happening routinely.

Bill Danoff

In 1965, Bill Danoff, a Georgetown University student working toward a career in politics, got a call from a friend asking Bill to rush down to the Cellar Door and fill in for the doorman who hadn't shown up. It was an urgent request because the headliner was tenor saxophonist Stan Getz, who also hadn't shown up yet. The crowd outside was getting restless. Bill recalls, "I turned into a comedian that night as I worked the crowd waiting for Stan, who finally slipped in to start his show."

Bill became the doorman at the Cellar Door for $15 a night. When then-seventeen-year-old Stevie Wonder played for a week, "I Was Made to Love Her" was his big hit. A DC government guy showed up to verify that Stevie was of age, and club co-owner Sam stalled the guy a few days until Stevie turned eighteen. Bill also recalls, "I had my ass handed to me when I inadvertently addressed him as 'Little' Stevie Wonder, as we all knew him. He was no longer being called that. I made the same error with 'Little Anthony' [and the Imperials], who was by then ten years older than me. To my credit, I only made each mistake once."

Danoff graduated to working the lights. "I broke in doing lighting for singer Nina Simone. Then-owner Charlie Fishman stood next to me to give me the lighting cues. Nina was terrific with a song, 'Mississippi Goddam,' that openly addressed racial inequality. Filmmaker Spike Lee's uncle Bill was her bass player. She was having her own personal battle with the white race, to be honest, and she was drinking a bottle of Old Grand-Dad bourbon during the first show. But I was just so impressed by the power of the stage that a commanding person could have. She was a powerhouse."

Georgetown was Bill's hometown in those days. He met his future wife, Mary Nivert, singing with the jukebox at the nearby Clyde's bar. Her nickname was Taffy, and when Jack Boyle returned as owner, he took a liking to them. Bill explains, "You know the business part of the music business is [often] a lot of crap going on. People taking advantage of each other. Some artists could be real assholes. Some acts work a week and then never get paid, that sort of thing. But Jack wasn't like that. He wanted things to be square. People should have a good time at the Cellar Door. Jack wanted the business side to be right."

Once in his office, Jack opened up a copy of *Billboard* magazine and asked Bill who he should book for the club. Contracts were negotiated three months in advance. Bill remembers, "Jack never seemed to know much about music himself, so he'd ask his musician friends. For example, he asked me what I knew about the Pointer Sisters. I'd never heard of them. The agents were pitching various acts all the time and Jack knew what their prices were. Jack said, 'I can get the Pointers Sisters for this amount. I see they have a great show with a new album coming out.' The other artist in this conversation was Carly Simon. So Jacked booked them both."

When the Pointer Sisters made their debut at the club in 1972, their *Yes We Can Can* album would make them international stars. Jack would later book them at the Kennedy Center (with comedian Martin Mull opening). When Carly made her club debut, also in 1972, her "You're So Vain" was a Number 1 hit song, her biggest ever. Like his poker playing, his winning bets on acts were remarkable.

The Next "Hey Jude"

Bill had met another student while at Georgetown named Jack Williams, also a guitarist. Jack was enthusiastic to play music with Bill. They slowly formed a band that included Taffy and Jack's friend, singer Margot Chapman, who had just moved from Haight-Ashbury in San Francisco. It has been reported that Bill abandoned Jack because he was "too loud on stage." Bill calls that "completely bogus." He sets the record straight here: "Jack had a childhood friend, Tim O'Brien, who was working with Columbia Records. We played him some of our songs and Tim was very critical: 'This sucks, this will never work, and so on.' And then Jack joined the National Guard, so Taffy and I became Fat City, playing the clubs like Emergency but especially Tammany Hall. Jack returned and we tried a trio but the three voices were never quite right. He'd often assign the parts, but when we'd sing, he would start doing my part."

Jack would form the band Breakfast Again and play the clubs. Taffy and Bill moved into a Q Street basement apartment in Georgetown. There, Bill wrote songs for Fat City's first album, *Reincarnation.* The album cover showed a photo of a kind-of Renaissance dinner scene with friends on the roof of their apartment building. Left to right, Bill identifies them: "Lucy Kirkland (her father was Lane Kirkland, head of the AFL-CIO); Raphael from Dupont Circle; best buddy, Bruce Adams, the Cellar Door bartender who first told me about Taffy at Clyde's; one of Taffy's friends, Susan Warren; Taffy's younger brother, Eddy; a great character, Norman Welles, who played drums with us; 'Big Jim,' who called himself the mayor of Dupont Circle; Taffy and me; Helen Dapney, a woman Taffy worked with; Phil Keats, who was my roommate at Georgetown; John Hall, from 'HFS, and Howard Freidman, a lawyer from downtown."

Meanwhile, Bill and Taffy/Fat City were often opening at the Cellar Door and making friends. One good pal was John Denver, who originally played in the Chad Mitchell Trio before going solo. Denver played the Door often and recorded a Danoff composition, "Guess He'd Rather Be In Colorado."

During Denver's return in December 1971, the Danoffs invited John back to their apartment to listen to some of Bill's new material. Thus begins the well-known story of how the three of them completed "Take Me Home, Country Roads." They played it as an encore at the Cellar Door a few nights later, singing the lyrics from notepaper. Their subsequent five-minute standing ovation is considered the longest applause in the history of the Cellar Door.

Taffy remembers that while they were recording the song in New York, Paul Stookey of Peter, Paul, and Mary—who had just broken up—dropped by the studio. "He listened to a playback and turned to Taffy and said, 'That's the next "Hey Jude".' Paul was recording his own solo album then and had he come back the next day, I would have put him on the record singing the chorus. The song has become an anthem, rerecorded by countless musicians, including Loretta Lynn, Lynn Anderson, Eddy Arnold, and Ray Charles."

Surfing the success of John Denver's hit, Bill put together his new group, the Starland Vocal Band. It would be Taffy, Margot Chapman, and a young musician named Jon Carroll, who had just graduated from Bishop Ireton High School in Alexandria, Virginia, and was off to the University of Miami, which had a strong music program.

"I called Jon and said I wanted him, but I didn't want to be responsible for him quitting college," says Bill. "So Jon agreed to transfer to Catholic University. He lasted a semester, so it was 'CU' later to college for Jon."

Bill continues: "Starland would play the Cellar Door New Year's Eve shows for many years. One I really recall is the day the Washington Redskins beat the shit out of the Dallas Cowboys to win the National Football Conference championship on December 31, 1972. I was a big Redskins fan and was friends with many of the players, including Jeff Bostic, John Wilbur, George Berman, and Terry Hermeling. Pedal steel guitarist Danny Pendleton—who became my best friend—and I were elated as we rushed to the club to play that night.

"My Redskin friends showed up for the second show, and upstairs Bryan Bowers, our opening act, was also very excited for the win and to meet the players. Bryan, who is a big, strong guy, said 'God damn, you guys played incredible' and slapped Hermeling on the back. Terry said, 'That's the hardest I've been hit all day.' We laughed."

When the Starland Vocal Band opened for Leo Kottke at DAR Constitution Hall on March 13, 1976, I had the pleasure of introducing them. "Afternoon Delight" had just been released. They would make four albums before their label, Windsongs, folded and the band broke up. Jon Carroll joined Mary Chapin Carpenter's band on keyboards and is still a good friend of mine today.

Bill has been generous to many musicians. Emmylou Harris was working the DC clubs when Bill helped her get a steady gig at Clyde's of Georgetown. He brought his own Shure Vocal Master PA system for her to use. Clyde's is where Chris Hillman of the Byrds and Flying Burrito Brothers discovered Emmylou and introduced her to fellow Byrds and

Burrito player Gram Parsons, who was looking for a female voice to harmonize with on his solo album, *GP*.

Coincidentally, Gram Parsons was a musical hero of Sageworth and Drums's Walter Egan. The Byrds's *Sweetheart of the Rodeo,* featuring Parsons, was a musical game changer for him. Today, he remembers that "Emmylou had never heard of Gram. So I invited her to the Sageworth group house in Georgetown and played her his music. In fact, the first time they really sang together was in my kitchen, and I was pretty much the only one there."

Georgetown's then student president Bill Clinton was also a frequent guest at the Sageworth house to hang out and listen to music, but I didn't ask Walter if Bill inhaled.

To make this story even cooler, Walter next wrote his first country song, "Hearts on Fire" (with Tom Guidera), and Gram liked it enough to record it on his next album, *Grevious Angel.*

Gram and Emmylou toured together to promote his album *GP* and formed a close friendship. Parsons, however, died of drugs and alcohol soon after, and Emmylou was devastated. Her unforgettable song, "Boulder to Birmingham" was co-written with Bill Danoff while she was grieving Parsons's death. Brimming with raw grief, the song's chorus finds the singer lamenting what she would do if she could only see [Gram's] face.

Bill also helped an unknown Mary Chapin Carpenter meet her guitarist/producer, the late John Jennings. Bill found her day-job work and a place for Chapin, as her friends know her, to write and rehearse songs. She and Jennings performed briefly with the Bill Danoff and Friends group in 1982. Jon Carroll led a host of musicians, including Mary Chapin Carpenter, playing a benefit for John Jennings at the Bethesda Blues and Jazz Supper Club in 2015. Area musicians and fans of Jennings were very saddened when he died later that year after a long battle with kidney cancer.

Looking back on his long career as a songwriter and performer with Fat City and Starland Vocal Band, Bill Danoff confesses, "I'm overwhelmed with the success we had and thankful for what we did. The fact that kids all over the world know "Take Me Home, Country Roads." I don't have any time to regret anything. So many artists struggle for so long before anything happens, before they finally get a break. For us, it was everything out of the box. John Denver has a smash hit with "Take Me Home, Country Roads." I put Starland together. We win two 1976 Grammy awards: Best New Artist of the Year, and Best Arrangement for Voices for "Afternoon Delight." So we sort of did the career thing in reverse."

Adele's Picks

"Many of the Cellar Door acts played the music we liked at 'HFS," says former DJ, Adele Abrams. "This was my go-to club for live music, along with the Childe Harold and Desperados. We were always hoping for the opening acts to get the brass ring from a national act that would notice them and then take them on tour."

Adele names Joan Armatrading, the British singer/songwriter known for an eclectic style that includes pop, blues, and even reggae, as her most memorable live show.

"Joan had a couple of albums out then which I was playing on my 'HFS show. I was surprised to see Joan being backed up by members of Fairport Convention [a pioneering band in the English folk rock movement]. And to see and hear her with artists like Fairport's David Mattacks was wonderful. I was friends with opening act Bill Holland and Rent's Due and met Joan that night. It was a snowy night and I almost didn't go because of the weather conditions."

Adele's other favorite show was by Warren Zevon, whose Jackson Browne–produced album *Excitable Boy* had just been released, a 1978 masterpiece chock-full of Zevon's most iconic songs. Adele recalls,

"Warren was blowing everybody away with his songwriting, and at the Door, he was everything everyone said he'd be, with a bag of chips thrown in. He was flying high that night. He tried to climb up on his grand piano and fell off, if I recall correctly."

Late Night's David Letterman was a fervent friend of Zevon's music. (Letterman also got his first national TV break when he did the Starland Vocal Band's short-lived summer variety series in 1977. One of the best scenes of that show was when Starland performed "First Rate Romance" at a Cellar Door private taping. "They wanted something live, and that song worked," says Bill Danoff.)

When Warren revealed he had inoperable lung cancer, Letterman featured him on his show as the evening's only guest. It was apparent in the interview that Dave was a huge fan, brimming with admiration for Warren's remarkable body of work and fondness for the man himself. Paul Schaffer, who is a revered musician and bandleader, also sang Zevon's praises that night. Warren himself gave an unforgettable interview, poking fun at his own terminal illness in a way that I'm not sure I could have pulled off. "I might have made a tactical error in not going to a physician for twenty years," he told Dave. It was an unforgettable interview with an incomparable artist.

9:30 Club

Although the Cellar Door is long gone, Washington audiences are more than fortunate to have Seth Hurwitz and his 9:30 Club to continue the tradition of "best place to see live music in DC." Originally at 930 F Street with a show start time of 9:30 p.m., the club's early advertising on WHFS was "9:30: A place and a time." It moved to current location 815 V Street N.W.—the old WUST Radio Music Hall—and celebrated its twenty-fifth anniversary on May 27, 2005.

The first concert Seth remembers was Peter, Paul, and Mary at the Carter Barron Ampitheatre with his parents. His first rock concert when he was thirteen featured Delaney & Bonnie, Roy Buchanan, Billy Preston, and Loggins and Messina at Gaithersburg, Maryland's Shady Grove Music Fair in 1972.

Seth began his rise to rock impresario by running kung fu movies at the old Ontario Theatre. Then, he and partner Rich Heinecke brought the Slickee Boys to the Ontario Theatre in 1980, a move that led to them creating the 9:30 Club.

The club has won consecutive awards as Nightclub of the Year by Pollstar, the concert industry trade magazine. A Who's Who of excellent performers have appeared there over the years, including Bob Dylan, the Beastie Boys, Adele, Alice in Chains, Red Hot Chili Peppers, R.E.M., Crowded House, Wilco, Nickel Creek, Punch Brothers, Steel Pulse, Marshall Crenshaw, the Ramones, Psychedelic Furs, the Police, Black Flag with then-local Henry Rollins, Courtney Love and Hole, and the Pixies. New location opening act was the Smashing Pumpkins, to name a few of many hundreds of others, spanning eras and genres.

Thank God for Seth.

In 2014, Seth told *Washingtonian Magazine*'s Benjamin Freed what a real rock concert is: "You used to show up and you didn't know what was going to happen—with the show, the music. It wasn't this planned set list. It wasn't Katy Perry. Katy Perry's a fantastic product, but it's a different show. Dave Grohl calling audibles—that's a rock concert. It's supposed to be this thing that takes a direction and has ups and downs, hopefully a crescendo. When I went to concerts as a kid, everyone was on the same roller coaster ride."

The historic 9:30 Club celebrated its thirty-fifth anniversary in 2016 by launching a music variety show on PBS. *Live at 9:30* is a "modern-day music variety show filmed at the club featuring live acts, comedy, interviews, and short films."

CHAPTER 17

Jackson Browne
and Kootch

first became aware of Jackson Browne through folksinger Tom Rush.
Rush had covered "These Days" in 1970. Budding blues singer Bonnie
Raitt recorded Browne's "Under the Falling Sky" in 1972 on her second
album, *Give It Up.*

Although other artists had recorded Browne's songs for several years,
his earliest notoriety as a performer came from his shows at Hollywood's
Troubadour Club in 1969. He made his local DC debut opening for Joni
Mitchell at Constitution Hall in late February 1972. He headlined at the
Cellar Door on September 5, 1972, promoting his first album, *Jackson
Browne,* on David Geffen's hot new Asylum label. We began playing
this album on 'HFS right after his show with Joni, but we mistakenly
called it *Saturate Before Using.* That's because those words are on the
cover. Barry Richards was the only other DJ then playing Jackson on
WHMC-AM 1150.

Our top five albums playing on 'HFS at that moment were: *Incredible!
Live!,* by Country Joe; *In the West,* Jimi Hendrix; *Jackson Browne; L.A.
Midnight,* B. B. King; and *Mother Earth,* Tracy Nelson.

Jackson Browne included three-soon-to-be classic songs, "Doctor
My Eyes," "Jamaica Say You Will," and "Rock Me on the Water." When
these singles began to chart, DC stations WEAM, WWDC, and WEEL

picked up on "Doctor My Eyes." *Rolling Stone* described Jackson as a "new face to look for . . . with mind-boggling melodies." The Nitty Gritty Dirt Band, whom Jackson had briefly played with before being replaced by John McEuen, also recorded some of his early songs, including "Shadow Dream Song."

Jackson made his first huge mark when the Eagles chose his song "Take It Easy" to be their first single, just a few months before his debut album was released. Co-written and sung by Eagle Glenn Frey, "Take It Easy" is one of the Rock and Roll Hall of Fame's "500 Songs that Shaped Rock and Roll."

The backstory is that Jackson and Glenn knew each other from playing in Los Angeles and lived in the same apartment building at that time. The Eagles could hear him composing songs like "Doctor My Eyes," for hours through the walls. Jackson shared the beginning of "Take It Easy" with Glenn, who continued hassling him to finish it. Jackson was working on his own album and wasn't planning to use "Take It Easy," so he told Glenn to finish it himself. Glenn added the second verse about standing on the corner in Winslow, Arizona, with a girl (my lord) in a flatbed Ford—and the rest is history.

When Jackson returned to DC as headliner in 1974, he brought Linda Ronstadt with him. Washington music critic Richard Harrington wrote, "What this city needs is a weekly dose of the kind of music that graced Georgetown University's Gaston Hall last night. The bill was shared by Jackson Browne and Linda Ronstadt and during both sold-out shows the air reverberated with crystal pure honest beautiful sounds. . . . It will be repeated for two more shows on Tuesday at Lisner Auditorium."

Clyde Jackson Browne was born in Heidelberg, Germany, in 1948 while his father, Clyde Jack, was stationed there as an army serviceman reporting for the *Stars and Stripes* newspaper. Jackson's grandfather, also a Clyde, was a very accomplished printer who built a very elegant and unusual stone house, the Abbey San Encino in Los Angeles's Highland

Park district. The Abbey resembles an old-style California mission. Jackson lived in this house from age three, and it is still in the Browne family. The house courtyard was pictured in the cover art for his second album, *For Everyman.*

I've interviewed and hung with Jackson since my days at 'HFS. I recently talked with him when he played the Warner Theatre about his long and celebrated career. I asked him about one of my favorite songs, "Running on Empty," recorded at Merriweather Post Pavilion in Columbia, Maryland, in 1977 and appearing on his album of the same name. I was there that night and did some announcing from the stage, mainly about 'HFS upcoming news. Jackson chose not to use any of my pearls of wisdom for his album. Many of us are proud of the success of the album, *Running on Empty,* and its local recording at the Post Pavilion. Maybe Washington will start to be famous for more than politics, is what I was hoping when that one came out.

There's a lyric, "In sixty-five, I was seventeen running up 101 . . ." and I wondered if Jackson ever thought then that he'd still be performing in his sixties. He answered, "I thought I might last until I was thirty. Whether I have a batch of songs or an album I'm thinking about making, it's really a product of desire. It's something that I need to still want to do."

Before this recent interview, I went back and listened to Jackson's earlier albums. *For Everyman* is just a stunning record. The power of his songwriting. His wisdom for such a young man. His ability to capture the longing and wistfulness of his generation and times. His honest introspection. *Rolling Stone* cites it is as one of 500 most important albums ever made. Jackson has also expertly combined music with political activism during his career. Jackson has been involved in such causes as No Nukes, Amnesty International, Farm Aid, and US involvement in Central America, to name a few, along with a lifelong commitment to environmental causes.

"I think for a while my audience wasn't sure if I was going to abandon writing the type of music that I did on my earlier records," Jackson explains. "It's not so much about if you talk about politics. But rather it's more how you do it. And whether or not you're able to engage people about what they really care about."

I mentioned his 1986 album *Lives in the Balance,* and how I thought it was as vibrant and relevant thirty years later.

Jackson and some of his musical cohorts like Bruce Springsteen and John Mellencamp have been such steadfast advocates for environmental and social justice, using their music and public visibility as a way of promoting awareness of issues close to their hearts.

Jackson thanked me for these thoughts and added, "It's part of the music that we grew up with, too. Bruce and John are good examples but they both have come to re-embrace traditional music as well. They may have grown up wanting to play rock and roll, but that music came from rhythm and blues, country, rockabilly, and Appalachian music. People wrote all that music about their lives. And the work that those musicians did and the troubles they had."

Jackson was inducted into the Rock Hall of Fame in 2004.

Danny Kortchmar

I've been following the career of guitarist, producer, and songwriter Danny "Kootch" Kortchmar since 1970 when I first noticed his guitar credit on James Taylor's breakthrough album *Sweet Baby James.* He's credited as Danny Kootch on that one. His name has seen lots of variations on record credits over the years, because his performer friends always call him Kootch.

A year later, he added acoustic and electric guitar, vocals, and conga on Carol King's *Tapestry,* one of the most successful recordings of all time. He's worked with David Crosby, Graham Nash, Carly Simon, and Jackson Browne, and was Eagle Don Henley's songwriting and

The Section: (L-R) Lee Sklar, Danny Kortchmar, and Russ Kunkel rehearse for the Carole King–James Taylor Troubador Reunion Tour.
Credit: © Elissa Kline

producing partner in the 1980s. You often saw Danny with fellow musicians Lee Sklar on bass and Russ Kunkel on drums backing these artists. They call themselves "The Section."

I first met him when he backed Jackson Browne during the recording of *Running on Empty*. We talked about that show and other things recently.

Danny's memories: "That was a tour with Jackson and our first show was at Red Rocks in Colorado. Merriweather was our second show, I believe. I had already played Merriweather that summer with James Taylor as had most of Jackson's backing band, and in the seventies with Crosby and Nash, and Linda Ronstadt. I knew that stage very well. And we really hit it on the *Running on Empty* show. Most of the live recordings on that album are from the one show. But the credit goes to Jackson for having the vision and the guts to make a live album of new material on the road. The audience responded brilliantly like they had heard the music before but they hadn't. No one had done that. *Frampton Comes Alive* was a live recording but it wasn't Peter Frampton's *new* material."

Speaking of Peter Frampton, I only have one personal story about Peter. It has nothing to do with Danny. I was vacationing once at La Samanna on the French side of St. Martin in the Caribbean. Someone had told me that Frampton was staying there too. I wasn't a huge fan then, although I have grown to appreciate his music more over the years. One morning while sitting on the beach, I saw Peter Frampton walking toward me from the distance. I stood up and yelled, "Hey Peter," with a friendly wave. He yelled back, "Fuck off," and kept walking. I guess I should have told him that I was a radio DJ, but the moment had passed.

Like many of us, Danny was inspired by The Beatles. He remembers, "As soon as I graduated high school, my father made me get a job as a mail boy, but I quit after a few weeks and started a rock band and never looked back. One of my influences was the late B. B. King. He was one of the first guys to play what we now call 'lead guitar.' So everyone who played the blues or lead guitar was in some way influenced by B. B. King. The other guy I absolutely adored was Steve Cropper from Booker T and the MG's. I was a huge fan of the Stax-Volt record label, which had Otis Redding, Sam and Dave, Wilson Pickett, Eddie Floyd, and all those great R&B performers. Steve Cropper was in Booker T.'s Stax house band, so Steve recorded on many of those sessions in the Memphis recording studio. I wanted to be exactly like Steve, and go to the studio every day and work on recording with great R&B artists."

Danny's first band was the King-Bees, who played their rhythm and blues in enough New York City clubs to get some attention.

"Peter (Asher) and Gordon (Waller) came to see us and asked us to back them up on a short tour on the East Coast. I became good friends with Peter," says Danny.

Danny and King-Bee drummer Joel O'Brien next hooked up with a then-unknown James Taylor to form the Flying Machine. Kootch had met James during a summer vacation at Martha's Vineyard in 1963 when they were both teenagers. They had played folk songs together around the Vineyard as "Jamie and Kootch." It was Danny who talked James into coming down to Greenwich Village to start the Flying Machine following James's first hospitalization for depression.

Danny remembers, "Greenwich Village was great. It was an exciting time. All the musicians knew each other and we'd see each other on the street. The folk boom had hit. John Sebastian and others were folkies. Now they were rebooting as electric bands, adding electric basses and drums. Sebastian's 'Summer in the City' by his band the Lovin' Spoonful really captures that time."

Soon the Flying Machine was a regular band at the popular Night Owl Café, playing with groups like the Turtles and Lothar and the Hand People.

Unfortunately, James Taylor became a full-blown heroin addict during this time, and went off for six months to clean up. That put an end to the Flying Machine. "Sweet dreams and flying machines, and broken pieces on the ground" is how Taylor noted this period in his first hit song, "Fire and Rain."

James Taylor Goes to Apple

Six months later James came back to New York City healthy. Danny introduced James Taylor to Peter Asher. "James went to England and visited Peter at his house and the rest is history," says Danny.

This set in motion The Beatles signing Taylor as a solo artist to Apple Records, the first non-Beatle artist to record for their label. Peter was the brother of Jane Asher, McCartney's girlfriend. Paul had given his song "A World Without Love" to Peter and Gordon to record after John Lennon heard the first line, "Please lock me away." John yelled to Paul, "Yes, please lock me away from this song."

Asher became Taylor's producer and manager. "Even though Peter was working for Paul McCartney," James Taylor said, "he was still in total control of his own destiny. I knew from the first time that we met that he was the right person to steer my career. Peter has this determination in his eye that I had never seen in anyone before."

Apple released *James Taylor,* which was not a big commercial success, but songs like "Carolina in My Mind" (with McCartney on bass) and "Something in the Way She Moves" were standouts. His next album on the Warner label, *Sweet Baby James,* was incredible. Danny's guitar on this album and many subsequent Taylor recordings, as well as on numerous tours, demonstrates their friendship and the important role he played in helping to launch Taylor's career.

The Fugs

Danny was also briefly in The Fugs, a political, satirical, early outrageous, and arguably the first honest-to-goodness underground rock band, with songs like "Fingers of the Sun," "Wet Dream," and "Turn On, Tune In, Drop Out" written with LSD guru, Timothy Leary.

"The Fugs were basically East Village poets and writers," says Danny. "But they wanted to do something in the area of music. Something that was "rock band–like." So they started playing at a theater on McDougal Street and hiring mostly out of work musicians in the area. I played on one of their albums, *Tenderness Junction.* We actually went into a real studio and made that album. Being in a real studio was unusual for me in the summer of 1967. We all had our pictures taken by the photographer Richard Avedon. It was exciting."

Songwriter

Danny describes another career milestone: "Don Henley invited me to work on his solo albums beginning with *I Can't Stand Still.* One of the first songs we discussed writing together was "Dirty Laundry," which was Don's prescient commentary on rumors and sensationalist news. We screwed around with that for months. One night at home, I came up with the music for it, which is that repetitive groove as the song starts. I realized the static nature of the groove would be the perfect vehicle for Don to speak his piece about the media. And we wanted the song to be a 'butt wiggler' as well as providing a message. You could dance to it or you could listen to it and get something out of the lyrics.

"Working with Don Henley in the 1980s was a transcendent experience for me. Going into the studio with someone as brilliant as Don and trying to achieve whatever we could think up was great. I had never worked on albums before where you could take your time and try whatever we could think of. I really enjoyed myself then."

I commented on how Danny had seen periods of creativity in the music scene much like I saw the radio scene morph and change over the years.

"Things change and have to change," Danny agrees. "But we have satellite radio now and people are doing creative things there. Little Steven's *Underground Garage* is a terrific station. So when one door closes another opens, we hope."

Danny has also played, produced, toured, or written songs for Warren Zevon, Bob Dylan, Cheech and Chong, Neil Young, Jon Bon Jovi, Stevie Nicks, Billy Joel, Hanson, Tracy Chapman, and others. Danny was also in the *This Is Spinal Tap* movie, playing bass on their "Gimme Some Money" video.

"I've been fortunate to play with absolutely great musicians and writers. I guess I was at the right time and the right place with the right stuff. Part of it is luck, but it was my dream to be committed to being the best that I could be," Danny says.

I asked Danny about his guitars: "I tend to play Fender Telecasters mostly. I still have my Telecaster that I bought in 1968 that I used to play on all those records. I still use it on gigs. My 1968 Tele was highly modified by Jeff 'Skunk' Baxter. Jeff was a guitar tech at that time in Los Angeles. He brought some brilliant electronics into my guitar and changed the pickup system. No Telecaster sounds like mine. It's unique."

Skunk is a native Washingtonian who played the guitar leads on classic songs by Steely Dan and the Doobie Brothers, to name a few. I see him in DC about once a year at benefits or special events at the Hard Rock Café. We have a Boston connection in that he was in the band Ultimate Spinach back in the day.

Skunk has also been a consultant for the US Defense Department. His knowledge of music compression and file storage were skills that made the Feds interested in asking him to help them in the fight against terrorism.

"Jeff 'Skunk' Baxter is brilliant," Danny says. "A great guitarist, musician, and diverse fellow."

Looking back on his outstanding resume, I asked Danny what has been the best part of his career. He says, "Working with Don Henley and doing so many different things on his records kind of got me kicked upstairs to be thought of as a record producer. However, I've always been a songwriter. My two favorite things are playing my guitar and writing songs. I wanted to play music with my heroes and I've been very fortunate to accomplish this."

CHAPTER 18

Life After WHFS

My WAVA experience was very positive. WAVA was locally owned, unlike the conglomerates we have now. Our slogan was "Rock the Nation." It was also interesting to me because, my God, they had modern equipment. The stuff at 'HFS had been welded together by Marconi when he invented the first radio. Seriously, some of it was that ancient.

The 'HFS studios were like a bunker. Unlike Steely Dan's "FM" song—with no static at all—the 'HFS signal was weak with tons of static. WAVA had a strong signal. And there were windows, with sunlight, where you could see trees.

Howeird Stern

Music was the driving force of radio when I joined WAVA. And whether it was the rich jazz that Felix Grant was playing from his personal record collection on WMAL-AM or the urban contemporary tunes that Donnie Simpson was airing on WKYS, the essential ingredient for thriving radio ratings was the music.

This dynamic of music-centric radio dramatically and unexpectedly changed in the nation's capital on the morning of March 2, 1981. Howard Stern, an iconoclast-on-steroids twenty-seven-year-old jock, made his DC debut on station DC 101. One of his first outrageous moves was to call several area police stations to ask for a parade and motorcade to welcome him to the city.

The next day, he phoned Bethesda–Chevy Chase High School to suggest they let students off to honor his new morning program. He did a song parody about President Reagan "playing with Nancy's gun" and invited female listeners to call in about what they liked and didn't like about boys. "Did you score?" he asked them.

This was different.

He told writer Dennis John Lewis of the *Washington Star* that he was strongly critical of rigid formatted radio. Stern said, "They think a non-talking non-thinking disc jockey is all listeners will stand for but I think that's nothing but robot radio. It doesn't relate and it's dishonest."

About fifteen months later, Howard was wildly popular and had tripled the ratings of DC 101. However, Howard was terminated shortly afterward by station president, Goff Lebhar, after signing a five-year million-dollar deal with New York City station WNBC. Howard's nickname for Goff was "Goof."

After his firing, we invited Howard over to WAVA to broadcast his farewell show to Washington listeners. I was there. My first impression on meeting him was that he was very tall: six feet four. I knew from listening to his morning show that he was very creative and funny.

During that farewell show I got a chance to see that he was also extremely introverted off the air. That never occurred to me from all the bits I had heard him do on DC 101, like the "Beaver Breaks" parodies of the 1950s *Leave It to Beaver* TV show. It became the Cleavage family with Howard as "Wally."

I thought, "How can this be? How could he be so over the top on the air but yet so reticent in one-on-one conversations?" He's usually in shades, so there's not a lot of eye-to-eye contact going on.

Our WAVA morning man, Steve Matt, and newsman Michael Del Colliano gave Howard full rein to give a final area radio performance. It was March 19, 1982, about three weeks after Howard was fired from DC 101.

Howard introduced his program producer, "Earth Dog" Fred Norris, as "the man who has been silent for the past six months" (DC 101 didn't like Fred talking on-air) and his "Think Tank" pals, "Crazy" Steve Chaconis and Harry Cole. His newswoman Robin Quivers wasn't there.

Robin, a Pikesville, Maryland, native with a nursing degree from the University of Maryland, was a consumer reporter on Baltimore radio station WFBR when she first heard a tape of Howard. Her first reaction was, "How do I meet this guy?"

In retrospect, Howard's farewell show was wacky yet bittersweet. "First off, Fred and I are going to apply for welfare because we are out of a job," Howard proclaimed, adding, "We're going to try to get some of those cheese grants." The latter was a reference to a government cheese program for welfare and food stamp recipients going on at the time.

Their first *imaginary* bit of the morning was TV's talking horse, Mr. Ed (Howard) making a phony phone call to someone impersonating the well-known spokeswoman for a clothing store where an "educated customer is our best consumer."

Mr. Ed wondered if she had a series of famous designers like Oleg Cassini and Yves Saint Laurent at the store. When the woman answered yes to each name, Mr. Ed asked, "Don't you get tired of having so many guys?" (Bada boom).

Howard took a listener's phone call requesting a bit about a drunk lady from his DC 101 show. Howard explained he wasn't allowed to play anything that aired on DC 101. "My attorney is listening and we're going to call him later to see how I'm doing. I don't want to get in trouble," said Howard.

He took the opportunity to heavily promote his satirical record, *Fifty Ways to Rank Your Mother*, playing "John's Revenge," a send-up of

John and Yoko's relationship, and "Havana Hillbillies," which goofed on immigration. Other tracks, like "I Shot Ron Reagan," he skipped. The record was recorded at DC's Studio 10 and mixed at the Ranch in New York City. Howard did many record signings at Penguin Feather and Kemp Mill record stores before he left town.

Howard declared, "I'm pushing the album because I want it to sell so I can make some money. You listeners owe it to me because I gave you such good radio. Fred has to pay his lawyer. Is this payola, playola, or plugola? Wait a minute. I'm a guest here so I can push this album. No problem."

After adding the music (Neil Young, Genesis, The Beatles, Blue Oyster Cult, and others) and commercials, Howard didn't have as much airtime at WAVA as he would have liked, but he wrapped up his farewell show with a heartfelt goodbye:

"Let me end this show right. I don't want to drag this out, but I love you people for what you've done for me. I've made fun of people but it's all in good fun. Washington will be my home now. I was born in New York but Washington is my home. And I love you guys."

I also helped host Howard's farewell party at the Numbers nightclub in the city. The "Theme from Rocky" heralded Howard's entrance to the party followed by his ass cheeks mooning the audience. "Do you remember where you were and what you were doing when you first heard Howard Stern?" I asked the clamorous Numbers crowd.

Despite the fun, Howard was without a doubt touched by his fans' loyalty and their regret that he was leaving the city.

He good-naturedly introduced his DC 101 replacement, Asher Benrubi, or "Adam Smasher," as we came to know him. The crowd loudly booed the Smash. "Tough act to follow" is how Adam dealt with the crowd dis.

"Hey, he's ad-libbing," said Howard. "You can get fired for that. I know."

Private Parts

Howard's production team contacted me when movie filming began for his *Private Parts* autobiography. They wanted to recreate the look of the DC 101 radio station, and I was happy to provide posters, buttons, and other artifacts from my collection to help them out. I even sent one of those plastic red hats that the band, Devo, wore. Everything was returned, insured, with a lovely thank-you note.

For many years, Howard would celebrate his birthday by broadcasting from the storied Tavern on the Green restaurant in Manhattan. I was invited and remember meeting and fist bumping Donald Trump, who evidently didn't shake hands back then.

As my relationship with Howard continued over the years, I came to appreciate what a warm-hearted guy Howard is. He always refers to me as "that hippie in DC," which is fine with me. He is grounded by all the years he has practiced Transcendental Meditation, and his family and success have given me a great respect for him.

(L-R) With Howard at his book signing for *Private Parts*, 1994.
Credit: © Bob Avicolli/Cerphe Archive

Howard is an American self-made success story. Today, Howard's net worth is estimated at $600 million. That's about $80 million more than Elton John, Tom Cruise, or David Lettermen have.

Unlike Howard Stern, I've never been a controversial broadcaster. But I did have somebody threaten my life once. In fact, he wrote me a letter: "It may not be this week. It may not be next week, but I'll be the guy in the bushes, and you won't see it coming." And he added his name, address, and phone number.

Yes, I was scared shitless.

I reported this to the Arlington, Virginia, county police and subsequently found out he was an older guy, living with his mother, and a clinical schizophrenic.

The Grease

After Howard left DC 101, the powerhouse station hired the brilliantly creative Doug Tracht, known as "The Greaseman," to take over the morning drive slot. I was hired away from WAVA to do afternoons, then evenings, at DC 101, and Adam Smasher was new there, too.

I'd never heard of Grease before he came to DC 101 in 1982, but I learned he had been on local station WRC a few years before. Born in the Bronx, Doug got his nickname while he was a student doing radio at Ithaca College. He began as Dougie T, but one day while riffing on "cookin with the Four Tops" he said he was "cookin' with heavy grease." The name stuck, and a new, bombastic personality emerged. His comedy bits became increasingly weird yet consistently funny. His stories about his alter ego, Nino Greasemanelli, were wild. He added slang words; for example "hydraulics" would substitute for the word "penis." Armed with a new raunchy vocabulary, the Grease could evade the censors. He began to work out in the gym and bulk up because he felt his listeners would want him to look more like a muscle guy. I marveled at his ability to think on his feet and use sound effects to conjure up "theater of the mind" bits

(L-R): Doug "Greaseman" Tracht, Asher "Adam Smasher" Benrubi, Bill Scanlan, Dave "Young Dave" Brown, and me at DC 101 in 1988.
Credit: © Cerphe Archive

every morning on the fly. Grease could weave a story, make you laugh, and bam, you're back in the music. This was a true gift, I thought. I had never heard anyone like him.

And for me, it was wonderful to be part of this DC 101 team. The people were cool, and the station was at 1150 Connecticut Ave and M Street, NW, downtown in the heart of the city and in the thick of things. As the population grew, Washington became more of an important radio market. Howard Stern had left us in very good shape ratings-wise, and the Grease picked up the baton and ran with it.

He became very successful. The *Washington Post* reported Doug was the highest paid radio DJ in Washington at $400,000 a year. He and his wife Anita bought a stately house in Potomac and frequently invited his friends, including Susan and me, out on his boat, the Good Ship

Grease. He'd wear his little white Captain's hat and troll about the waters of DC. He would go out of his way to make sure everyone was well fed, their glasses filled, and were enjoying themselves. He was good-natured, jovial, and a fine host.

The one thing I would notice that annoyed me on those outings (although Grease would tolerate it) was when guests would want him to do comedy bits. They wanted entertainment.

However, real trouble for Grease began in 1986 when, during a bit that included a reference to the new Martin Luther King holiday, Doug said, "Kill four more and we can take a week off," as reported in the *Baltimore Sun*.

The negative reaction was swift. Many advertisers canceled. Hundreds of thousands of dollars in ad money went away. What DC 101 management had to do was obviously redeem that business and establish that Grease had made a mistake. He said the wrong thing. And this mistake cost him. He was suspended for five days and made numerous apologies. He donated money to Howard University for a scholarship.

Infinity Broadcasting Corporation would syndicate his show nationally, but it wasn't as successful as they had hoped. In 1999, at station WARW in DC, he made a second racist joke related to the murder of a black man, James Byrd, who was killed by three white men who chained him to a pickup truck and took off. The Grease played a sound bite of singer Lauren Hill, commenting, "No wonder they drag them from trucks."

Some were willing to forgive one disgraceful slur, but the second racist incident sealed his fate. He was immediately and appropriately fired and his career abruptly ended. He has spent the last seventeen years seeking forgiveness. His is a terrible example of the perils of being a shock jock, paid to say outrageous things while ad-libbing live and crossing the line, twice.

WJFK

I left DC 101 when Ken Stevens, general manager of Infinity Broadcasting's WJFK hired me. Infinity was a young, aggressive radio company that owned many successful stations like WCBN in Boston, WXRK/K-ROCK in New York, and KROQ in Los Angeles. We tried a few different radio formats at WJFK, including a hybrid of classic rock and an adult contemporary "smooth jazz" format minus the urban slant. We ended up with a hipper, deeper rock tracks approach, although we were never hipper than WHFS.

While at WJFK, I attended several Radio and Records (R&R) conventions, which are always much more play than work. One in Dallas in 1987 was particularly fascinating and entertaining, when Geffen Records hosted a party and rounded up a bunch of us staying at the uber-posh, iconic Mansion on Turtle Creek. Stretch limos were packed with the almost-rich and nearly famous music industry heavies and radio folks and then headed into the late Texas night. Much later, we ended up at a bowling alley, and I got to knock over candlepins with Cher and Robbie Robertson. I know. It is Fellini-esque.

Ken and I found out that Don Geronimo and Mike O'Meara might be available. Their show *The Morning Zoo with Don and Mike* had debuted on WAVA in 1985. I knew Don (real name is Michael Sorce) from his WPGC days, and had been at WAVA just before they flipped to a Top 40 format when they were hired. I was familiar with their work. Ken and I met with Don and Mike at a very nice Fairfax, Virginia, restaurant for lunch, and they agreed to join us at WJFK.

I was impressed with Geronimo's creativity and on-air timing. A Rockville, Maryland, native, Don with partner Mike (also a very talented guy) created some truly memorable radio. They once took a group of listeners to an Intercourse, Pennsylvania, motel where they commented on the sexual activities (presumably) taking place. They ran a "What Your Wife Doesn't Know" quiz in which the listener would confess some crazy personal secret, and then they'd call the wife on-air to share his secret with her. Another bit was "Honk for Cash" in which a listener driving in a left-hand turn lane refuses to move when the light changes. Then we'd hear how many of the drivers behind the listener would honk in protest. Don would come up with crazy stuff that really caught on. Don and Mike's delivery made them funny and unforgettable.

In his book *Something in the Air: Radio, Rock, and the Revolution that Shaped a Generation,* author Marc Fisher, a *Washington Post* columnist, reported that "FM's niched version of Top 40 contemporary hit radio featured jingles, fast-talking deejays, and pop music, but this was a wholly new animal. It was not designed to attract a huge and varied audience by playing the top-selling records. Rather, like the other new formats, it was crafted through research, with songs selected for their appeal to eighteen to thirty-four-year-olds . . . Geronimo moved from station to station as managers pushed to minimize the role of deejays in the 1970s. Geronimo insisted on taking listener calls and developing the games and bits that would one day turn him into one of radio's most inventive talk hosts."

G. Gordon Liddy: G-Man

The political scandal called Watergate began when George Gordon Battle Liddy, then the general counsel of President Nixon's Committee to Re-elect the President (CRP), presented an "intelligence plan" to Nixon's attorney general, John Mitchell. This plan was to dig up some dirt to use against Nixon's opponent, Senator George McGovern, in the upcoming 1972 presidential election. So the Democratic National Committee (DNC) headquarters at the Watergate office complex in DC was burglarized twice, but no dirt was found.

The burglars, however, were caught in the act with their third break-in by a lone security guard, Frank Wills. Frank noticed tape had been applied on the Watergate door locks to keep them open. He ripped off the tape. Later that night, he saw that someone had reapplied the tape. That's some stupid burglars. Only then did Frank call the DC police.

When the secret of Liddy's intelligence plan started unraveling, Nixon staged a cover-up. Thanks to investigative work by *Washington Post* reporters Bob Woodward and Carl Bernstein, along with their editor, Ben Bradlee, the story broke wide open, and after televised hearings and mounting national disgrace, Nixon resigned. Forty-eight Nixon administration officials went to jail for various crimes like perjury and obstruction of justice. Gordon Liddy was sentenced to twenty years in prison for burglary.

Liddy was released from prison after four and a half years. Far from his career being over, he bounced back immediately. He wrote a huge bestselling autobiography, *Will*, and hit the lecture circuit. He also did TV shows like *Miami Vice* and appeared in a number of movies. When he tried his hand as a radio broadcaster, I became his first program director at WJFK and, along with John Popp and Cameron Gray, launched his syndicated show on Westwood One. In 2010, Gordon retired from radio and today is living a quiet life.

We already knew a lot about the G-Man when he arrived at WJFK in 1990, but as we worked together, we discovered more about his background.

For example, at twenty-nine years old, he became the youngest bureau supervisor for the FBI. I once asked him what working for the infamous director J. Edgar Hoover was like.

Gordon said, "It was an extraordinary experience. J. Edgar Hoover was the kind of person that let you know exactly what he thought. He had a feud going with [Attorney General] Bobby Kennedy that went back and forth. Bobby Kennedy had a dog named Rufus and he let the dog walk up and down the halls of Hoover's section letting the dog do his business."

With the G-Man at WJFK in 1994.
Credit: © Cerphe Archive

I asked him if he saw the movie *J. Edgar*. He said, "I didn't because I heard they had some assertions that he dressed in women's clothes. That is absolute nonsense."

Liddy left the FBI to practice law in New York City, and then went on to become prosecutor for Duchess County, where he arrested LSD guru Timothy Leary. I asked him about that: "Leary and I toured college towns debating issues. He was basically a romantic comedian. I arrested him twice," Liddy says. "The interesting thing is that he was a highly intelligent man, unlike that other guy I used to hate. The gonzo guy, Hunter Thompson. Hunter was a bright guy, too. When he was sober, he was sharp as a tack. But he was an alcoholic and cocaine addict. We appeared together on the college lecture circuit but he would end up sitting on the stage with a bottle of whiskey. Eventually, I ended up debating myself."

Gordon regarded Richard Nixon as his "forever commander in chief." The day Nixon died in 1994, I saw Gordon weeping. When the G-Man was sent to prison, I thought that had to be hard on him, as he had a wife, Frances, and five young children.

"It was harder on my wife than it was on me. Years later, after I had long-since got out of prison, Frances would refer to this period as when she was left doing all the work while I was off having fun in prison."

So secrets, leaks, and revelations after-the-fact are all part of life here in Washington. I asked him if he thought we would ever learn more about Watergate.

"I don't know because just about everybody but me is dead," he said.

Govinda Gallery

The first art gallery that focused on music-oriented art was the Govinda Gallery at 34th and Prospect Street in Georgetown. New Yorker Chris Murray became friends with fellow students Bob Colacello and Christopher Makos at Georgetown University. When they graduated, they became friends with artist Andy Warhol. Chris launched Govinda in 1975, showcasing Andy Warhol's work, but when *Rolling Stone* photographer Annie Liebovitz held her first Washington art show at Govinda, Chris began to see his future. He has called it his epiphany.

Chris told Annie that he wanted to buy the first print of her portrait of the naked John Lennon curled up with Yoko that graced the cover of *Rolling Stone* in January 1981, shortly after Lennon was murdered in December 1980. Annie told Chris the picture was taken on the day that Lennon was killed.

Chris didn't know that at the time, but he knew it was a significant photo. Fusing his love of music with his recognition of an emerging and exciting art genre, he decided to dedicate his career to the promotion and care of important rock and roll photographs and art. He was one of the first gallery owners to do so.

Ronnie Wood of the Rolling Stones released a book of his artwork, had a book signing at Govinda in 2009, and displayed some of his work. It turns out that Ronnie is a pretty good graphic artist. One of Murray's favorite shows wasn't music-related. It was in celebration of Govinda's twentieth anniversary, when photographer Howard Bingham shared his *Thirty Years with Ali*. Muhammad Ali attended the show and enthusiastically signed autographs and talked with the attendees.

Govinda was the place to be when these shows opened. The party would spill over to the nearby Halcyon House, owned by one of Murray's friends, sculptor John Dreyfuss. The first secretary of the navy, Benjamin Stoddert, built this majestic house in 1797. Washington, DC, city designer Pierre L'Enfant created the gardens. It is one of the most impressive houses I've ever been in. The singer Donovan would stay there when he was in town. Susan and I also had the pleasure of staying there the night of President Obama's inauguration in 2009. I was emceeing the Blue Diamond Inaugural Ball with Jackson Browne and Graham Nash at the Smithsonian Museum of Natural History, and John, knowing the streets and bridges would be blocked, invited us to stay at his home. Our room was across the street from the Francis Scott Key house on M Street in Georgetown. It wasn't lost on us that we were overlooking the house of the man who wrote our national anthem while America was ushering in its first African-American president.

Chris organized over two hundred exhibitions at Govinda. The brick-and-mortar gallery closed its doors in 2011, but Chris is as busy as ever arranging major art shows in America, Europe, and Cuba. As we write this, he has a Bob Dylan photo show opening in Manchester England, and a Tom Waits show in Los Angeles. His website is www. govindagallery.com.

CHAPTER 19

Hall of Famers

first saw the Rolling Stones on TV in 1964. I loved them. Like The Beatles, they had the intangible mojo. They had the 'it" factor. I didn't know exactly what that was, but I knew I wanted some of it. I saw them live at the Boston Garden in 1969. This was their first American tour since 1966, and the first with Mick Taylor, who replaced Brian Jones after Jones's swimming pool accident (categorized by the British police as "death by misadven-

ture") three months earlier. Their 1970 live album, *Get Yer Ya-Ya's Out!*, was recorded during their Madison Square Garden shows on this tour. They opened with "Jumpin' Jack Flash" and closed with "Street Fighting Man."

Their opening act was the Barbarians, a Cape Cod, Massachusetts, band that had the hit "Are You a Boy or Are You a Girl?" The drummer, Victor

With Keith Richards at DAR Constitution Hall in 1988.
Credit: © Cerphe Archives

Moulton, nicknamed "Moulty," lost his hand as the result of a pipe bomb explosion when he was a teen.

We ran a contest for listeners to win tickets to the Stones 2002 "Licks" tour show at FedEx Field when I was at CBS radio, 94.7 The Globe. For listeners to win tickets to a concert is one thing. A ticket to get backstage is another thing. But a ticket to see and meet the Rolling Stones is the mother lode. This contest was a big deal.

It was also my chance to see Keith Richards again. We first met at DAR Constitution Hall in 1988 when he toured with his side group, the X-Pensive Winos. That was a tight show. Keith had guitarist Waddy Wachtel, saxman Bobby Keys, and drummer Steve Jordan, among others. This was during one of the big fall-outs between Keith and Mick over where the Stones were heading. Mick was chasing current trends

At FedEx Field with 98 Rock's Sarah Fleischer, WRNR's Bob Waugh, and others, 2002. Credit: © Cerphe Archive

while Keith was protecting the band's blues legacy and roots. One of the show's tunes, "You Don't Move Me," was a shot at Mick. The only Stones songs the X-Pensive Winos played that night were "Time Is on My Side" and the very cool "Connection" from their fifth studio album, *Between the Buttons,* one of my favorites.

The Globe shared the contest with two other radio stations, so DJs 98 Rock's Sarah Fleischer and WRNR's Bob Waugh were with me. We each hosted five winners and their guests, and there were other label guys and press attending. A group photo was taken before the show (my head looks like it was Photoshopped in) and the Stones met and shook everyone's hand. It was kind of like a wedding line. The Stones seemed happy to do this meet-and-greet, and were guardedly nonchalant. My observation was "they don't need to do this," but they'd been doing this kind of promotion for forty years. They've seen it all. They practically invented this rock and roll lifestyle.

The room lighting was superb, casting shadows on the curtain swags. Incense was burning. Near the end of the meet-and-greet, the door opens and Washington Redskins football team owner, Daniel Snyder, walks in, carrying a football. The listeners all recognize him. Dan opens his jacket and pulls out a Sharpie pen, autographs the ball, and hands it to Mick Jagger.

Jagger had no idea who Dan was. Nobody introduced him. Mick looks at Dan and looks at the football. No words were exchanged. Snyder departs, and Mick leaves the football on a table. I'm watching this in real time thinking, "You can't make this up."

The Ox

The Who were inducted into the Rock and Roll Hall of Fame in 1990. I met the Who's bass player, John Entwistle, in 2001, several weeks after they performed at the Concert for New York. John's bass playing style and signature sound really punched through on Who tracks, and influenced many musicians. Bill Wyman, original bassist for the Rolling Stones, once described him as "the quietest man in private but the loudest man on stage." Who leader Pete Townshend said John played loud so he could be heard over drummer Keith Moon's rapid-fire drumbeats.

He and high school classmate Pete Townshend began making music in a Dixieland band, with John on trumpet and Pete on banjo. Their first rock band, the Detours, included another school pal, Roger Daltry. They wore matching red jackets and played Top 40 hits. However, Pete soon discovered bluesman John Lee Hooker, and the band became the Who. This was 1963.

I learned that John collected suits of armor, guns, and medieval weapons. He didn't write many songs but the ones he did write stood out for their quirky and often dark side: "Boris the Spider," "Silas Stingy," "Cousin Kevin," and "Fiddle About" are examples.

He said he wrote "My Wife," arguably his best song, while he was walking his dogs after a fight with his wife. John also alluded to not being thrilled with the way his songs were presented by the Who, but he didn't elaborate.

John died on June 27, 2002, in a Las Vegas hotel room. Cardiac arrest and cocaine. It was one day before the Who were scheduled to begin an upcoming world tour. After four days, the Who took the stage with a replacement bass player, Pino Palladino, who has played with the Who ever since.

Robert Plant

"It's not hard to suss that Led Zeppelin are well on the way to becoming a 'Supergroup,' in the best tradition. . . . The gent who really has that mysterious something, both as an artist and as a person, is Robert Plant and I can well see him causing a severe outbreak of knicker wetting."

—Led Zeppelin debut album review,
International Times, April 1969

The three surviving members of a band that has earned its place in rock aristocracy, Led Zeppelin—Jimmy Page, John Paul Jones, and Robert Plant—were in Washington, DC, in December 2012 to accept the thirty-fifth annual Kennedy Center Honors. Coincidentally, there were Zep connections to two other Kennedy Center honorees that year; Buddy Guy's astonishing Chicago blues guitar work was inspirational to Jimmy Page, as it was to the rest of the blues guitar gods like Clapton, Beck, and Hendrix. David Letterman also was honored that night. Coincidentally, one of Robert Plant's post-Zep group works, *The Honeydrippers: Volume One,* included pianist Paul Shaffer and trombonist Tom "Bones" Malone from Letterman's CBS Orchestra.

At the Kennedy Center gala, Heart's Anne and Nancy Wilson performed an emotional rendition of Zeppelin's signature song, "Stairway to Heaven." On drums was Jason Bonham, the son of the late John Bonham, Led Zep's drummer. The song moved Robert Plant to tears, partly because he and John were friends at age sixteen, long before Led Zeppelin was formed.

On a side note, I talked recently with Nancy Wilson about my appreciation for Heart's live performances, especially their versions of Led Zeppelin songs like "The Battle of Evermore" and "Black Dog." I asked Nancy how the band decides on cover songs.

Nancy explained, "It changes with every tour. I sit around and play guitar a lot when we're not performing, and certain songs kind of rise to the top. They are songs we learned growing up and people love and remember them. We're doing two Led Zep songs, "Kashmir" and "The Rain Song," back to back on the current tour." For Nancy, a kick-ass guitarist, I was surprised to learn that it is Robert Plant's lyrics that have always been her favorite part of Led Zeppelin.

Ever since the band broke up in 1980 following drummer John Bonham's death from alcohol poisoning, Robert Plant has refused to slow down. From his solo work, including collaborations like the

Grammy-winning 2009 Album of the Year *Raising Sand* with Alison Krauss, to his collaborative Band of Joy and now the Sensational Space Shifters—who play a kind of Americana roots music mixed with just enough of his ethereal croon—Robert remains one of the best voices in rock. He is blessed with the kind of endless curiosity that can't be faked, and a humility that is a rare commodity in rock. I caught up with him when he played DC's DAR Constitution Hall in February 2011. I had been listening to his box set, *Nine Lives* (featuring early rare singles and cuts from the nine studio albums released by Robert between the years of 1982 and 2005). I was taken by the number of covers he did, like "Hey Joe," "Sea of Love," "If I Were a Carpenter," and so on. That's how we started our discussion.

Cerphe: I've been playing your music since 1973. You've sung a lot of cover songs.

Plant: I really didn't start writing songs until 1968. But I also wasn't doing "Tie a Yellow Ribbon." I was looking for something else. I made a choice between the mainstream path of music and something new. There was a huge movement in Britain at that time to hook up with the Chicago blues music, that sort of thing. I really dug that kind of music. There really wasn't a lot of stuff left to write. But I got it. I learned how to do it.

Cerphe: You definitely did. The amazing thing about your music is that no one has ever sounded like you.

Plant: Well, you can recognize styles. For example, you and I, because we are involved in music, can hear the difference between a [Fender] Telecaster or [Gibson] Les Paul guitar, or different amps on a record. You can recognize Jimmy Page's playing. So it's true that you do develop your own way. That's how it goes, thank God.

Cerphe: What a wonderful tour you had with Alison Krauss. Amazing.

241

Plant: Thank you. We are very, very proud of it. We did some work on it in America. We went down to Austin, Texas, to the South by Southwest music festival and did some great shows there. Good place to be!

Cerphe: That 2007 album, *Raising Sand,* with Alison won six Grammies. The album you did before that one, *The Mighty ReArranger.* You were saying how proud you were of that album and that it had the same intention as Led Zeppelin's record, *Physical Graffiti.* That's very powerful. Look at the amazing impression that you've had on all of us, and in music in general. What a great legacy, Robert.

Plant: The whole deal about music was much less commercialized in those early years. There was a little more mystery to it. These were times before music television and before there were many magazines that glorified people for one reason or another. There were only a couple of music magazines back then. These were different times back in those days. And because music was less optical, it was more enchanting, I think.

Cerphe: Are you going to come back to the Washington area this summer?

Plant: Ain't got a clue. [Laughs.] It's all right. I ought to know where I'm going.

Cerphe: That would be a good thing.

Plant: Normally, they give me a list of places and ask me, "Hey, do you want to go there?" and I say, "Yeah."

Cerphe: I've got a poster of the movie *Almost Famous.* That's one of my favorite rock movies. Did you see that?

Plant: I certainly did. I loved it. It was superb, and pretty close to how it all was.

Cerphe: I thought so, too. I thought it really captured 1973.

Plant: There was a general sincerity about those times and a general will, with the ideology that we were going to someplace new, and we were taking the whole society with us. And we were going to have our own culture that was free of "Tricky Dicky."

Cerphe: For our young listeners, "Tricky Dicky" was a name we used to call Richard Nixon, who was president of the United States during the time we're talking about here. And while we are on the subject of youth, Mr. Robert Plant, what advice would you give to young musicians today?

Plant: Stay off of drugs and have a good time.

Cerphe: Wait a minute. You invented that lifestyle.

Plant: No, that was Fatty Arbuckle. [Laughs.] But I know now that you have to keep it light, have a really good time, and you have to keep it inventive. Don't take the easy way.

Cerphe: Being inventive kind of describes what you did with Band of Joy, and now with the Sensational Space Shifters. You're performing about half a dozen or so Led Zeppelin songs now, with revamped versions of some of your classic songs like "Ramble On," "Tangerine," "Houses of the Holy," "Thank You," "Gallows Pole," and "Rock and Roll." How do you decide which songs to do, given your incredible body of work with Led Zeppelin, plus all your solo stuff?

Plant: Well, I have actually been doing all of this since 1968. But I choose things that I can rearrange. To personalize it now is interesting, and they are very exciting adaptations.

Cerphe: Of course, Led Zeppelin broke up a long, long time ago. While you were with Zeppelin you guys sang a lot about hobbits. What's the deal about hobbits?

Plant: I was seeking approval from the guys. In those days, *Lord of the Rings* was quite a mysterious place to be and place to go long before any movies were made. And it was also like a morality play and I liked that. The weak can triumph over evil and that sort of thing. And also when you're twenty, you're much more compelled to hobbit-dom than you are when you're in your forties.

Cerphe: I remember reading J. R. R. Tolkien as a kid and I loved it. But I think I'm really more into hobbits now than I was back then. Is that true for you, too?

Plant: I guess that's my excuse. It was a nice place to go and I can't get out of it now. There it was.

Cerphe: I just had to ask you that. Every time I played "Ramble on" or "The Battle of Evermore" on my radio show, hobbits came up. So I wanted to go to the source.

Plant: "The Battle of Evermore" is really about the Welsh borders and the turmoil of pre-medieval Britain. And that's what Tolkien did. He went to those very same places, and in the very same area of Canty and Shire that I went to. But of course he got it right. I [only] mused around for two-and-a-half minutes.

Cerphe: Yeah, Robert, but that two and a half minutes of musing changed rock and roll forever. I'll see your show tonight. Go on to the sound check.

Plant: Thanks. We're really on fire and the band is pumping like mad.

Talking Heads: Chris Franz

In November 2015, Music Planet Radio helped promote a unique performance event showcasing gifted military veteran artists. This show was produced by the 501(c)(3) nonprofit Veteran Artists Program (VAP), based in New York City. Military brats and Rock and Roll Hall of Famers, Chris Franz and Tina Weymouth of Talking Heads and the Tom Tom Club, graciously volunteered to emcee the evening. The lobby of the theater hosted a fine arts exhibit curated by Veterans Art Foundation. I got the chance to interview Chris and help promote this special affair.

In 1974, Chris, on drums, and his then-girlfriend Tina (mainly providing instrument transportation) began playing music together with lead vocalist and guitarist David Byrne while they all were attending college at the Rhode Island School of Design. They called themselves the Artists. They later added Jerry Harrison on guitars and keyboards, and Tina learned bass as the band evolved to become Talking Heads.

By 1977, Chris and Tina were married and the band released their first eponymous album, *Talking Heads: 77* with "Psycho Killer" an acclaimed hit song, the only one from the album to reach the charts.

Chris and Tina also formed a dance band, the Tom Tom Club, and had considerable success with album releases. Here's my conversation with Chris:

Cerphe: It's a pleasure to talk with you, Chris.

Chris: Likewise, Cerphe. Tell me, did we ever talk in person back in the heyday of WHFS and the Talking Heads? Because I know I went to the station a few times.

Cerphe: We passed in the hallway and said, "Hi, how are you?" but we at WHFS were so into your music from the very, very beginning. But you know what? It sounds as good today as it did then. It really does.

Chris: Thank goodness for that. It would be so embarrassing if it sounded bad.

Cerphe: Well, you know and I know that some music from that era did not necessarily translate very well over the decades and for very good reasons your music did.

Chris: Yeah, I feel very fortunate to be part of Talking Heads and Tom Tom Club. Those were good times.

Cerphe: They were great times. And you and Tina being the rhythm section of the Talking Heads: best rhythm section out there. And I know there's been a lot of time, water under the bridge, changes. There is such a lot of interest and love for your music. And who knows? You never say never. If there was ever going to be a time for a Talking Heads reunion, I think there'd be so much interest from the media, radio, and the listeners. And I don't think it would be reviewed or considered as part of a nostalgia kind of reunion. Part of it would, but your music is so alive and vital and in the moment. This is just one guy's opinion, but I would love to see that happen.

Chris: It would be nice if the Talking Heads could take advantage of the fact that we are all still kind of with it and alive and well.

Cerphe: I am such a fan of your wife's bass playing. She is on a short list of great women bass players.

Chris: She is amazing and I'll tell you what. It is sometimes maddening. She is not a bass player who plays the same thing on every song. She treats each new song like it's reinventing the wheel. She doesn't revert to her old stylistic devices. She is always trying to do something new that surprises everyone. She really does a good job at that.

Cerphe: She really does. And with bass guitarists, it's a very much male-dominated scene. So few women like Carol Kaye of the Wrecking Crew or women who have played bass for Jeff Beck, like Tal Wilkenfeld and Rhonda Smith. But Tina rocks. Always has.

Chris: Yes, I have the utmost respect.

Cerphe: As you should. You are a very wise husband. This project you are involved with is so great, seeing the music community support our veterans. You and Tina are military brats, aren't you? Your dads were lifelong military men. Am I right?

Chris: My father was in the army. Tina's father was in the navy. He's a retired admiral. She's visiting him right now in New Hampshire. He's ninety-eight years old but still very active in the Veterans for Peace organization.

Cerphe: That New Hampshire air and water keeps you healthy.

Chris: That's right, although he spends his winters in New Orleans. He says, "Some of my friends like to spend their winters in Florida but I prefer New Orleans."

Cerphe: A man after my own heart.

Chris: He's a smart man.

Cerphe: Part of the mission of this project is how to reintegrate veterans back into our community. There are so many vets coming back. Art is a great option for them. And if you look back, as you know, many of our great musicians have been veterans. Johnny Cash, Jimi Hendrix, Clint Eastwood, Richard Pryor, Julia Child. All of them military veterans.

Chris: That's correct. And let's not forget Glenn Miller. [Laughs.] But you know that the arts are great for anyone who has been under duress. I must say that our vets that were in Iraq and Afghanistan have been under extreme duress. I'm glad to be able to participate in this project to help them.

Cerphe: I think it's wonderful that you and Tina and your brother Roddy are doing this and helping vets. The music community has always risen up to help, especially in recent years. You and Tina, along with Bruce Springsteen, Joe Walsh, Stevie Nicks, Roger Waters, Sheryl Crow, and many others have all visited the Walter Reed Hospital here in Washington, DC. Thank you for this effort.

Chris: It is really us who should be thanking our veterans.

CHAPTER 20

Our House

My wife, Susan, is a kick-ass Texas girl and by all accounts should never have gone for a buttoned-down Bostonian like me. Ask any marriage counselor: North and South usually pair about as well as oil and water. But it was love at first sight, and for sixteen years, we've weathered our cultural differences just fine.

What to say about Susan, the absolute love of my life? It's her laugh, the shape of her face, her green eyes, the smell of her skin, her spiritual grounding, the way she makes sense of things, her beautifully wild hair in the morning, the way she makes me laugh so hard I shoot water out of my nose, her hot berry-soup pies—all of it I can't live without.

Susan lives to travel. Me, not so much, but I have been with her to some of the most amazing places on earth. The ruins of Rome, the medieval city of Elba, France, which clings to a cliff overlooking the Mediterranean, the Tuscan countryside to look at a statue Francis of Assisi, the beaches of Cannes in the summertime, a seventeenth-century chateau in Aix-en-Provence, hiking in Sedona, Arizona, a dude ranch in Tucson—too many cool places to list. And she puts up with my need to put down homebody roots. Once in a while, her wanderlust gets the better of her and she'll burst into a room with her laptop to show me where we're going next.

It feels as though she and I were meant to live this life together and that all the misfortunes, bad relationships, missed opportunities, and bumps in the road were just the universe, in its infinite wisdom, moving people, places, and things to lead us to the exact moment in time that we laid eyes on each other.

There's a Charles Aznavour song from the movie soundtrack of *Notting Hill* that Elvis Costello sings. It's about why a man is alive and survives. It is the care for his love. She is the meaning of his life. Whenever I hear it, I think of my impossibly beautiful green-eyed Irish girl from Midland, Texas—the one who stole my heart. Just to live in her light makes me a better man.

Susan on Me

Susan Colwell: "The first time I laid eyes on Cerphe, I knew he was the one for me. Unfortunately, I had just been married three months before.

"In 1989, I was the news director and straight man half of the morning show team Owens and Butler in the Morning on WMJR (a tiny Manassas, Virginia, FM station) when I got a call from Ed Levine, then program director at WJFK. I had only been on radio for more than a year. He was offering a part-time, overnight position. I jumped at the chance to work for Infinity Broadcasting, then one of the largest and most powerful broadcast companies in the world.

"When I arrived at WJFK, I was told I would be sitting in with Cerphe to learn how to work their radio board before my shift started later that night. Music director Mike Wolf walked me down the corridor to the studios. Like most people who listen to Washington radio, I knew who Cerphe was, but I've never been the star-struck type. I was more eager to learn the job than to meet the legendary DJ. There was a large window between the hallway and Cerphe's studio. I took one look at him through that glass and *bam!* Bolt of lightning!

"I sat in with Cerphe for several hours that first day. When our hands accidentally brushed, I knew he had felt a jolt, too. He played Van Halen's 'Oh Pretty Woman' and dedicated it to 'the pretty woman with him in the studio.' I was a goner.

"We worked different shifts during my year-and-a-half stint at WJFK, but we did see each other at work functions, meetings, and the occasional bar promotion. We had one of those flirty, sexual tension things that TV shows make plot lines out of, but neither of us acted on it.

"One night, not too far into my new overnight gig, I called in sick. I was the kind of sick that comes with hallucinations, greasy hair, and that overwhelming feeling of 'kill me now and be done with it.' My then-husband had gone with his buddies on a sudden camping trip. It was early evening and I was lying on the couch watching the news. I remember thinking that Sam Donaldson was speaking directly to me. How is he doing that, I wondered? The phone rang. It was Cerphe and he asked if I was all right. He knew my job meant so much to me that I either would have to be dead or on life support to miss a shift. He was right. Sam had gone and the angels were now singing me home. 'I'm coming over,' he said, 'but I'm going to stop at the health food store first. Can you get up to let me in?'

"Cerphe, loaded down with grocery bags soon arrived and went to work in the kitchen whirring, stirring, and mixing. He mixed a hot lemonade/bee pollen drink and spoon-fed me soup and natural remedies for hours. He stayed with me until my fever broke early the next morning. I'd never felt so cared for.

"It wasn't the first time the universe conspired to put us together. In 1986, before I was married, I lived in a condo overlooking a pretty row of houses on Lake Audubon in Reston. I would often sit on the deck looking down at one place in particular and wondered who lived in that lovely house on the water? Although I never saw him, later I would learn it was Cerphe's house.

"Cerphe and I have since compared notes on other things, too, an ongoing game of 'where were you when?' We found that on several occasions, we were at the same events at precisely the same time. 'You were at that promotion by the cars? I was in a radio kiosk by the entrance!' There was too much serendipity to be coincidence.

"Cerphe and I grew closer at work, both secretly longing to be together. One day, a local production company, who had seen our chemistry onstage at a couple of radio promotions, approached us about doing a TV show together. The idea fell apart when I announced I was moving to San Francisco. But I remember how excited I was to be going on business meetings with Cerphe, and having him pick me up at my house was heady beyond words.

"In 1990, my husband and I moved to the Bay Area for his work. I managed to secure a transfer to Infinity's San Jose rocker KOME, whose famous DJ at the time was a fellow introvert named Dennis Erectus. KOME's program director was Ron Nenni. He knew Cerphe. Everybody knew Cerphe. He was three thousand miles away and I missed him like crazy.

"I worked at KOME and landed a TV gig at the California Music Channel in Oakland as a video DJ. When my marriage began to end, I moved back to Washington in 1993. The first person I called was Cerphe.

'How are you?' I said, relieved to hear his voice.

'I'm great!' he said, 'Are you and Brad home for good?'

'Just me,' I said, 'Brad stayed in California. What are you up to?'

'I live in Philly now. I'm doing mid-days on WYSP and I got married about a year ago. What about you?'

"My heart sank. 'Oh, well, um, I'm getting divorced. I've moved back to DC for good and I'm looking for work.'

'I'll make some calls,' he said.

'No, I think I'm done with radio, but thank you,' I said, wanting to end the call.

"We exchanged a few pleasantries and hung up.

"Two years later, I was dating a mutual friend. It was Christmas time and I was at his house when the mail came. And there it was, a Christmas card from the Colwells. And oh, look! It's a picture of Cerphe's house, a gothic church turned residence on Philadelphia's Main Line with a massive wrought-iron door and a bell tower, the house where he lives with his wife. How lovely. I resisted the urge to throw it into the fire.

"In 1996, I was living in Old Town Alexandria with a roommate, Jim, who worked for an up-and-coming tech company. We got along well. I dated a little and worked too much. Jim worked all the time and dated seldom. It was a typical Washington singles existence and it suited me fine. On a random Tuesday, the phone rang. It was Cerphe. He told me that he'd gotten my phone number from my mother. My overly protective mother, who even if someone was calling to give me huge sums of money, would pretend not to know how to contact me. After Cerphe and I were married, I asked her, 'Why that time, Mom?' She said in a slight, leftover Texas drawl, 'Well, he had a nice voice.'

"The conversation was light and easy, like we'd never been apart.

'What are you doing these days?' he said.

"I updated him on my life, trying to make it sound more interesting than it was.

"He told me that he had been divorced for almost two years. 'Are you seeing anyone?' he asked.

'Yes, but nothing serious,' I said, holding my breath a little.

'Well, we'd better start dating before one of us gets married again.'

"Two hours later, we were sitting in a bar near my house, holding hands for the first time. We were married six months later.

"With only close family and friends in attendance, our ceremony took place at the Thomas Law House in Southeast DC (Martha Washington's granddaughter's house overlooking the Potomac River) with hundreds of votive candles perched on windowsills, mantels, and tabletops. I still can't believe they let us have all those burning candles in a centuries-old house that, when mixed with alcohol and celebration, could have so easily burned to the ground. It's something we marvel at to this day. But hundreds of candles there were just as we wanted. It looked like a Sting video.

"The day of our wedding, the skies opened up and it rained without mercy. The grounds were soaked. My family was fighting. The caterers weren't cooperating. I was an hour and a half late because the limo driver got lost. Both Cerphe and I remained eerily calm. We knew we were destined to be married. I walked down the aisle at 9:05 p.m. on a wet Saturday night in October 1999 in a historic house lit only by candlelight to meet my forever husband.

"The early days of our marriage were bittersweet. We were deliriously happy to be together, but sickness and death and the challenges of living with someone new presented an obstacle course to be navigated. After losing his mother five years earlier, Cerphe's beloved father, Chet, had just passed away. I never got to meet him. He was living in Massachusetts and died in the early days of our courtship. My mother was very sick here at home and my sister and I took turns spending one week on and one week off living with Mom to give her the round-the clock care she needed. I had just started a new business and Cerphe and I, both set in our ways, wondered how we would ever be able to live with someone who left the toothpaste cap off (me) and insisted the toilet seat be down at all times (him). Little things that, to most couples, are simply the first year of marriage were amplified by grief and stress.

"A few months before we were married, I accompanied Cerphe on a trip to his hometown in Massachusetts to collect his father's remaining belongings. We climbed into his Jeep for the nine-hour ride to Winchester. I, an insomniac all of my life who could never nap in the daytime or fall asleep in cars, and sometimes took over-the-counter sleeping pills at night, slept on and off the entire trip up and back. It was the first time I had ever felt safe enough to do so.

"We arrived at a friend's home and drove around for hours. Cerphe showed me where his childhood home used to be (there's now a large luxury home on the site where his modest family home once stood) and Sixten Erickson's farm next door where Cerphe spent most of his early years splashing in streams, chasing butterflies, and collecting rocks. Sixten had built the Colwell house next door to his own property. By sheer coincidence, Sixten had also built the house in Arlington that Chet and Mabel Colwell brought a one-week-old baby Cerphe home to and where he would later climb out of bed (at the age of three) in the wee hours to eat all the candy in his Easter basket in one sitting. And where, on a separate occasion after one of his mother's evening china painting classes, he would wake to paint her studio with all the precious paste-gold paint she had.

"We drove to Mount Auburn Cemetery in Cambridge to pay our respects to Cerphe's parents. As an aside, Mount Auburn is one of the most beautiful cemeteries in the world and was inspired by Père Lachaise Cemetery in Paris. Poet Henry Wadsworth Longfellow, landscape painter Winslow Homer, psychologist B. F. Skinner, Supreme Court Chief Justice Oliver Wendell Holmes, and the founder of Christian Science, Mary Baker Eddy, are also buried there. It is breathtaking.

"As I write this, it's another rainy day in October and Cerphe and I have been married for sixteen years. Like all couples, we fight over petty things: who unloaded the dishwasher last; overfeeding the cat; whose turn it is to go to the grocery store. He can drive me absolutely mad at times, but we love each other deeply.

"Since we both work from home, most days are spent in full togetherness, sunup to sundown. Cerphe is charming as hell, witty, and is the only person who makes me laugh daily. There's always something funny. We hug in grocery store aisles for no particular reason and Cerphe says when he wakes me from a dead sleep, I most always laugh although I never remember. I think it's my soul's way of saying 'It's you! It's you! I found you!' and being so overcome with joy, there's no other thing to do but laugh."

CHAPTER 21

Music Planet Radio

One example of good fortune in my career is that radio management never pressured me into interviewing any performer that I didn't particularly like. There was no "Hey, Cerphe. We've got Nicky Nostril and the Nose Pickers waiting for you on line two. Please interview them." Either I would set up interviews with whomever I wanted, or the record label would ask me if I'd like to interview someone. My choice.

Therefore, there weren't many disappointments. I also have a habit of forgetting negative things, but one bad interview with the Soft Machine, a jazz-rock fusion group from England, stands out. Three of the four band members were chain smoking in our small studio. I was dying. And their answers were insipid.

Cerphe: So tell me what it was like opening for Jimi Hendrix?
Soft Machine: It was great, mate [silence.]

Some interviews I've done do not translate to the page very well. You had to be there in real time and hear it. Philip Proctor and Peter Bergman, for example, were part of the surreal comedy troupe, Firesign Theatre. When they came on my show in 1975, Springsteen's album *Born to Run* was completed but hadn't been released yet. WHFS had an acetate copy given to us personally by a member of the E Street Band. Their label, Columbia was pissed off that we had it, as were other DC radio stations. We didn't care. This was before corporate lawyers would send "cease and desist" letters.

So Proctor and Bergman were in the studio doing their very stream-of-consciousness humor and knew we had Bruce's record. They asked me if they could do a bit. I said, "I think so," not knowing what to expect.

I played the opening song, "Born to Run." After Clarence's sax solo, Philip Proctor lifted the tone arm. He stopped the record and began a commentary: "You know, I'm not sure if I would have played the sax that way."

Bergman chimed in, "Is he playing an alto sax? I wonder if that's a Selma sax."

I start laughing while the phones lit up. Listeners were irate. They were not used to hearing humor this droll if they even got the joke. Understandably, they wanted to hear the song. Springsteen was surging and we had an exclusive. So I tried to start the record where it was interrupted. About forty-five seconds later, the funny guys stopped the record again: "Did you hear that lyric? I don't think I would have written *that*."

Although I was laughing, I had mixed emotions. Was this great performance art or were we just pissing in the wind? It didn't go over well with most listeners. But the memory of it sure is funny.

Goodbye, Hello

When I left 94.7 The Globe in 2009, the *Washington Post* ran the news on their front page with the headline "D.C. Radio's Last Rock Overturned; DJ Cerphe Signs Off as 'Classic' WTGB Switches to Pop." The article by writer Paul Farhi's quoted Michael Hughes, then vice president of programming for CBS Radio's four local stations saying I was "one of the most knowledgeable and respected musical experts (he's) known."

At that time WTGB was the city's only remaining classic rock station. The *Post* said I was "arguably the voice of Washington's rock generation." I told Paul that I had an amazing run. Most people in radio don't get to stay in the same job, or on the air, for a very long time. The only business with a higher turnover is Taco Bell.

But I still believed that the classic rock format had worth. People like to go back twenty years. When they hear a song and they remember what was going on in their lives back then, it takes them back to a kinder, gentler time.

Paul asked me if I thought I could have transitioned to the new WTGB Fresh 94.7 hit-maker format. I told him yes. I really love radio, and I really love Washington. But I'm really not a Kelly Clarkson kind of guy. I'm more of a Springsteen, U2, and Coldplay guy.

We ended the WTGB classic rock format with "The End" by The Beatles. A few days later, the *Washington Post* published a letter to the editor from a District Heights, Maryland, listener commenting on my demise. In his letter, he included this passage:

"Many of us grew up listening to Cerphe. For more than thirty years, Cerphe gave us insight and reported on rock news and facts that we heard nowhere else. He did not talk endlessly as most of today's DJs do. He did not try to be funny or cute. Cerphe shared the music news and kept it short and to the point. When Cerphe reported on the music scene or concert news, it was gospel."

I appreciated this very much. But it would not be my last goodbye to radio.

I did afternoon drive on Classic Rock 105.9 The Edge when Mike O'Meara and Kirk McEwen were on mornings. The entire air staff left when Cumulus Media flipped their format to simulcast talk sister station WMAL.

This kind of format flipping became the norm. WHFS switched to Latin music in January 2005—rebranding as El Zol 94.7. The Globe switched from Classic Rock to Adult Alternative and then to Hot Adult Contemporary in a matter of several years. Back when I was on WHFS, if you'd told me that one day, radio stations would fire all the talent and play music (programmed by an out-of-town consultant who has no idea of the local market) from a focus-group-driven, computer-generated playlist with a guy six states away doing traffic and weather, I would have said you were nuts! But that's exactly what happened.

I've never liked change. When I was eight years old and had outgrown a pair of beloved cowboy boots, I Vasolined my feet to keep from having to get a new pair. So when big shifts started happening at the stations I worked for, I was a bit out of sorts. Susan, sensing my growing angst, suggested that I start my own online radio station, and in 2009, we did.

We launched in September that year with the blessing of CBS Radio (my employer). The only goal for our station was to be a creative outlet for playing music that Susan and I liked, artists that FM stations weren't playing, new songs from classic rock artists, deeper tracks, and Tom Waits—gotta have Waits.

About a year in, a techie friend of Susan's asked what our numbers were? We didn't have a clue and asked how to go about checking them. We figured we might be the only two people on the planet listening. The web stats said we were two of 10,000. Susan watched the numbers while I continued doing my on-air thing, turning people on to great music and interviewing guests like Robert Plant, Coldplay, Stevie Nicks, and others. Our audience began to climb without any promotion on our part, 20,000, then 30,000. When it hit 40,000, we knew we had something.

Susan called a friend, Helen Kruger, who had just left her high-powered job at the Ritz Carlton. As the two caught up, Helen asked and Susan shared the story of the little Internet radio station that could. We decided that day to turn Music Planet Radio into a serious business, with Helen becoming the station's general manager (sales and marketing),

Susan steering the ship as station manager, and me programming the music and hosting shows.

Our first paying client was the Town of Leesburg, Virginia, which hired us to promote their events, the Air Show, the Flower and Garden Festival, the Halloween Haunted House Tours, and the Annual Car Show. Susan and I decided that we never wanted to have hyped-sounding ads like you find on FM. She suggested we go the gentler public radio route with segments of content being "brought to you by . . ." I loved it immediately. It reminded me of the days at 'HFS when we were a community-minded station.

Susan and Helen focused on what they called "infotainment" and began crafting content marketing around our sponsors—creating custom music and lifestyle shows and features and building a theme relative to the sponsor. I'm happy to say that many people who have listened to me in the DC area for years and who are now disenchanted with music on FM love what we're doing on Music Planet Radio. New listeners are finding us online, too and it's fun to watch the audience grow.

While we keep our content focused on the DC Metro, we have listeners worldwide. Our format is music intensive, and our playlist includes gifted local singer-songwriters like Don Chapman, Jon Carroll, Prescott Engle, Cal Everett, Cassidy Ford, Stilson Greene, Johnny Kasun, Mary Ann Redmond, Michael L. Sheppard, Gary Smallwood, Mark Williams, and Todd Wright along with classic rock and modern rock icons—all of them flowing together seamlessly as if they had always belonged in the same format. We also feature lifestyle segments on home renovation and home-buying tips and have cooking and wellness features scheduled.

To date, we have done promotions for Wolf Trap National Park for the Performing Arts, Live Nation, I.M.P./9:30 Club, Crown Publishing/ Random House, Reston Town Center, International Record Store Day,

Earth Day Network, The Smithsonian Institute, Duke Ellington School of the Performing Arts, Wounded Warriors, Juvenile Diabetes Research, Acoustic on the Green, Jingle Jam, and many others.

Music Planet Radio streams 24/7 at MusicPlanetRadio.com. My "Cerphe's Progressive Show" showcases artists from yesterday, today, and tomorrow. Bands you grew up with and artists on the rise.

It's free to listen, there's always something unique and cool going on, and we don't plan on switching formats, tweaking our playlist based on focus groups, or hiring a guy six states over to do DC traffic and weather. We are freeform radio that's taken the best of FM from its earliest, progressive days and shaped it into a twenty-first century listening experience. I love what we have become and where we're going.

An example of one of my Music Planet Radio shows from October 2015 included world-class rock from the Fixx, Joan Armatrading, the Pretenders, Ringo Starr & His All Starr Band, and new Jeff Lynne and Electric Light Orchestra. Progressive Show Flashbacks with UB40, Garbage, and the latest Hozier and more! Since it was Halloween week, I played a theme set that included Warren Zevon's "Werewolves of London," Tom Petty's "Zombie Zoo," Donovan's "Season of the Witch," a spooky lecture on witchcraft by the late horror actor, Vincent Price, and the haunting song about a Welsh witch, "Rhiannon" by Fleetwood Mac. You can't do that on FM anymore!

Like back in the WHFS days, I get to play what I want and interview who I want. Here are some recent chats I've had with old friends:

Rod Stewart

"Instead of getting married again, I'm going to find a woman I don't like and just give her a house. . . . You go through life wondering what is it all about but at the end of the day, it's all about family."

—Rod Stewart

Cerphe: Rod, I have a confession to make to you. It's been bothering me for years so I have this confession. I saw you back in 1972 at the Alexandria Roller Rink here in suburban DC.

Rod: Oh, behave yourself.

Cerphe: Now you're going Austin Powers on me.

Rod: It's so funny because I remember that show like it was last year. That was the second Faces tour of America. I remember it well.

Cerphe: I snuck into that show, Rod. I owe you three dollars and fifty cents.

Rod: You can't get anything for three dollars these days.

Cerphe: I've owed you that three-fifty for all these years. And your shows with the Faces back in the day were legendary.

Rod: We are always so drunk in the Faces, but I do remember Washington, DC. It was one of our favorite places to be because the women were so pretty.

Cerphe: You know I'm married to one of those pretty women and there's a whole a lot of pretty women who want to see you the next time you're in concert here. You also have aged so well.

Rod: Thank you, but I don't feel so good right now because I just got off an international flight and those trips really wipe you out.

Cerphe: Are you at home?

Rod: Yes, I'm in Los Angeles, which is home for me, but I love England and try to go back for about three months out of the year.

Cerphe: Your Los Angeles home is beautiful. I've seen it in *Architectural Digest* magazine. Not too shabby. From the time I saw you in 1972 you have been so consistent. So many bands have come and gone. Decade after decade, you just keep coming back, reinventing yourself. I saw you recently on *American Idol.* What's your secret? How do you do it?

Rod: That's one thing that a lot of the kids asked me when I did the *American Idol.* I said boringly that I have lived a pretty clean life as far as drugs are concerned. I've seen many of my fellow musicians fall by the wayside because of drugs. I was never that heavily into drugs. And I think you have to have a distinctive voice. God has given me the instrument of distinct voice. You don't need a technically great voice but I think all the great musicians of our generation are not technically great singers but they have have that wonderful distinction.

Cerphe: Well you've got that in spades. Nobody sounds like Rod Stewart. I sound a little bit like you when I get a cold.

Rod: [Laughs.]

Cerphe: I love that album you did back in 2006, *Still the Same . . . Great Rock Classics of Our Time* where you did a bunch of great covers by artists like Van Morrison, Bob Seger, John Fogerty, and Dylan. You did a really cool cover of "It's a Heartache" recorded by Welsh singer Bonnie Tyler. We used to say Bonnie Tyler was the female Rod Stewart.

Rod: Yes, I remember it was 1977 when my mum called me up and said, "There's somebody over here trying to sound like you." I have been waiting to get my teeth into that song ever since.

Cerphe: You did a really good job on that. Who would you like to work with as a writer or collaborator on a song?

Rod: If I wanted to write with somebody or have somebody write my songs, it would actually be Tom Waits.

Cerphe: That's so wild that you said that because Tom Waits is one of my favorite musicians.

Rod: He's a genius lyricist.

Cerphe: That he is and he rarely tours but we got to see him recently on TV when David Letterman signed off his show. And we rarely see him on TV.

Rod: With all due respect to you on the radio, TV is how we get exposure and Tom Waits needs to sell some more records, as he is a phenomenal talent.

Cerphe: Yes, he was a guest on my radio show on WHFS. He's amazing. Have you ever met him?

Rod: No, I've never met Tom, believe it or not. I've done two or three songs of his and I would dearly love to meet him one of these days.

Cerphe: Tony Bennett just turned eighty-nine. Do you think you're going to be doing this when you're eighty-nine?

Rod: As long as I can keep my waistline and have air my lungs, I'll probably keep on doing it. Even if I don't have a waistline. I love it to death. I really do love singing.

Cerphe: I've been playing your music on the radio for a very long time from the beginning and you know a lot of your cohorts haven't done so well. You've managed to stay out of trouble. You've lived a really good life.

Rod: I do live a good life. I have six children now. I couldn't be happier.

Cerphe: And we couldn't be happier either. When I see you next time I'll give you that three-fifty I owe you.

Rod: All right, Cerphe. Thanks, mate.

The Demon of Screamin'

"I was on the junior Olympic team in high school for trampoline. I could do twenty-six back flips in a row."

—Steven Tyler

I first interviewed Steven Tyler, lead singer of Aerosmith, on my WAVA-FM radio show in 1980. I most recently caught up with him when his 2011 book *Does the Noise in My Head Bother You?* came out.

He told me that his publicist said he had to talk to this radio guy about his book, and Steven asked him who it was. The publicist said, "Cerphe" and Steven said "Oh, my God!" He was happy to hear from me. I let him know, "You can't lose me, even after thirty-five years, buddy boy. I'm like a bad penny."

Steven writes on the first page of his memoir, "If you're a hammer, everything looks like a nail. If you're a singer, everything looks like a song. Life is short. Break the rules. Forgive quickly. Kiss slowly. Love truly. Laugh uncontrollably. And never forget anything that makes you smile."

This sums up Steven Tyler, although he's definitely had his problems over the years. In 2008, he lost his mother, and in 2010, his dad. Their deaths and other personal problems put him back in drug rehab. Steven talks about his excessive-even-by-rock-standards drug use (twenty million dollars worth by his own estimate), and while he has been a frequent and vocal proponent for clean living, he has been in and out of rehab eight times. But just like one of the titles of his band's albums, *Nine Lives,* Steven is a survivor and a dear friend. One of the things I like about him is that when you see or talk with him, you get an immediate sense of what he is really all about. He's funny. He's self-deprecating. A lovable and honest guy.

As you might expect, Steven's story is a wild ride. He was born Steven Victor Tallarico on March 26, 1948, in Yonkers, New York. His father of German and Italian descent was a classical musician who taught high school music. His mom, a secretary, was English and Polish. He spent his summers in Sunapee, a New Hampshire resort town about 90 minutes from Boston. He says his closest neighbor was a mile away. The deer and the raccoons were his friends, and he'd spend time walking through the woods, looking for the most beautiful tropical thing that can survive the winter in the woods of New Hampshire.

His childhood friend in Sunapee was Joe Perry, who lived there year round. Both of them grew up listening to rhythm and blues and rock and roll music and formed various bands in Sunapee (Joe Perry with bassist Tom Hamilton) and New York (Steven). The three went to the Woodstock festival together in 1969. A month later they decided to move to Boston, and there they became a power trio with Steven on vocals and drums. Joey Kramer took over drums so Steven could focus on singing, and Brad Whitford came in on rhythm guitar. Aerosmith was formed. They've been rockin' ever since, with estimated worldwide sales of 150 million albums. Inducted into the Rock Hall of Fame in 2001, I still call them the Bad Boys from Boston.

I asked him about their early days. Aerosmith's fourteenth album, *Honkin' on Bobo*, tracks through eleven cover songs of classic blues tunes like "Road Runner" by Bo Diddley, "Eyesight to the Blind" by Sonny Boy Williamson, and "You Gotta Move" by the Reverend Gary Davis. Younger Aerosmith fans might not know that the band were always titanic fans of the blues.

"Bingo. We were always blues fans, first and foremost," Steven concurs. "*Honkin' on Bobo* was supposed to be a studio album but then we thought we had never put something like this out that we love. It always has to be new [Aerosmith songs], with another kind of 'Jaded' or 'Walk This Way.' But what if we do a record that pays homage to the kind of stuff that helped us write 'Jaded' or 'Walk This Way'? I mentioned it [to the record company] and told them the title and they said, 'No, you can't do that.' I said, 'Yeah, it's an old blues phrase.'

"The very first song I saw Joe Perry play in his own band [the Jam Band] in New Hampshire was a blues song, 'Rattle Snake Shake,' by Fleetwood Mac. That's all I had to hear. I threw my hands in the air and said, 'That's it.' I quit all the other bands I was playing with for four years in New York and joined him. The rest is history."

I talked with Steven about his 2005 *Rockin' the Joint* live album. He told me: "We recorded *Rockin' the Joint* at a small club called The Joint in Las Vegas, where many bands have played. We do some classic Aerosmith and also 'I Don't Want to Kiss Your Thing,' um, I mean 'Miss a Thing'," Steven joked. "It's a little like *Honkin' on Bobo*. The audience went out of their minds. It was a perfect situation."

The quintessential rock megastar, Steven Tyler helped define rock and roll and continues to entertain and influence with his unbridled irreverence. I told him that I considered him to be on the short list of the best front men in rock bands ever.

"You know what?" he replied. "It's because of people like you who were there at the beginning, and I mean this very sincerely and honestly. You liked us and passed it on. You turned people on to a good thing, and it is. I'm grateful to be in this band and have a voice. I'm walking around Los Angeles and I bump into Barbra Streisand, and she says, 'I love your music,' and I say, '*What?*'"

I answer him. That's because Aerosmith songs are like buttah.

Emotionally Yours

Music and community started this conversation between us forty-five years ago. It's been such a pleasure to share these stories with you and I hope you've enjoyed reliving them with me.

My accidental radio career has given me a good life. Along the way, I have tried to adopt the best qualities of those I love: my mom's tenacity, my dad's honesty, and my wife's passion for life.

You, my friends, have given me the freedom to share new artists and music. Without you, there would be no story, no book, no Music Planet Radio. Thank you for being part of this musical life.

Be Cool	Vaya Con Dios
Chin Chin	Hasta la Vista
Cerphe's Up	Gidday
Bonzai	Adios
Cheerio	Aloha
Cowabunga	Addio
Namaste	Adeus

Dovidjenja

Do Svidaniya

Bon Soir

Au Revoir

Sayonara

TTFN

Ayoayo

Ciao

Tung Tung

Totsiens

Muhnak Parov

Bhalo Thakben

Agur

Tot Ziens

Kaliméra

Bless Bless

Selamat Tinggal

Slán

Aveto

Annyeong

Hágoónee

Kwaheri

Paálam

Nana

Zàijiàn

Khoda Hafez

Le'hitra'ot

La Revedere

Na Shledanou

Auf Wiedersehen

Shalom

Arrivederci

Mañana

Rock on Baby. You rock only once!

Acknowledgments

Every good story needs a cast of interesting characters, just like every fine band needs compelling musicians. Fortunately, this book includes both.

I am foremost grateful to my wife, Susan, who helped me throughout this project. Her empathy, insight, and expertise greatly assisted the organization and execution of this book.

My coauthor, Steve Moore, has been a friend since my WAVA radio days and was an 'HFS fan at the University of Maryland. He's worked with both actress Helen Hayes and broadcaster Johnny Holliday on their autobiographies, oversees research technologies at Georgetown University, and plays in a cover band, the Razors.

Steve and I have greatly benefited from the creative and dedicated editing and contributions of our good friend Patty Johnson Cooper, also an ardent 'HFS fan since 1969. Special mention also goes to Michael Oberman, music writer and nature photographer extraordinaire, and Marc Fisher, *Washington Post* reporter and author of *Something in the Air: Radio, Rock, and the Revolution that Shaped a Generation* (Random House), an outstanding radio history book. Their early support and contributions are enormously appreciated.

Others who helped make this book possible include Adele Abrams, James "J B" Allison, Laura Balducci, Dixie Dee Ballin, Dick Bangham, Jack Boyle, Charlie Bragale, Josh Brooks, Jackson Browne, Peter Bonta, Roy Buchanan, Barbara Carr, Bob Coleman, Tom Collins, David Crosby, Bill Danoff, Gene Davis, Donovan, Michael Del Colliano, Walter Egan, Damian Einstein, Jake Einstein, Cal Everett, Paul Farhi, Chris Franz, John Friedman, Richie Furay, Danny Gatton, Lowell George, Elliot Gilbert, Jonathan "Weasel" Gilbert, L. Suzanne Gordon, Stilson Greene, Thom Grooms, John Hall, Richard Harrington, Jim Herron, Johnny Holliday, Seth Hurwitz, Len Jaffe, Michael Jensen, Terre Jones, Steve Jordan, Ed Kalicka, Paul Kasko, Howard Kaylan, Jill Timmons Kennedy, Danny Kortchmar, Elissa Kline, Donal Leace, Joe Lee, Dennis John Lewis, G. Gordon Liddy, Jeff Lodsun, Nils Lofgren, Stevie Nicks, Suzanna Moore, "Buzz" McClain, Roger McGuinn, Dennis McNally, Chris Murray, Graham Nash, Tracy Nelson, Stevie Nicks, Taffy Nivert, Dave Nuttycombe, Danny O'Keefe, Bill Payne, Robert Plant, Chris Phillips, Andrew Ratliff, Mary Ann Redmond, Earl Rollison, Biff Rose, "Big Al" Sevilla, Mark Seagraves, John Sebastian, Mike Shreibman, Stephen Stills, Kirk Sillsbee, Fred Sirkey, Bruce Springsteen, Charles Steiner, Howard Stern, Rod Stewart, Patrick Thornton, Joe Triplett, Steven Tyler, Charles Young, Steven Van Zandt, Tom Waits, Mark Wenner, George F. Will, Mark Williams, Kenny Wilson, Frank Zappa, Dweezil Zappa, and Tom Zito.

Appendix

Childe Harold Players

Here is an attempt at a complete listing of Childe Harold performers, courtesy of authors' memories and our friends in the '70s DC Area Music Scene Facebook group.

1 Shot
4 Out of Five Doctors

Al Jarreau
Alan Holdsworth
Alvin Crow
Amos Garrett
Andy Newmark
Anthony Braxton
Art Blakey
Arthur "Big Boy" Crudup
Asleep at the Wheel

Babe
Bad Brains
Balloons for the Dog
Berline, Crary, and
   Hickman
Big Walter "Shakey"
   Horton
Bill Blue Band
Bill Harris Trio

Bill Holland & Rents Due
Bill Troy & Rubber Band
Billy and the Shakes
Billy Evans
Billy Hancock
Billy Price
Blue Jug Band
Bob "Catfish" Hodge
Bob Lawson (mime)
Bobby Radcliff
Bonnie Raitt
Boys of the Lough
Breakfast Special
Brian Auger
Bruce Springsteen Band
Bryan Bowers (autoharp)
Buckeye
Byron Berline
Captain Beefheart
Casse Culver & Belle Star
   Band
Central Park Sheiks

Cheek to Cheek Allstars
Chicken Legs
Child's Play
Chris Bliss
Chris Moquin (juggler)
Chuck McDermott
Clarence "Gatemouth"
   Brown
Clovers, The
Club Wow
Coasters, The
Country Gazette
Coup de Grass
Cryin' Out Loud
D. Ceats with Martha Hull

Dale Miller
Dale Stein
Dan Hicks
Danny Denver
Danny Gatton Band

Dave Allen Romance Band
Dave Van Ronk
David Allan Coe
David Bromberg
David Newman
David Olney
David Sanborn
De Dannan (Irish band)
Delbert McClinton
Diane Davidson
Dick Heintz
Dick Pinney
Dillards, The
Diversions, The
Dixie D. Eastridge
Dogmatics
Doug Sahm
Down Child Blues Band
Downchild Blues Band
Drifters, The
Dude Brown

Earl "Fatha" Hines
Earl Scruggs
East Coast Offering
Eddie and Martha Adcock
Ellen McIllwaine
Elvin Jones
Emmylou Harris
Eric Kloss
Eric Quincy Tate
Ernie Steel Band
Este Boys
Evan Johns & H Bombs
Evernow

Fabulous Touchtones
Firefall
Flora Moulton
Flying Burrito Brothers
Ford, Robben
Four Out of Five Doctors
Freedom Train
Funky Kings

Gamble Rodgers
Gary Apple
Geoff Muldaur
George Gritzbach
George McWirter
George Thorogood
Gove Scrivenor
Greg Artzner (Magpie)
Grits
Grow Your Own
Guy Clark

Happy & Artie Traum
Happy the Man
Hickory Wind
Holy Modal Rounders
Horace Silver
Houston Stack House
However
Hubert Sumlin

Illusions of Fantasy
Insect Surfers, The

J. S. D. Band
James Talley
Jamie Brockett
Jeffrey Fredericks Clamtones
Jeremiah Samuels
Jerry Prell (mime)
Jim Clark
Jim Hall
Jim Kweskin
Jim Post
Jim Ringer
Jimmy Ley Blues Band
Jimmy Thackery
Joanne Dodds Band
Joe Zauner
John Denver
John Hammond, Jr.
John Hartford
John Hiatt
John Lincoln Wright
Johnny Barnette

Johnny Nash
Johnny Nicholas
Johnny Shines
Jonathan Richman
Jonnie Barnett Nelson
Jorge Calderon
Jr. Cline & the Recliners
Juice Newton
J. W. McClure

Keltner, Jim
Kenny Definis Quartet
Keystone Rhythm Kings
Kinky Friedman

Lamont Cranston Band
Larry Coryell
Larry Gatlin
Larry John Wilson
Last Chance
Len Jaffe
Leon Redbone
Little River Band, The
Liz Meyer w/Midnight Flyers
Long Hall String Band
Lonnie Pitford
Lou London
Luther Allison

Mac Bogart Band
Magpie
Mama Scott
Mama's Pride
Margot Chapman
Mark O'Connor
Marshall Chapman
Marshall Keith
Martin Mull
Martin, Bogan, and Armstrong
Mary McCaslin
Max Collie's Rhythm Aces
Meg Christian
Michael Hurley

Mike Bloomfield
Mike Cotter Band
Mike Reid
Mirabai
Mississippi Fife & Drum
    Band
Mose Allison
Mother Earth
Muffins, The
Murray McLaughlin
Musica Orbis

Napoleon Strickland
Natural Bridge
New Grass Revival, The
New Morning String
    Band
Night Sun w/Jeff Wisor
Nighthawks, The
Norman Blake
Northstar Band, The
Nurses, The

Odetta
Oliver
Original Fetish

Pat Metheny (solo)
Patrick Sky
Paul Geremia
Paul Seidel
Paula Lockhart Trio
Persuasions, The
Pete Kennedy
Pete Ragusa
Peter Bonta
Peter Ecklund
Peter Lang
Pharaoh Saunders
Phil Woods
Pinetop Perkins
Pits, The
Pleasant Valley Boys
Pleasure
Potstill Band
Powerhouse Blues Band

Professor Longhair
Puppets, The

Rahsaan Roland Kirk
Ramblin' Jack Elliot
Ramones (10/24/76)
Randy Burns
Razz
Reactions, The
Red Sails in the Sunset
Red Shoes Walkin'
Rhythm Masters, The
Rhythm Rockers
Ritchie Cole
Robert Jr. Lockwood
Robin and Linda Williams
Robin Williamson
Rocket 88 Band
Rocket 88 Blues Band
Roland Hanna Trio
Ron Carter
Ron Crick
Roomful of Blues
Root Boy Slim
Rosslyn Mountain
    Boys
Roy Bookbinder
Roy Buchanan
Ruben Brown Trio
Scott, Tom
Slickee Boys
Small Talk
Son Seals
Sonny Fortune
Sour Mash Boys
Southern Wind
Southside Johnny
Stains, The
Star Spangled Washboard
    Band
Stephane Grapelli
Steve Bassett
Steve Miller (sat in)
Steve Wolf Jazz Trio
Stormin' Norman
Strokers, The

Sun Ra
Sunnyland Slim
Swingshift

Tears
Teresa Gunn Group
Terry Chandler
Terry Leonino (Magpie)
Terry Reid
Tex Rubinowitz
Texas Tornados
Thunderbirds
Tim Craven
Tim Eyermann
Tom Jans
Tom Principato
Tom Rapp
Tommy Lepson
Tony Perkins & the
    Psychotics
Tony Williams Lifetime
Townes Van Zandt
Tracy Nelson
Travis and Shook
Tru Fax & Insaniacs
Tut Taylor

Um-Babe
Uncle Josh Graves
Unholy Modal Rounders
Unknown Maracas
Urban Verbs, The

Waz
Wendy Waldman
Wheat Straw
Widespread Jazz
    Orchestra
Willie Dixon

Yellow Rose

Index

Unless otherwise specified, entries in *italics* indicate album, book, TV, or movie titles. Those in quotes indicate song titles.